BETWEEN HOMELAND
AND MOTHERLAND

BETWEEN HOMELAND AND MOTHERLAND

Africa, U.S. Foreign Policy, and Black Leadership in America

Alvin B. Tillery Jr.

CORNELL UNIVERSITY PRESS   ITHACA AND LONDON

Copyright © 2011 by Cornell University

All rights reserved. Except for brief quotations in a review, this book, or parts thereof, must not be reproduced in any form without permission in writing from the publisher. For information, address Cornell University Press, Sage House, 512 East State Street, Ithaca, New York 14850.

First published 2011 by Cornell University Press
First printing, Cornell Paperbacks, 2011
Printed in the United States of America

Library of Congress Cataloging-in-Publication Data
Tillery, Alvin B. (Alvin Bernard), 1971–
  Between homeland and motherland : Africa, U.S. foreign policy, and Black leadership in America / Alvin B. Tillery, Jr.
    p. cm.
  Includes bibliographical references and index.
  ISBN 978-0-8014-4897-3 (cloth : alk. paper)
  ISBN 978-0-8014-7734-8 (pbk. : alk. paper)
  1. United States—Foreign relations—Africa. 2. Africa—Foreign relations—United States. 3. African Americans—Relations with Africans—History.
4. African American leadership—History. 5. African diaspora—History. I. Title.
  DT38.T55 2011
  327.7306—dc22   2010040740

Cornell University Press strives to use environmentally responsible suppliers and materials to the fullest extent possible in the publishing of its books. Such materials include vegetable-based, low-VOC inks and acid-free papers that are recycled, totally chlorine-free, or partly composed of nonwood fibers. For further information, visit our website at www.cornellpress.cornell.edu.

Cloth printing   10 9 8 7 6 5 4 3 2 1
Paperback printing   10 9 8 7 6 5 4 3 2 1

For Maferima and Norah, who live between America and Africa, and keep my heart with them in both places

Contents

Preface ix

Introduction 1

1. "Not One Was Willing To Go!": The Paradoxes of "Liberia's Offerings" 14
2. "His Failure Will Be Theirs": Why the Black Elite Resisted Garveyism and Embraced Ethiopia 43
3. Protecting "Fertile Fields": The NAACP and Africa during the Cold War 72
4. "The Time for Freedom Has Come": Black Leadership in the Age of Decolonization 99
5. "We Are a Power Bloc": The Congressional Black Caucus and Africa 125

Conclusion 149

Notes 157
Index 195

Preface

This book is about the complex ideational dynamics that shape the behavior of black politicians, social movement activists, and intellectuals as they engage with issues in U.S. foreign policy toward Africa. My journey to complete this project was rooted in some of the same ideas that pushed the subjects of this study to either embrace or reject an association with the continent of Africa in the U.S. foreign policymaking arena. Fortunately, I always had the benefit of several dense networks of support as I confronted the dialectic process of understanding the ties that bind black Americans to their historical motherland.

There is no doubt that my initial interest in Africa was stoked by the many reassuring and rich conversations that I had about race relations with my immediate family in the shadow of the Civil Rights Movement. Indeed, I first discovered that I was both black and a descendant of Africa when my parents, Alvin B. Tillery Sr. and Jacquelyn Peterson Tillery, sat me down in the living room of my maternal grandparents, Millar ("Jack") Peterson and Thelma Peterson, to watch the premiere of the *Roots* miniseries on ABC. Even more vividly than the gruesome depiction of the "seasoning process," in which the overseer forces LeVar Burton's character, Kunta Kinte, to adopt the name Toby, I remember that the miniseries evoked long-buried oral traditions of African ancestry among my family members.

I carried these stories of my African nobility back to my school in the integrated Penrose Park neighborhood of West Philadelphia the following week, where they eventually blended in with the narratives my cohorts brought to school in the run up to St. Patrick's Day and Columbus Day. Ironically, it was not until my parents, seeking better housing options, moved our family to a suburb in New Jersey that my African ancestry reentered the forefront of my consciousness. This time, however, my real connection to the continent emerged through the perpetual chants of "spear chucker" that I heard throughout the day from those who resented my presence in their formerly all-white space. I owe a debt of gratitude to my parents for countering this psychological assault by exposing my brother, Julian Ethan Tillery, and me to very tangible information about the realities of Africa through books, museums, and art in our home.

My formal education about both black politics and Africa began at Morehouse College in 1989. At Morehouse, I was fortunate to encounter highly competent and caring professors in both these fields. Professor Tobe Johnson taught me what it meant to do serious empirical research on the black presence in U.S. political institutions and was the first person to encourage me to view political science as my vocation. Professor Hamid Taqi, who was himself a political refugee from Sierra Leone, gave me my first sense of the realities of African postcolonial politics and economics.

I was also fortunate to encounter many faculty members at Morehouse who embraced modes of thought about racial identity in the United States and Africa that challenged the mainstream paradigms of my two primary mentors. Professor Hassan Crockett was the first person to expose me to ideas that now fall clearly within the field of black diaspora studies. I also owe a debt to Professor Aaron L. Parker, who sprinkled important readings on the debate over Afrocentricity into his courses on religion and philosophy. These experiences prepared me well for the robust debate that I would find raging over these issues when I arrived at Harvard University to begin my doctoral studies.

My interactions with classmates and friends at Morehouse and the entire Atlanta University Center opened my eyes to how deeply ambivalent black Americans were about both their status as Americans and relationship with Africa. Indeed, daily debates would break out on the "yards" of Morehouse, Spelman College, and Clark-Atlanta University about whether we as a people in the United States should call ourselves *Black, Afro-Americans, African-Americans,* or *Africans* and what obligations we owed to the race and the motherland. We never really resolved any of these issues, but the fact that we took as much joy from Nelson Mandela gaining his freedom as we did watching Douglas Wilder, the grandchild of slaves, win the governorship of Virginia in 1990 points to our shared baseline orientation toward pan-Africanism. I thank William O. Generett Jr., Brian Nelson, Edward Thomas, Melvin D. Smith II, Julian Tillery, Nicole (Hunt) Strange, Jennifer (Williams) Ben, Otis Moss III, Michelle (Hughis) Flagg, Shaka A. Rasheed, Ardythe (Williams) Mitchell, Thomas Espy, Lawrence Humphreys, Jamal Bryant, Deidre Bailey, Seldon Peden, Afi Davis, Philip Edmonds, Torre Jessup, and Nima Warfield for helping me navigate these debates.

When I entered Harvard University to pursue my doctoral studies in political science in 1993, my plan was to study comparative politics with a focus on state formation and democratic transitions in Africa. I am thankful for the warm reception and excellent training that I received from the distinguished Harvard community of Africanist scholars: Robert Bates, Kwame Anthony Appiah, Martin Kilson, Jennifer Widner, and Emanuel Ackyeampong. I am particularly grateful to Professor Bates for becoming my primary advisor as I prepared a proposal for a study of the restoration of traditional monarchies in transitional Uganda and pursued a grant from the Social Science Research Council (SSRC) to fund the project. Moreover, the support that I received from Professor Bates when

I finished in the "honorable mention" pile of the SSRC competition gave me the courage to stay in the Ph.D. program and shift directions to the project that ultimately became the foundation for this book.

I also thank Professor Bates for urging me to ask Professor Kwame Anthony Appiah, who had collaborated with him during their overlapping tenures at Duke University, to serve on my committee for the project. Professor Appiah's *In My Father's House: Africa in the Philosophy of Culture* (New York: Oxford University Press, 1992) had been the key text in helping me (and most of my cohorts in the Harvard African studies seminars) shed essentialist thinking about Africa.

As any graduate student knows, just because one has the option of working with a faculty member does not mean that it will happen. I thank Professor Appiah for taking me on as a student in the midst of his frenzied schedule as a writer, teacher, and public intellectual. Whatever I know about the historiography of the Pan-African movement, I learned from him. I am also grateful to Professor Appiah for maintaining an open-door policy with me as I finished the project and for continuing to provide encouragement as I generated the revisions that led to this book. Finally, I am deeply indebted to him for providing me with a host of professional development experiences during my Harvard years, including my first teaching assistantship and lecture opportunities.

Whereas Professors Bates and Appiah helped me nail down the dimensions of the project in terms of African politics and Pan-African history, Professor Michael Jones-Correa was the one who ensured that this project fit within the subfield of American politics. Indeed, it was through my interactions with Professor Jones-Correa that I gained exposure to the core theories that animate the study of U.S. racial and ethnic politics. His multimethod approach to these issues in U.S. politics was also a great source of inspiration. Moreover, the almost daily conversations that I had with him about the project and his meticulous attention to my chapters kept me on pace in the final stages of writing. Finally, I owe him thanks for urging me to reconceptualize (and not abandon) the project when it became clear that two important works published in the same year that I graduated from Harvard mirrored my approach.

I also thank Professors Louise Richardson, Peter Hall, Richard "Dick" Neustadt, Morris Fiorina, Ken Shepsle, Keith Bybee, Peter Berkowitz, and Nathan Glazer for supportive comments and conversations during my six years at Harvard. Interactions with my cohort—Eric Narcisse, Jason Needleman, Kira Sanbonmatsu, Claudine Gay, Joao Resende-Santos, J. P. Gownder, Ben Berger, Kanchan Chandra, Stephen Marshall, Shirley Thompson-Marshall, Naunihal Singh, Lawrence Hamlet, and Jacques Hymans—during my Harvard days and beyond have also enriched the project. Finally, I would have never survived my days in Cambridge without the support of Daniel Victor Alexandre, Jimmy Price,

Allison Carter-Marlowe, Bit (Bingham) Alexander, Betty Bingham, Hafsat Abiola, D'yetra (Hall) Mendes, Pamela Boone, Carter Morse, Giana Eckardt, Chris Douglas, and Ayanna (Hudson) Higgins.

I completed most of the research that gave this project new life during my six years as a junior faculty member at the University of Notre Dame. Obviously, the most significant experience of my time at Notre Dame was meeting my wife, Maferima (Touré) Tillery, a native of Côte d'Ivoire in West Africa. Merging our two families and bringing our daughter Norah into the world has only reaffirmed my belief that Africa is a second home front for black Americans. I thank Maferima and Norah for their enduring patience as I worked through many evenings and weekends to complete this book. I also thank Mariam (Mama) Touré for providing so much support to all of us during this time.

Beyond my family, I am also grateful for the many supportive voices that I found among my faculty colleagues during my Notre Dame years. I am particularly indebted to Rodney Hero, Eileen Hunt Botting, Layna Mosley, Peri Arnold, David Nickerson, Alexandra Guisinger, Ruth Abbey, Dianne Pinderhughes, Michael Zuckert, John Roos, Richard Pierce, Hugh Page, Neal Delaney, Toni Irving, Tom Guglielmo, and Emily Osborn for their feedback and encouragement. Angela Ingram, Maria Mota Monteiro, Christy Fleming-Greene, Alan Greene, T. D. Ball, Mariana Sousa, Anabella Espana-Najera, Cheri Gray, Keir Lieber, Carolina Arroyo, Kathy Johndrow, Gina Shropshire, Reanna Ursin, Josh Kaplan, Shawtina Ferguson, and Charles Hedman provided me with a dense social network of support. Finally, the Notre Dame McNair Scholars program and Institute for Scholarship in the Liberal Arts provided me with funding to hire an excellent corps of research assistants that included John Biel Henry, Michell Chresfield, Meagan Brittain, William David Williams, Andrea DeVries, Shanida Sharpe, Angela Huang, Jazmin Garcia, Vanessa Allen, Dagoberto Garcia, and Cora Fernandez.

During my fourth year at Notre Dame, I was fortunate to win the Du Bois-Mandela-Rodney Postdoctoral Fellowship from the Center for African and African-American Studies at the University of Michigan in Ann Arbor. The center provided me with generous financial support and space to complete the archival research that distinguishes this book from the original project. I am grateful to James Jackson, Kevin Kelly Gaines, Penny Von Eschen, Lori Brooks, Julius Scott III, V. Robin Grice, Derrick "Chuck" Phillips, and Don Simms for their incredible hospitality during my year at the center.

I completed the book during my transition to a teaching post at Rutgers University. Conversations with my new colleagues, Jane Junn, Dennis Bathory, Lisa Miller, Dan Tichenor, Beth Leech, Rick Lau, and Kira Sanbonmatsu, kept me focused and filled with confidence in these last days. I also thank Hanes Walton, Paul Frymer, Janelle Wong, Shayla Nunnally, Niambi Carter, Chrissy Greer,

Dorian Warren, Ira Katznelson, Thomas "Tim" Borstelmann, Mary Dudziak, John Skrentny, Dennis Chong, Desmond King, Phil Klinkner, Mark Sawyer, Reuel Rogers, and the anonymous reviewers of the manuscript for insightful and supportive comments on the work.

I would be remiss if I did not thank Roger Haydon, Peter Wissoker, and Michael McGandy for shepherding the manuscript through the process at Cornell University Press. I am also grateful to Candace Akins, Julie Nemer, and the incredibly efficient Cornell University Press copyediting and production team. Finally, I thank Reanna Ursin, Julie Brunneau, Jennifer Molidor, and Sophie Cox for the freelance copyediting services they provided at various stages in the development of the manuscript.

Part of the section in chapter 3 titled "Keeping Africa Safe from the Reds" is drawn from my essay "G. Mennen 'Soapy' Williams and the American Negro Leadership Conference on Africa: Rethinking the Origins of Multiculturalism in U.S. Foreign Policy," which appears in Hanes Walton and Robert Louis Stevenson, eds., *The African Foreign Policy of Secretary of State Henry Kissinger* (Lanham, Md.: Lexington Books, 2007). Similarly, the sections in chapter 5 titled "Welcome to the House" and "The Diggs Plan" were published as part of my article "Foreign Policy Activism and Power in the House of Representatives: Black Members of Congress and South Africa, 1968–1986," which appears in *Studies in American Political Development* 20, no. 1 (2006): 88–103.

BETWEEN HOMELAND
AND MOTHERLAND

INTRODUCTION

> **Just as we were called colored, but were not that, to be called black is just as baseless. Every ethnic group in this country has reference to some cultural base. African-Americans have hit that level of maturity.**
>
> —Jesse Jackson Sr., speech in Chicago, Illinois, 1988
>
> **All politics is local.**
>
> —Thomas P. ("Tip") O'Neill (D-Mass.), speaker of the House, 1977–1987

On February 23, 1999, Representative Jesse Jackson Jr. (D-Ill.) took the floor of the U.S. House of Representatives to deliver a speech in support of his signature legislative priority in the 106th Congress—the Human Rights, Opportunity, Partnership and Empowerment (HOPE) for Africa Act. In the speech, Representative Jackson urged his colleagues to embrace his HOPE bill to defend African nations against burgeoning "trade pressures" imposed by the United States and the World Trade Organization (WTO). In short, Jackson argued that the U.S. government should be working to extend more aid to the continent rather than forcing these nations to sign on to a "NAFTA [North American Free Trade Agreement] for Africa."[1]

For more than two generations, political scientists and diplomatic historians have maintained that transnationalism is the best lens through which to understand the way that the elite members of minority groups mobilize on behalf of their ancestral homelands in the U.S. foreign policymaking arena.[2] Social scientists use the term *transnationalism* to refer to an orientation that leads individuals and groups living in one nation to engage in behaviors that maintain active linkages with their ancestral homelands.[3] Most researchers see transnationalism as rooted in rich affective ties to "families, communities, traditions, and causes" in the ancestral homeland.[4] Moreover, there is broad consensus within the literature that most transnationalist behaviors are signaling games designed to reinforce collective identities.[5] Under this view, measures such as Representative Jackson's HOPE bill are expressive behaviors aimed at emphasizing and strengthening affective ties to ancestral homelands.[6] This theory is so popular among scholars of political science and history that it holds the status of a universal explanation, or covering law, within these disciplines.⁷ In other words, whenever most researchers in these fields see the elite members of ethnic and racial groups mobilizing around an issue in the U.S. foreign policymaking arena that affects their ancestral homelands, they assume that commitments derived from affective ties to these homelands are the *sole* explanation for this political behavior.

On first glance, Representative Jackson's behavior does seem to conform to the predictions generated by this dominant paradigm. After all, Jackson was a rising star within the Congressional Black Caucus (CBC), an organization with a long-standing history of advocacy on behalf of Africa, when he introduced his HOPE bill. Moreover, Jackson, the eldest son of the veteran civil rights activist Jesse Jackson Sr., used his own formidable oratorical skills and the symbols of the civil rights movement to play up the transnationalist dimensions of his support for the bill in his speech and his subsequent contacts with the press.⁸

When we delve a little deeper into the legislative history of the HOPE bill, however, an empirical puzzle emerges that confounds the dominant paradigm. Jackson's reference to NAFTA in his speech was a thinly veiled attack on the African Growth and Opportunity Act (AGOA), a rival measure designed to promote greater free trade between the United States and the African continent. Although the AGOA was by no means a perfect compact, all forty-seven African governments recognized by the United Nations were enthusiastic about the legislation and had spent considerable financial and diplomatic resources during the 106th Congress working to secure its passage.⁹ Moreover, many of these same governments had pushed for decades for greater access to U.S. products and markets through trade relationships.¹⁰ So, why would Representative Jackson introduce legislation to protect African nations from trade relationships that they openly courted? More important, how would Jackson forge closer ties with the ancestral homeland by opposing the AGOA?

The fact of the matter is that Representative Jackson probably knew well before he introduced the measure that his HOPE bill had little chance of altering the course of U.S. relations with Africa. Indeed, Jackson introduced the measure to provide ideological cover for himself and other black members of Congress who opposed the AGOA because they feared that it would have a deleterious effect on either their constituents or powerful political allies on the home front. In other words, Jackson's HOPE bill was really a strategic move designed to advance his interests in the domestic political environment and not an expressive act borne of affective ties to the African continent.

This narrative is just one of many that I will recount in this book that demonstrate the necessity of pushing beyond the expressive behavior model of the motivations of ethnic and racial groups in the U.S. foreign policymaking arena. This is not to say that the expressive behavior model holds no analytical or predictive power for understanding the motivations of the elite members of these groups when engaging with U.S. foreign policy toward their ancestral homelands. On the contrary, we have a wealth of empirical evidence that suggests that emotive commitments derived from a transnationalist orientation do often play an important, and sometimes even *necessary*, role in the equation. At the same time, there is clear evidence that such commitments are rarely *sufficient* to lead black activists, intellectuals, and politicians to take up the work of advocating for their ancestral homelands in the U.S. foreign policymaking arena.

The decisions that minority elites make about mobilizing in the foreign policymaking arena on behalf of their homelands emerge from strategic calculations balancing the value of the engagement against the costs accrued in the domestic arena. In short, the behavior of the majority of the black intellectuals, politicians, and social movement leaders—whose activism takes center stage in this book—conforms to the logic of two-level games first articulated by scholars of international relations in the 1960s.[11] Black leaders tend to make their most robust transnationalist (or Pan-African) expressions in the U.S. foreign policymaking arena when such activism dovetails with the goals that they are pursuing in the domestic arena.[12] By contrast, when expressions of transnationalism hold the potential to generate cross-pressures—such as the ones Representative Jackson and some of his colleagues faced around the AGOA—or threaten goals that they are pursuing on the home front, black elites typically disengage from serious foreign policy efforts on behalf of their ancestral homelands.

Over the past several decades, scholars of voting behavior and legislative studies have repeatedly demonstrated that the long history of systemic antiblack racism in the United States has created special bonds among black Americans.[13] In this book, I present numerous cases in which these bonds magnified the effect of the representational imperatives that typically lead the elite members of ethnic and racial groups to privilege their commitments in the domestic environment over transnationalist activities in the foreign policymaking arena. Moreover, these same bonds also help us to understand why transnationalist initiatives in the foreign policymaking arena have occasionally become domesticated issues in black politics.[14]

This model of black elite behavior in the U.S. foreign policymaking arena holds many advantages over the dominant paradigm. First, it allows us to account for the fact that the expressions of transnationalism made by black elites have waxed and waned over time. Second, it brings domestic politics back into the equation, which helps us to adjudicate recent debates among scholars of black politics about how black leaders' engagement with issues in African affairs shapes their ability to represent their constituents on the domestic policy arena. Third, by demonstrating that black elites filter their decisions about mobilizing on behalf of Africa through a heuristic derived from calculations of their domestic interests, it provides a strong challenge to those who argue that such behavior is irredentist.

Theoretical Context and Core Arguments

It is easy to understand why so many scholars subscribe to the view that transnationalism drives the behavior of the black elite on issues in African affairs. The vast majority of studies took place in the wake of the civil rights and black power movements; this means that social scientists and historians turned their attention to this issue at a time when the identification of black Americans with Africa was near its zenith.[15] With so many black politicians and activists extolling the importance of affective ties to Africa during that period,[16] transnationalism appeared to provide the perfect covering law to explain the actions of the black elite in the U.S. foreign policymaking arena. Moreover, this explanation dovetailed with findings about the behavior of elite actors from European-descent ethnic groups, which added further credibility to the model.[17]

But, unlike covering laws in the field of experimental physics, which are ironclad, even the most well-established theories of political behavior are only probabilistic in nature.[18] This means that counterexamples will always present challenges to the validity of theories that we use to make sense of political life. Despite the fact that many social scientists advocate that we strive for the same degree of validity that physical scientists achieve in their work, those who support the dominant theory of black elite behavior have been slow to acknowledge cases that call that theory into question.

This is so for two reasons. First, most of the studies used to support the dominant theory focus on a very short time period—the twenty-nine years between the emergence of Ghana as an independent nation and the Comprehensive Anti-Apartheid Act of 1986—when black politicians, intellectuals, and activists were hypermobilized around African affairs. Thus, the first qualitative studies of black elite engagement with Africa were based on samples in which respondents overwhelmingly attributed their behavior to transnationalism rooted in affective ties to the continent.[19]

It is tempting to accuse these scholars of the type of selection bias that methodologists such as Barbara Geddes have demonstrated frequently undermines single-case designs.[20] Geddes rightly argues that "selecting on the dependent variable" leads to "pitfalls" in case-study research by "overestimating" the role that a causal variable plays in explaining an outcome.[21] To get around this problem, Geddes urges researchers to "examine a wider range of cases."[22] The problem for the scholars who conducted the first wave of studies of black elite engagement with U.S. foreign policy toward Africa is that knowledge about previous epochs was extremely limited. Indeed, the majority of historical accounts of black elite behavior in the U.S. foreign policymaking arena did not appear until several years after the first social science studies.

Moreover, and this is the second reason why the dominant theory has not been vigorously challenged, the majority of the historical literature focuses on black elite behavior between 1935 and 1960. During this period, according to these studies, the Cold War context forced black elites to suppress their natural tendency to mobilize on behalf of Africa in the U.S. foreign policymaking arena to avoid persecution on the home front. In short, the consensus within the historical literature is that exogenous shocks are the major source of variation in black elite behavior.[23]

My goal in this book is not to overturn the view that transnationalism is an important force motivating the black elite in its attempts to shape U.S. foreign policy toward Africa. On the contrary, many dimensions of the analytic narratives presented here provide confirmation of this theory. But, at the same time, the narratives show that transnationalism alone is typically insufficient to mobilize the black elite to try to influence U.S. foreign policy toward Africa. Moreover, a transnationalist outlook does not guarantee that black politicians and activists will work constructively on behalf of what they understand to be the interests of the African continent. Consider, for example, that Representative Jackson and many of the other fifteen CBC members who were against the AGOA frequently professed to hold transnationalist commitments at the same time that they were working to kill the bill.

Recognizing that black politicians and activists view their activities in the foreign policymaking arena as fundamentally bound up with their activities in the domestic environment is the best way to resolve this conundrum and the many others presented in the substantive chapters. In short, members of the black elite strive to strike a balance between their political activities in the domestic arena and their activism in the U.S. foreign policymaking arena. Indeed, scholars of international relations have long argued that U.S. foreign policy is often rooted in domestic sources. Many of the early works in this literature simply demonstrated that U.S. policies tended to reflect the values of the U.S. public as expressed through opinion surveys.[24] Other studies traced the origins of U.S. foreign policy back to a remote cause in the domestic sphere through detailed "policy histories."[25]

In 1978, Robert D. Putnam presented the first systematic evidence of a link between the domestic sphere and the behavior of the governmental officials who control the formulation of U.S. foreign policy. After observing several rounds of international negotiations, Putnam concluded that U.S. diplomats consider what is best for powerful domestic interests when negotiating international treaties. Putnam referred to this tendency of diplomats to seek to balance their commitments to abstract principles against the demands of powerful domestic interests as the "logic of two-level games."[26] The analytic narratives presented in this book demonstrate that the engagement by the black elite with issues in U.S. foreign policy toward Africa conforms to this same two-level logic. In other words, black activists and politicians pay considerable attention to how their actions in the U.S. foreign policymaking arena will play with their constituents and affect the entire black community in the domestic environment.

The historians who documented the way that groups such as the National Association for the Advancement of Colored People (NAACP) reduced their rhetorical attacks on U.S. allies that held colonies in Africa during the Cold War to avoid persecution during the Red Scare were certainly aware of this underlying dynamic. The limitation of these studies, however, is that their focus on the exogenous nature of the repressive climate that accompanied the rise of the national security state under Harry Truman obscures that this balancing between the priorities of U.S. foreign policy and the demands of the home front is the equilibrium position for black politicians and activists. In other words, the Cold War was not an exception to the rule but, rather, merely an instance of the two-level game that leaders have played since the early nineteenth century. Moreover, an examination of black elite engagement with African affairs over a longer period shows that dynamics internal to the black community play a large role in shaping its ability to pursue transnationalist initiatives in the U.S. foreign policymaking arena.

In the wake of the landmark National Black Election Studies (NBES) conducted by Patricia Gurin, Shirley J. Hatchett, and James Jackson in 1984 and 1988, public opinion scholars reached a consensus that upper- and middle-income blacks think very differently about racial group membership than do their white counterparts.[27] In short, upper- and middle-income blacks demonstrate a strong sense of linked fate with other blacks. Michael Dawson claims that this finding is a function of the fact that "until at least the late 1960s, individual African Americans' life chances were over determined by the ascriptive feature of race."[28] In light of this regularity, Dawson argues, black Americans developed a "black utility heuristic" to "economize" the decision-making process about both policies and political candidates.[29] "This heuristic," he continues, "suggests that as long as race remains dominant in determining the lives of individual blacks, it is rational for American Americans to follow group cues in interpreting and acting in the political world."[30] In addition, Dawson asserts that the "tendency of African Americans to follow racial cues has been reinforced historically by institutions developed during the forced separation of blacks from whites during the post-Reconstruction period."[31]

Several scholars have argued recently that black members of Congress rely on a similar schema to guide their behavior as legislators.[32] "The Congressional Black Caucus," Katherine Tate writes, "would declare its mission as national with a primary focus on the needs and interests of Black Americans."[33] Similarly, Richard Fenno writes that black legislators see themselves as "representing a national constituency of black citizens who live beyond the border of any one member's district, but with whom all black members share a set of race-related concerns."[34] The tendency for black leaders to exhibit a strong sense of linked fate with their constituents did not start with black members of Congress serving in the Post–Civil Rights Era. On the contrary, as Kevin Gaines demonstrates in his seminal historical work on black leadership, *Uplifting the Race,* this norm has been deeply rooted among black activists and politicians since at least the late nineteenth century.[35]

Building on this body of work, I show that the strong sense of sharing a group identity with the black masses leads black elites to privilege the domestic context over the international when trying to balance their political portfolios. As a result, black leaders have the most freedom to engage issues in U.S. foreign policy toward Africa when such mobilization either bears no costs or generates positive benefits on the home front. Moreover, members of the black elite sometimes mobilize in the foreign policymaking arena primarily to generate these externalities. Indeed, this type of behavior—which proponents of the two-level game model in the international relations literature call second-image effects—is frequently in evidence in the narratives presented in this book.[36]

The importance of transnationalism as a force that sometimes motivates members of the black elite to engage with issues in U.S. foreign policy toward Africa is undeniable. It is also clear, however, that black leaders set limits on how far they will go in the U.S. foreign policymaking arena based on calculations about what is expedient for black Americans on the home front. There are times, as several scholars have pointed out, when the black community becomes hypermobilized around events in Africa and the distinction between the domestic and international arenas becomes blurred.[37] Yet these periods when issues in U.S. foreign policy become so domesticated[38] within the black community that they are transposed into just another racial group interest are exceedingly rare. Indeed, black politicians receive cues from their constituents, demonstrating Representative Thomas P. ("Tip") O'Neil's maxim that "All politics is local." This finding presents a significant challenge to those, such as Samuel Huntington, who argue that that the tendency of ethnic and racial groups to mobilize around the concerns of their ancestral homelands in the foreign policymaking arena portends the Balkanization of the United States.[39]

Although black elite members generally work very hard to stay in line with the preferences that their constituents communicate through these cues, they are by no means completely subservient to public opinion in the black community. Indeed, some of the most dramatic episodes presented in the analytic narratives unpack conflicts that erupted between black leaders and the rank-and-file over issues in U.S. foreign policy toward Africa. As shown in chapter 1, the black elite's hostility toward the grassroots exodus movements that swept through black communities in the Counter-Reconstruction period is undoubtedly the most notable example of this type of conflict.

Some scholars have argued that the existence of such ruptures demonstrates that black leaders are often out of touch with the concerns and demands of their constituents. This argument cuts two ways in the literature on black leadership and representation. On the one hand, scholars such as Nell Painter, a historian, suggest that black leaders sometimes break ranks with their constituents in the U.S. foreign policymaking arena because they are interested in preserving their positions of privilege within the U.S. government.[40] On the other hand, Carol Swain, a political scientist, argues in her work on the CBC that black leaders often push foreign policy initiatives against the wishes of their constituents to generate second-image effects.[41] No matter how we parse the particulars, the bottom line is that both these scholars (and many others) assert that these conflicts between the masses and black leaders over transnationalist goals are evidence that the latter are failed representatives.

Building on Gaines's work, I show that these conflicts are more illustrative of the paternalism that often informs the black elite's commitment to uplifting their lower-class brethren than a complete abrogation of leadership. In short, the U.S. foreign policymaking arena sometimes becomes a theater in which black politicians and activists perform deeply flawed morality plays aimed at demonstrating to the masses that they know what is best for the race. Ironically, then, even on the few occasions when they have ignored the preferences of their constituents during these episodes, black leaders have seen themselves as fulfilling the representational imperatives dictated by the black utility heuristic. This interpretation aligns this book with studies by scholars who argue that black elites (though imperfect) have been mostly sincere brokers on behalf of their constituents in U.S. politics.[42]

Approach, Methods, and Data

The quantitative revolution that took place in American political science in the 1960s and 1970s had its most pronounced impact on the subfield of American politics.[43] Over the past two decades, the tolerance for multimethod research has grown dramatically within the subfield. This shift—which is still in process—is undoubtedly a product of the intense period of contestation over epistemology that has taken place within the entire discipline since the beginning of the twenty-first century.[44] At the same time, it is clear that two communities of scholars within the subfield, the American political development (APD) and race, ethnicity, and politics (REP) movements, have been at the cutting edge with regard to this issue for several decades.

Both groups of scholars pushed for greater methodological pluralism because they found quantitative approaches based on large data sets—which tend to present mere "snap-shots" of attitudes and institutional trends—insufficient for understanding the development of political dynamics over long periods.[45] Despite this common concern, cross-fertilization between APD and REP scholars has been minimal because APD scholars are generally interested in macro-level developments whereas REP scholars tend to focus on political behavior at the group and individual levels. Recently, scholars in both fields have called for greater integration between the two traditions.[46] For example, Hanes Walton, one of the deans of the study of black political behavior, has suggested that we would gain greater clarity about the connections between the concept of race and political outcomes if scholars working in the REP subfield eschewed their recent obsession with the individual and paid greater attention to institutions and social context.[47]

Taking up Walton's charge, in each chapter I situate the efforts of black leaders to exert influence in the U.S. foreign policymaking arena within the political context of the historical period under study. I do this by reconstructing elite discourse and mass opinion through analyses of archival materials and by taking stock of major shifts in institutional structure, partisan alignments, and the law that were of special concern to the black community during each period.[48] I then consider how some of the arguments that APD scholars make about institutional stability and temporality shed light on the behavior of the black elite in the U.S. foreign policymaking arena. Karen Orren and Stephen Skowronek, for example, have argued that we should pay greater attention to critical junctures that either reinforce the stable elements or puncture the equilibriums within institutions.[49] Looking at the historical record of black Americans' engagement with Africa in this way allows us to see the considerable continuity that has defined the behavior of the black elite in the U.S. foreign policymaking arena.

The analytic narratives approach I employ here anchors the research enterprise and synthesizes the insights developed by both APD and REP scholars. In other words, I test the deductive theory outlined through detailed narratives that span the period from 1816 to 2000. This approach, first developed by proponents of rational choice theory, holds several benefits over the available alternatives.[50] First, the approach facilitates the kind of congruence testing that is necessary to demonstrate the existence of the empirical puzzles under investigation.[51] The analytic narratives approach also enables the process tracing (the identification of new causal chains and mechanisms) required to establish the validity of the alternative theory of black elite behavior that I posit.[52] Social scientists use process tracing to, in the words of Stephen Van Evera, international relations scholar, "unwrap" and "divide into smaller steps" the links between causes and effects.[53] In short, process tracing is a search for causal mechanisms.

I use multiple sources of data to recover the narratives examined in this book. First, following in the footsteps of many eminent scholars in APD, comparative political development, and sociology, I use published secondary materials as the primary source of data.[54] The vast majority of the data used to make causal inferences about black elite behavior in the U.S. foreign policymaking arena, however, is the product of primary materials from archives,[55] public records, and human subjects.

Then, I employ several qualitative methods and statistical modeling to analyze these data.[56] I use content analysis of documents and print sources to develop proxies for elite attitudes and public opinion about issues in U.S. foreign policy toward Africa. The systematic analysis of media representations has long been a tool employed by social scientists to gain traction on questions in both public opinion and institutional research.[57] Moreover, political scientists interested in understanding racial dynamics in the United States have become particularly adept at using content analysis to arrive at richer explanations of political behavior and institutional dynamics.[58]

The Road Ahead

In chapter 1, I explore the ways that black elites engaged with U.S. foreign policy toward Africa between 1816 and 1900. Some scholars have argued that the behavior of the black elite has never held more significance for black Americans' domestic struggle for equality than it did in these years.[59] This is so because the federal government frequently promoted policies that encouraged black emigration to Liberia as a means of reconstituting the United States as an all-white republic. For the most part, during this period the black elite rejected any association with the African continent and worked hard to block policies that sought to stimulate the growth of Liberia. There are, however, several notable cases in which the black elite broke from this pattern and worked to assist the development of Liberia. The conventional wisdom is that the black elite's commitments to a transnational sense of community trumped their concerns about their black U.S. citizenship status during these periods.[60] But my analyses of the archival materials undermine this assertion. Indeed, I find that members of the black elite entered the foreign policymaking arena in support of Liberia only when they calculated that doing so would shift the national discourse about the capacity of the black race for U.S. citizenship.

In chapter 2, I examine the ways that black elites responded to Marcus Garvey's Universal Negro Improvement Association (UNIA) movement and the grassroots protest movement that emerged in black communities during the Italian-Ethiopian War. I focus on the question: Why did the black elite oppose Garveyism, perhaps the most successful mass movement with Pan-African goals in U.S. history, at a time when most black leaders were also committed to transnationalism in the U.S. foreign policy? Some studies maintain that the black elite members worked against Garvey because they viewed his rapid success in building a mass movement as a threat to the survival of their own organizations.[61] The majority of the literature, however, suggests that the rift between Garvey and the black leadership class was due to a clash of personalities.[62] The research presented in chapter 2 shows that black leaders shunned Garvey because they viewed his movement as an attempt to resurrect the long-repudiated ideology of emigrationism. Moreover, their strong sense of linked fate with the black masses made most of the leading activists, politicians, and intellectuals in the black community hypersensitive to the exploitative dimensions of the Garvey movement. In addition, the black elite feared that Garvey's high potential for failure would damage the credibility of the black masses in the public sphere.

The literature dealing with the black elite's engagement with issues in U.S. foreign policy toward Africa focuses primarily on the activities of the NAACP between 1935 and 1955.[63] According to most of these studies, during the interwar period the NAACP entered the foreign policymaking arena on behalf of Africa as part of a strategy to build a global movement against racism and colonialism.[64] The rise of the Cold War then forced the NAACP to set aside its political commitments derived from transnationalism to avoid persecution by the national security state of the Truman administration.[65] The conventional wisdom within this body of scholarship also sees this strategic shift as facilitating the collapse of anticolonial politics in the black community during this period.[66] In chapter 3, I challenge all of these assumptions. As I show, the NAACP (and other mainstream civil rights organizations) always saw its anticolonial agitation as an extension of its politics on the home front. As a result, the shift of the organization to an anticommunist anticolonialism was well in line with its behavior before World War II. Most important, the NAACP was able to use this anticommunist frame as a political means to push the Truman and John F. Kennedy administrations on the issue of colonialism in Africa. There is, in fact, evidence that bureaucrats within the Kennedy administration invited these groups into the policy formulation process to gain a greater degree of autonomy within the executive branch. This finding provides a strong challenge to the view that bureaucrats within the national security state have viewed black elite activism on behalf of Africa with antipathy.

In chapter 4, I demonstrate how the political context of black politics shifted in response to the decolonization movements that swept across Africa beginning in the 1950s. My main finding is that both the black elite and the masses rewrote their prevailing notions of black authenticity in response to these African decolonization movements. This new black authenticity grew out of the notion that Africa was now a place to look for models to challenge white supremacy on the home front. Due to this transformation, black Americans now saw their collective fate as linked with the new nations in Africa. Although, the black elite and the rank-and-file generally agreed on the terms of this new authenticity, the paternalistic notion held by members of the black elite that they were in control of the civil rights movement did sometimes lead to conflict between these two segments of the community. These occasional breaks, however, were far less frequent than the scholarly literature suggests. Indeed, for the most part, there was widespread agreement within the black community about the importance of Africa for the domestic movement by the close of the UN Year of Africa.

In chapter 5, I focus on the role that the CBC has played in the formulation of U.S. foreign policy toward Africa since the 1960s. The pivotal role of the CBC in passing the Comprehensive Anti-Apartheid Act (CAAA) of 1986 (which placed sanctions on South Africa) forms the backdrop to my account. Previous studies tend to view the activism of the CBC on this issue as a function of its deep commitments to striking down the last vestiges of settler colonialism in Africa and to forging ties with the ancestral homeland.[67] My analyses of archival materials and interviews with important members of the black elite confirm that affective ties to black South Africans living under apartheid were an important force motivating the CBC during its long campaign to pass a sanctions bill. I also demonstrate here that strategic calculations about what was expedient on the home front played an even larger role in pushing the CBC to initiate sanctions legislation; moreover, the black legislators' domestic orientation is crucial for understanding the contours of CBC activism in African affairs since 1986. Both the statistical analyses and interviews with CBC members presented in chapter 5 demonstrate that affective ties to the African continent remained robust within the group. These same data also reveal, however, that those CBC members who worked to defeat the AGOA did so because they feared that the bill would generate dire economic consequences for their constituents. Thus, the same logic that pushed the entire CBC to enter the U.S. foreign policymaking arena on behalf of South Africa in the 1980s encouraged many black legislators to oppose the AGOA in 2000.

Following the tests of my core arguments in the narrative chapters of the book, in my concluding chapter I evaluate the contributions of the strategic behavior model of black elite activism in the U.S. foreign policymaking arena. The first broad contribution is the way in which the model helps us to resolve the problems associated with the fact that the commitments of black leaders to mobilize on behalf of Africa waxes and wanes over time. Indeed, were the expressive behavior model an accurate depiction of reality, we would expect the majority of black elites to remain constantly mobilized around the stated preferences advanced by the governments of their ancestral homelands. On the contrary, as the behavior of Representative Jackson and many other figures who take center stage in this book illustrates, black leaders often take policy positions that stand in opposition to the goals that the governments of their ancestral homeland pursue in the U.S. foreign policy. As I show, the two-level games metaphor at the heart of the strategic behavior model gives us greater theoretical purchase on the behavior of the black elite in the U.S. foreign policymaking arena because it is clear that black leaders jealously guard their interests and those of their constituents in the domestic arena. This model, in addition, has broad applicability to other racial and ethnic groups. Finally, I show how this alternative theory also helps us resolve recent intellectual debates about the impact of transnationalism on U.S. foreign policy and the quality of black representation in U.S. politics.

1

"NOT ONE WAS WILLING TO GO!"
The Paradoxes of "Liberia's Offerings"

> **We want colored men, when colonizationists press upon them the propriety of emigrating to Liberia, or anywhere else, to give them this simple and decided answer: We will not go!**
>
> —J. D., editorial in the *North Star*, September 14, 1849

> **The Negro-hating disposition of the General Government is also seen in its ungenerous, dishonorable and despicable conduct toward Liberia.... The United States has steadily and persistently refused to acknowledge their independence.**
>
> —Ohio, letter to *Frederick Douglass' Paper*, March 16, 1855

The U.S. Congress established formal diplomatic relations with Liberia in February 1862. A little less than one year later, on January 13, 1863, a delegation from the new ally disembarked in Washington, D.C., to pursue two goals. First, the Liberian envoys wanted to shore up diplomatic relations with the Abraham Lincoln administration; second, they hoped to stimulate interest in emigration among the black population of the United States. The historical record is largely silent about whether the delegates achieved their first goal; there is no evidence that the delegation met with Lincoln or any of his high-ranking deputies. We do know, however, that the delegates toured free black communities with a stump speech and pamphlet on Liberia entitled "Liberia's Offerings" and that they had widespread contacts with members of the black elite. We also know that the delegates came away from this tour disappointed that free blacks did not receive the call of their fledgling nation to join in cultivating "Liberia's offerings" with the enthusiasm that they had predicted.[1]

Alexander Crummell, the only U.S.-born member of the delegation, wrote to a friend with great sadness about his people's "diminutive" interest in the "resources of Africa."[2] In his view, the troubles that he and his fellow delegates had in selling their new nation to black Americans were rooted in the fact that generations of slaves had learned to "repudiate any close contact and peculiar connection with Africa."[3] Nevertheless, Crummell also held out hope that subsequent missions would raise black Americans' consciousness to the point where they would recognize their "duty" to "labor for the salvation of the mighty millions of their kin" in Africa.[4]

Crummell lived to see the day when a sizable number (and perhaps even the majority) of black Americans took a greater interest in Liberia. Indeed, Liberia Fever ran rampant among the poor and abused victims of the Hayes-Tilden Compromise of 1877. Unfortunately, Crummell also suffered the heartbreak of watching men and women of his own social class in the United States squelch the grassroots exodus movements that sought to translate this interest in Liberia into tangible streams of emigration. "The chief obstacle to a healthy emigration from America," Crummell wrote to a member of the Liberian Senate in 1878, "is the unhealthy meddling of the *better classes* among the Freedmen [*sic*]."[5]

Previous studies of the engagement of the black elite with U.S. foreign policy toward Africa during this period have largely concurred with Crummell's assessment. Indeed, the conventional wisdom within the fields of social history and African American studies is that the members of the black elite quashed the exodus movements because they viewed them as a threat to their own ability to extract patronage positions from the Republican Party.[6] Other scholars take a more benign view of the black elite by suggesting that their opposition to the exodus movements was a function of a bifurcated class structure that made them unaware of the hardships that most blacks faced under the Counter-Reconstruction regimes.[7]

Both these arguments cut against the grain of the vast majority of the political science literature on black representation since the publication of Michael Dawson's influential *Behind the Mule: Race and Class in African-American Politics*. Dawson argues quite persuasively that members of the black elite have maintained deep bonds of attachment to low-status blacks since at least the rise of the abolitionist movement of the early nineteenth century. This sense of linked fate, Dawson asserts, has been the *modus operandi* of the black elite when they have sought to represent the interests of lower-class blacks in the public sphere.[8] Although some important studies in the field of black politics have recently questioned whether the black elite act on this imperative when dealing with marginalized members of the black community,[9] few political scientists question the general validity of the theory or Dawson's decision to locate the origins of linked fate in the politics of the abolitionist movement.

In this chapter, I reconcile the opposition of the black elite to the exodus movements of the late nineteenth century with the traditional understandings of the dynamics of black representation in political science. The qualitative and quantitative analyses of archival materials presented here demonstrate that black elites saw themselves as defending the interests of the black lower classes when they entered the U.S. foreign policymaking arena to quash emigrationism. Moreover, the research I present also reveals that lower-class blacks embraced Liberia not as a primordial homeland but as a safe haven from the hardships of the

Counter-Reconstruction. Thus, contrary to both Crummell's analysis and the conventional wisdom in the literature on Pan-Africanism, the black masses did not exhibit a greater commitment to the view that Africa was, in the words of Elliot Skinner, "the land of their nativity."[10]

Paul Cuffe's Movement

Any discussion of black elite engagement with Africa in the U.S. foreign policy-making arena in the late nineteenth century must begin with Paul Cuffe. A free black man and a wealthy merchant, Cuffe launched the most noteworthy of the many back-to-Africa movements that emerged in the antebellum North after the framers enshrined black inequality in the U.S. Constitution.[11] It is for this reason that many historians regard Cuffe as the "father of Pan-Africanism."[12]

Cuffe's movement began in earnest when he sailed one of his commercial vessels to Freetown, Sierra Leone, in 1811.[13] The British government had established the tiny hamlet on the western coast of Africa in 1787 to serve as a homeland for freed slaves from both the British Isles and the West Indies. Cuffe was so enamored of what he saw in this colony for "returned" blacks that he informed British authorities that he intended to encourage the "finest characters" among the free black population in the United States to resettle in Sierra Leone.[14]

Cuffe was apparently a very skilled salesman during his tours through the free black communities of Boston, New York, Philadelphia, and Baltimore. Indeed, less than a year later he had recruited enough volunteers to organize a return voyage to Freetown.[15] The strict embargo that the U.S. Congress placed on all intercourse with Great Britain during the War of 1812, however, prevented Cuffe from transporting this first wave of would-be emigrants to Freetown.[16]

Because the War of 1812 was primarily about access to the shipping lanes that linked the Old and New Worlds, the safest course of action would have been for Cuffe and his followers to delay their plans until after the conflict subsided. For the indefatigable Cuffe, however, a war on the high seas was no reason to put off a scheme that would eventually bring about the demise of slavery in the United States.[17] Thus, Cuffe decided to petition the Congress for a special dispensation from the embargo law.[18]

Cuffe's request for relief from the embargo passed the Senate on January 25, 1814;[19] this made him the first black American to win the support of the upper chamber on a policy matter. When the House of Representatives took up the matter two days later, Representative Timothy Pickering (F-Mass.) took to the floor to speak on behalf of his constituent's position. His comments, however, exposed his racist orientation more than any genuine support for the Cuffe plan.

Pickering's basic argument was that the House should support Cuffe's plan because it promised to "remove a population that [the United States] could well spare."[20] Despite the fact that many of his colleagues agreed that Cuffe's plan represented an excellent opportunity to rid the United States of free blacks, the majority of the House ultimately voted against the petition on the grounds of national security.[21]

When the conflict between the United States and Britain subsided in 1815, Cuffe immediately set sail for Sierra Leone with forty free blacks from Boston, New York, and Philadelphia.[22] Cuffe viewed the completion of this mission, which was the first time that anyone had successfully repatriated black Americans to Africa, as a great victory for the race. Moreover, his personal correspondence suggests that he expected the free black community in the United States to celebrate this victory with him. When Cuffe returned to the United States to begin recruiting a new crop of emigrants, however, he found that public opinion within free black population centers was hardening against his movement.[23] This shift in public opinion was a function of the activities of the American Colonization Society (ACS) in the black community during Cuffe's absence.[24]

Black Opposition to the American Colonization Society

The notion of repatriating free blacks to Africa had figured very little in mainstream political discourse before Cuffe emerged on the national scene.[25] But this changed dramatically after Cuffe's campaign to win an exemption from the U.S. government embargo against Great Britain during the War of 1812. Scholars of the black experience have frequently used the phrase *Liberia Fever* to describe the spike in emigrationist sentiment that took root among the freed blacks during the Counter-Reconstruction period.[26] The historical record suggests, however, that the very first outbreaks of Liberia Fever took place among the white men who roamed the halls of power within the U.S. capital in the wake of Cuffe's petition. Moreover, it is clear that many of the governmental officials who came down with Liberia Fever during this period nurtured a vision of a compulsory program that would eventually remove the entire free black population to West Africa.[27]

At the conclusion of the war, Henry Clay (DR-Ky.), who was in his second term as speaker of the House of Representatives, called a number of these men together with a few prominent members of white civil society and formed the ACS, with the express purpose of making this vision a reality.[28] Within weeks of its founding, the ACS initiated an aggressive campaign to raise funds and garner the necessary political support to establish a colony on the western coast of

Africa to serve as a dumping ground for the free black population. Not surprisingly, given the wealth and prestige of its founders, the ACS had very little trouble raising funds. Indeed, Philip J. Staudenraus, who has written the definitive history of the ASC, reports that in the its first month in operation "thousands of dollars flowed into the society for the purchase and charter of ships to transplant African-Americans to Africa."[29]

The quasi-governmental nature of the ACS also facilitated its ability to make quick gains on the political front. After just two weeks in operation, for example, the Virginia House of Delegates passed a bill that endorsed the efforts of the ACS and called on the White House to cooperate with the group.[30] On January 14, 1817, just one month after Henry Clay had organized the first ACS meeting, the House of Representatives began to debate the merits of extending the organization financial and logistical support.[31]

Historically oriented scholars in working the field of comparative politics and APD researchers use the concept critical junctures to, in the words of Paul Pierson, "mark a point [in a causal chain] at which their cases begin to diverge in significant ways."[32] The formation of the ACS was undoubtedly the critical juncture that turned the black elite against the ideology of emigrationism. Indeed, as the ACS gained momentum on Capitol Hill, boisterous protest meetings sprang up in free black population centers.[33] Moreover, like other critical junctures that comparativists and APD scholars have documented within institutions or during democratic transitions, the formation of the ACS and the protest movement that grew up in response to it had an enduring affect on black elite behavior in both the domestic and foreign policymaking arenas.[34]

Previous researchers have identified the primary source of free black opposition to the ACS as a strong sense of connection—what Dawson calls linked fate—with their kith and kin held in bondage.[35] There is certainly a wealth of evidence in the documentary record to support this interpretation. Consider, for example, the account by James Forten of how ACS activities soured public opinion toward repatriation to Africa in the Philadelphia black community. Writing just three days after the Congress took up the ACS petition for support, Forten reported to his old friend Paul Cuffe that black Philadelphians were so convinced that the organization was about continuing the "misery, sufferings and perpetual slavery" of their people that "not one was willing to go to Africa" under their auspices.[36]

The opposition of the free black community to the ACS was also rooted in a desire to defend their own stake in the United States. This fact comes across quite clearly when we examine the documents that emerged from the mass demonstrations where free blacks registered their disapprobation with the ACS. For example, the resolutions passed by the gathering of 3,000 free blacks who met at the Bethel African Methodist Episcopal (AME) Church rebuked the ACS for attempting to deny them their "birthrights" as descendants of the "first successful cultivators of the wilds of America."[37] Similarly the hundreds of free blacks who met in a protest meeting at Baltimore, Maryland, asserted that the fact that many black Americans had "rallied around the standard of *their* country" during the Revolutionary War had earned the community the right to be free from the harassment of the ACS.[38]

The free black community also demonstrated an equal commitment to defending the rights of enslaved blacks. Indeed, virtually all the protest documents that survive to this day also assign the inalienable rights of the Declaration of Independence to the enslaved. These statements were, however, often quite paternalistic in nature. Here, too, the Philadelphia resolutions are instructive. "Nor do we view the colonization of those who may become emancipated by [the ACS] operation among our southern brethren," Russell Parrot, the secretary of the Philadelphia protest convention, wrote, "as capable to produce their happiness."[39] This paternalism, grounded in a sense of linked fate, remained a major ideational force shaping the behavior of the black elite in the U.S. foreign policymaking arena throughout the nineteenth century.

The Black Abolitionists and U.S. Policy toward Liberia

The protests of the free black community against the first ACS petition for federal support for its colonization program yielded mixed results. On the one hand, the protests wounded the ACS by making it more difficult to raise funds among reform-minded white Americans.[40] On the other hand, the protests failed to influence the debate on Capitol Hill over the merits of the ACS program.[41] Within two years of its founding, the ACS was able to realize its goal of establishing a colony for the resettlement of black Americans on the territory that would eventually become the republic of Liberia. Over the next fifty years, the ACS helped transport more than 1,000 black Americans, mostly the manumitted slaves of their members who had to leave the United States as a condition for obtaining their freedom, to the tiny African republic.

Despite these facts, historians continue to see the protest meetings that erupted in black communities in response to the formation of the ACS as a watershed moment in black political history. It is easy to see why this is the case. After all, the decision of the delegates at the Philadelphia protest convention to appoint an eleven-member correspondence committee to lobby the Congress to reject the ACS petition represented the first time that such an effort had been undertaken on the federal level.[42] More important, the independent black newspapers that sprang up in the 1820s were initially developed for the express purpose of "countering the slanders of the ACS" against the free people of color.[43] In short, the protests provided the foundation for the emergence of the abolitionist movement.

Historians have long viewed the black-controlled newspapers that emerged between 1827 and 1863 as a resource for gauging black elite opinion on Liberia and a range of other important issues.[44] Because the resulting studies have generated largely impressionistic accounts of public opinion during this period, I conducted a systematic content analysis of the six black periodicals that had the greatest circulation in the black counterpublic between 1827 and 1863.[45] The results of my analysis support the conventional wisdom that the black elite held largely negative predispositions toward Liberia during this period. Indeed, 434 (50 percent) of the 868 items examined in the analysis had a decidedly negative tone when reporting on events in Liberia, emigration movements, or U.S. policies designed to aid Liberian development.

Surprisingly, 234 (27 percent) of the items contained language that exhibited favorable attitudes toward Liberia and the movements that aimed to stimulate its development. This finding suggests that blacks freely debated the merits of "Liberia's offerings" within their segregated public sphere. In other words, the editors and owners of the black abolitionist papers did not censor viewpoints that favored emigration to Liberia.

But the most striking finding is that 199 (23 percent) of the items that reported on Liberia during this period did so with a neutral tone. This content category contains two types of items. The obituaries of missionaries and other notables who spent their lives working for the betterment of Liberia during this period constitute 11 percent of this category; the remaining 177 items are editorials and articles that simultaneously repudiate black American emigration to Liberia and portray developments in the nation in a favorable light.

Why would so many of the correspondents to these newspapers engage in this peculiar rhetorical strategy? Figure 1.1, which charts the frequency of these items in the abolitionist papers published between 1855 and 1863, holds the answer to this question: 169 of the 177 items with neutral tone appeared in abolitionist newspapers during these years. These were crucial years in both the sectional crisis in the United States and the development of Liberia. On the U.S. side of the equation, the destabilization of the citizenship status of free blacks in the wake of the infamous Supreme Court decision in *Scott v. Sanford* (1857) provoked a new debate about the merits of emigration within the black community. Content analysis reveals that 72 (39 percent) of the items with neutral tone reflect the black elite's response to this ruling.

The vast majority of the neutral items appeared in 1862 and 1863, suggesting that this category is really about the black elite making an important statement

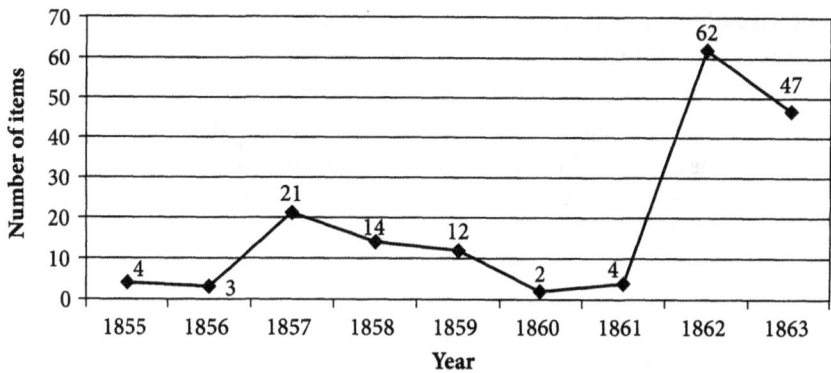

FIGURE 1.1 Periodical items with neutral tone, 1855–1863.
Sources: *Frederick Douglass Paper; Anglo-African Magazine; Christian Recorder*

about U.S. policy toward Liberia. It was during this period that the wartime 37th Congress conducted a heated debate about the merits of extending diplomatic relations to Liberia. Moreover, the abolitionist movement (including members of the black elite) supported Liberia's quest for recognition. Indeed, Senator Charles Sumner (R-Mass.; 1851–1874), undoubtedly the most committed abolitionist in the Republican Party, was the one who introduced the bill that carried the day for Liberia in the Congress.[46]

Some scholars suggest that affective ties to the Americo-Liberians and the continent of Africa created a drive within the black elite to protect the gain for black nationality that Liberia represented.[47] Although some black leaders may have possessed these sentiments, it is clear from the historical record that most black abolitionists supported the bill because of its implications for their struggle for freedom in the United States. On January 11, 1862, for example, Frederick Douglass, who for more than a decade had been the most outspoken critic of emigration to Liberia, opined in his monthly newspaper that Sumner's bill would "strike a blow" for black citizenship rights in the United States. He also argued that Sumner's getting the bill through the Congress would be tantamount to the institution's "endorsing" black Americans' fitness for self-government.[48]

Douglass was by no means the only member of the black elite to see that the Liberian campaign for recognition was crucial to the black struggle for U.S. citizenship rights. On the contrary, the majority of the 122 remaining items with neutral tone (or 89 percent of the category) focus on the Liberian campaign for recognition. Moreover, the other 11 percent of the items are articles and editorials that celebrate the arrival of the Liberian delegation in 1863.

In light of this dimension of the coverage, it is easy to see why the Liberian delegation was so surprised by the cold shoulder they received from black

Americans. Moreover, there was no way for the Liberian delegates to recognize that the support they had garnered from the black elite a year earlier was the secondary part of a two-level game that blacks and their allies were playing in the U.S. policymaking arena. On the other hand, it is also clear that had they consistently read the black abolitionist press even just one year before their arrival they would have come to the same conclusion that modern scholars have—the black elite engaged Liberia as Americans and not Africans in diaspora.

Liberia Fever

Only twelve years after the Liberian delegation set sail from the shores of the United States with heavy hearts due to their inability to recruit emigrants to their homeland, a new bout of Liberia Fever broke out among black Americans. As in the case of Paul Cuffe's movement fifty years earlier, the primary factor stimulating black interest in repatriation to Africa in the late nineteenth century was white backlash. Unlike Cuffe's movement, however, the participants in these exodus movements of the 1870s and 1880s were disproportionately southern and lower class.

It is easy to understand why this was the case. After all, the newly freed blacks suffered unspeakable violence and oppression at the hands of the white terrorist organizations that took control of the postbellum South during the Counter-Reconstruction. The Counter-Reconstruction grew from seeds sown at the beginning of President Ulysses S. Grant's second term in office. Grant had been a strong defender of black rights during his first term.[49] Indeed, one of his first acts in office was to use his influence to push the Republican-controlled Georgia legislature to reseat the black delegates whom a coalition of conservative white legislators had purged unlawfully from the 1869 state constitutional convention.[50]

As his first term began to wind down, President Grant found himself an increasingly isolated defender of black rights within his own party. This was so because many party leaders began to turn away from their commitment to protect the freed blacks in the wake a white backlash movement that swept through the North during the midterm elections of 1870.[51] Grant's reluctant decision to join his partisans in their retreat from the tenets of radicalism left rank-and-file southern blacks (and their allies) vulnerable to the terrorist violence of the Democratic Party's Counter-Reconstruction.[52] Most of these atrocities focused on black men who were attempting to exercise the voting rights guaranteed to them by both the Fourteenth and Fifteenth Amendments. On August 31, 1874, for example, the White League, a paramilitary organization sponsored by the Louisiana Democratic Party organization, summarily executed two would-be black voters in Red River Parish.[53]

Undoubtedly, one of the most horrific acts of terrorist violence directed at black voters occurred in Eufaula, Alabama, in 1874. In the midst of a local election, a group of Confederate veterans decided to try to suppress the vote in the tiny black community of the town. On the day of the election, the group marched on the local polling station under the banner of their newly formed White Man's League. Within a few hours, the group had murdered seven unarmed black voters and critically wounded seventy-five others (many as they tried to flee the carnage).[54]

These outbreaks of terrorist violence were by no means limited to locales and states where there were white majorities. On the contrary, the uprisings that have come to define the Counter-Reconstruction for modern historians took place in areas with large black majorities. The notorious White Line campaign that took place in Mississippi is a prime example of these backlash movements in majority black areas.

Beginning in 1874, the Mississippi Democratic Party decided that it would try to topple the administration of Governor Adelbert Ames and reconstitute a racial dictatorship in the state. Governor Ames, who was one of the few radical Republicans to remain in power in the South during Grant's second term, made several public appeals for federal intervention. When it became clear that the Grant administration was not going to send federal troops to preserve order in Mississippi, the emboldened white-liners embarked in the months leading up to the election of 1875 on a terror campaign that claimed the lives of several high-ranking members of the Ames administration and dozens of black citizens. The White Line movement was so effective in driving black voters away from the polls that the Democrats won the election by 30,000 votes despite the fact that Republicans had an advantage of at least 25,000 registered voters on the rolls before the election.[55]

Although this survey of terrorist violence refers to the experience of blacks and their allies in only three states, it is clear that these patterns were prevalent throughout the South during Grant's second term in office. Several historians have demonstrated that the White Line movement became a model for other terrorist groups throughout the South. Indeed, there is even evidence that southern Democrats talked openly about their desire to put the Mississippi Plan to work in their own states in the years leading up to the federal elections of 1876.

The frequency and widespread nature of the violent dimensions of the Counter-Reconstruction undoubtedly made many blacks feel like Elias Hill, an infirm teacher and minister from South Carolina, who lived in a community consistently terrorized by the Ku Klux Klan. When asked by members of the Joint Select Committee to Investigate Affairs in the Late Insurrectionary States how he felt about the white race, Hill simply remarked that he was "afraid of them now."[56] Hill also told the committee that many of his neighbors joined him in this sentiment and that they were exploring "means" by which they could be transported to Liberia.[57]

Hill's testimony should not lead us to believe that these white terrorists cowed blacks into submission. On the contrary, some blacks, particularly those living in majority population centers, did attempt to organize vigorous defenses of their communities. Unfortunately, inferior military technology and insufficient numbers typically left these grassroots self-defense movements unprepared to provide a response to the likes of the Ku Klux Klan, the White Man's League, and other paramilitary groups that fueled the Counter-Reconstruction.[58] The tendency of these groups to single out black victims; strike at night; and exact reprisals against women, children, and the elderly also worked to keep resistance-minded black men under control.

Testimony from black survivors of the period reveals that their vulnerability in the "free" labor economy of the New South was also a major lever of control at the disposal of the Counter-Reconstructionists. Henry Frazier, a survivor of the Eufaula Riot of 1874, reported to a Senate panel charged with investigating the incident that the White Man's League significantly reduced the ability of blacks to respond to their activities by forcing black agricultural laborers and tenant farmers (or sharecroppers) to choose between signing pledges to vote for the Democratic Party or unemployment.[59] These threats undoubtedly made the cotton, sugar, and rubber plantations of Liberia look more attractive to many downtrodden blacks.[60]

We also see this reality reflected in the narrative of Henry Adams of Caddo Parish, Louisiana. Adams was in many ways an archetype of a black man predisposed to resist the Counter-Reconstruction. As a soldier in the Union Army, Adams had acquired both combat experience and a formal education. After the war, he, like so many of his fellow black veterans, worked as an organizer among the free blacks. At the beginning of the Counter-Reconstruction, Adams gained notoriety among both blacks and whites in Caddo Parish when he forced a group of white men to back down from threats to him and a female companion by threatening a fight to the death.[61]

Not even Adams's extraordinary valor, however, was a match for the economics of oppression as practiced by the leaders of the Counter-Reconstruction in Louisiana. As Adams told the Joint Select Committee in 1880, the White Man's League forced all his potential employers in the parish to ban him after his heroic standoff with the white highwaymen. "I think a heap of you as a man; I know you are a true man, and that you will do what you promise to do, but under this order I cannot employ you," Adams reported that his long-time boss, W. C. Hambleton, told him shortly before the election of 1874.[62] The loss of his economic livelihood did to Henry Adams what the threats of white violence could not—it forced him from his home parish and turned him into an emigrationist.

The harsh realities of these dual means of social control were the source of Liberia Fever among rank-and-file blacks in the postbellum South. As one historian writes:

> Liberia fever followed fast on the heels of Reconstruction in the Carolinas, Mississippi, and Louisiana.... In the aftermath of the violence surrounding the campaign of 1876, many Afro-Americans admitted that they would never be first class citizens in this country. They might as well emphasize their African identity and emphasize their African descent. Turning to the most American part of Africa—Liberia—they envisioned building a perfected America, free from racial hatred and color disabilities.[63]

Unfortunately for the would-be emigrants, their expressions of affective ties to the continent did not translate into direct passage to Monrovia. Moreover, neither they nor their principal ally, the ACS, had the resources to fund the transatlantic crossing for the torrent of freed blacks who expressed a desire to go to Liberia during the Counter-Reconstruction.[64] This lack of resources led the proponents of emigration to turn once again to the federal government for support for their ideals.

Paternalism, Not Patronage

In 1875, the ACS embarked on a new lobbying effort to secure federal funds to provide financial aid for those freed blacks who sought passage to Liberia, but this campaign met with stiff resistance from the black elite. Ultimately, the Republican establishment decided to take its cues on this issue from the latter.[65] As a result, the vast majority of would-be emigrants to Liberia remained locked in the oppressive environs of the Counter-Reconstruction South. Indeed, no more than 1 percent of the estimated 100,000 blacks who sought assistance from the federal government in arranging passage to Liberia ever made it to Monrovia.

Previous researchers have attributed this apparent schism between the black elite and rank-and-file blacks on emigration policy to the spoils system. In other words, the conventional wisdom holds that members of the black elite became so enamored of the patronage positions that they had attained in the Reconstruction administrations of the South that they lost touch with the concerns of rank-and-file blacks.[66] Nell Irvin Painter goes even further by suggesting that the hostility of black leaders to the grassroots exodus movements of the 1870s and

1880s was a function of their conscious desire to protect their ability to compete with white carpetbaggers for patronage posts; in other words, Painter argues, black elites blocked emigration because they knew that the repatriation of the black masses in Africa would jeopardize their claims to represent a sizable interest bloc within the Republican Party.[67]

This viewpoint emerges from detailed analyses of primary documents and the testimony of the black Americans who were involved in building these grassroots movements. The *Charleston News and Courier*, for example, reported that class tensions within the black community prevented the local exodus movement from forming a steamship line to carry would-be emigrants from South Carolina to Liberia.[68] The U.S. Senate testimony of Henry Adams, whose frustrations with the climate for blacks in Caddo Parish led him to initiate an exodus movement, also offers great insight into these class dynamics. When asked by Senator William Windom (R-Minn.) to describe the composition of his Louisiana Colonization Committee, Adams replied that:

> No politicianers didn't [sic] belong to it, because we didn't allow them to know nothing about it, because we was afraid that if we allowed the colored politicianer to belong to it he would tell it to the Republican politicianers, and from that the men that was doing all this to us would get hold of it, too, and then get after us. Nobody that held an office by the votes of the neighborhood could become a member.[69]

The richness of these historical sources makes it impossible to reject the view that the bifurcated class structure of the black community played at least some role in motivating the black elite to work against the emigration movements.

On first glance, the behavior of at least some members of the black elite during the Reconstruction period also seems to confirm the standard interpretation within the extant literature. After all, patronage had been an important issue for black leaders since the end of the Civil War. Indeed, ensuring that they received their fair share of appointments from Republican administrations at both the federal and state levels was a constant fight for black politicians and activists. Ironically, the position of minister resident to the Republic of Liberia—the only diplomatic post in Africa—was among the two or three opportunities coveted most by members of the black elite.

Martin Delany, the most prominent black emigrationist in the decade before the Civil War, led the most public and vocal campaign for this position. Having traveled widely in Africa before the war, Delany believed that he was more qualified for the job than most of his rivals.[70] Delany also believed that the sterling reputation that he had earned as both the first black commissioned officer in the Union Army and as an agent of the Freedmen's Bureau in South Carolina after the war should have given him an inside track for the job.⁷¹ Thus, in the aftermath of the election of 1868, during which he had worked tirelessly to turn out the black vote in South Carolina for Grant, Delany began to solicit recommendations for the post from Republican bosses and elected officials throughout the South.⁷²

Despite the glowing recommendations that his allies forwarded to President Grant and Secretary of State Hamilton Fish on his behalf, Delany did not receive the coveted appointment as the administration representative to Liberia. Instead, Grant selected Francis E. Dumas, a white Republican operative from Louisiana, to fill the position.⁷³ Deeply disappointed by his inability to secure the position, Delany set out on a nationwide speaking tour to mobilize the black community to press for more high-level patronage posts. Delany began this campaign with a speech that he delivered in New Orleans's Congo Square in April 1869. "Any political party appealing to blacks," Delany told the crowd, "should share the patronage of public office on a pro-rata basis."⁷⁴ Continuing along these lines, he argued that it was particularly important that this policy take root in the South, where blacks comprised "a third to one half of the population."⁷⁵

The response of the black elite to Delany's provocative calls for a quota system in the federal civil service challenges the view that this segment of the black community was chiefly concerned with its ability to secure the spoils of office. Indeed, despite the facts that the black vote had helped deliver both the White House and control of Congress to the Republicans in 1868 and that there was widespread evidence of racial discrimination in patronage appointments, few black leaders rallied behind Delany's campaign. On the contrary, some of the most notable black leaders pilloried Delany's argument. Given his esteemed position in the black leadership class, it is not surprising that Frederick Douglass was one of the most vocal critics of Delany's line of argument. "The fact is[,] friend Delany," Douglass wrote in an editorial in his newspaper the *New Era*, "these things are not fixed by figures, and while men are what they are they cannot be so fixed."⁷⁶

Most scholars have attributed Douglass's conservative stance in this debate to his optimism about the Republican Party.⁷⁷ The historical record certainly supports this interpretation. Douglass, after all, had just led a successful lobbying campaign to get President Grant to expand the number of federal positions he awarded to blacks. Douglass referred to this campaign in one of his exchanges with Delany when he wrote that the "present Republican administration" had already appointed "at least two dark-skinned clerks to serve in federal departments."⁷⁸

It is also likely that Douglass feared that Delany's confrontational approach to the patronage issue would place even greater stress on the already fragile coalition between the black community and the Republican Party. Indeed, Democrats and some conservative Republicans were already using the appointment of blacks to patronage positions in the Reconstruction governments as an issue to unite white voters.[79] If black politicians and activists were as preoccupied with their own economic well-being under the spoils system as previous studies suggest, it is likely that they would have sided with Delany and not Douglass in their debate over patronage.

There are two other reasons to question whether the testimonies of figures such as Henry Adams provide a complete picture of the motivations of the black elite during the Counter-Reconstruction. First, there is ample evidence that members of the black elite already saw themselves as locked out of the spoils system in the Reconstruction governments long before the rise of the exodus movements in the middle of Grant's second term.[80] Second, the areas of the South where Liberia Fever hit the black population the hardest were already under the control of Counter-Reconstruction regimes by 1876. In short, there were almost no patronage opportunities for black politicians to even covet, let alone protect, once the Democrats began to regain control of the South.

So why did the black elite work to squelch the exodus movements that sprang up after the Hayes-Tilden Compromise? The deep-seated paternalism that the black elite exhibited toward low-status blacks in the first half of the nineteenth century provides an answer to this question. In other words, members of the black elite continued to view themselves as the only capable defenders of the interests of downtrodden blacks in the public sphere. The fact that low-status blacks were now organizing themselves and expressing a desire to go to Liberia did not alter the view among members of the black elite that they were the rightful spokespeople for this segment of the black community. On the contrary, many members of the black elite believed that the exodus movements were a prime example of why downtrodden blacks needed their representation.

We see these attitudes reflected quite clearly in the statements on the exodus movements that members of the black elite bandied about the black counter-public sphere between 1876 and 1880. Moreover, most of these statements recycled the arguments against emigration that had formed the basis of the black elite response to the rise of the ACS in the 1830s. In short, members of the black elite continued to argue that their race had a birthright to equal treatment in the United States, that the ACS was a front that represented the forces that wanted to deny black Americans these rights, and that conditions in Liberia were far worse than those in the postbellum South.

Consider, for example, the open letter on emigration that Senator Blanche K. Bruce (R-Miss.), the first black American to serve a full term in the U.S. Senate, published in the *Commercial* in March 1878. Bruce pointed out that the United States was the homeland of black Americans and the "scheme to colonize" them in Liberia "assumed that there was no future for the Negro here." Bruce also argued that emigration to Liberia was a "venture" that would "jeopardize" all that blacks had "accumulated" by "slow and painful processes" in the South.[81]

Bruce's talk of progress does not mean that he was oblivious to the hardships that downtrodden blacks faced in the South. On the contrary, he "maintained" the "truth" that black Americans had been "made the sufferers of exceptional and inexcusable violence" throughout the South. Ultimately, however, Senator Bruce believed that a "stern sense of justice and sentiment of humanity" would wash over white southerners and allow blacks to "assert and exercise" their rights "without hindrance and without danger." Because, in his view, "[n]one of the conditions" existed in Liberia "as to make a general exodus of the Negroes of the South either desirable or practicable," Bruce urged blacks to stick it out until whites realized that there was a "perfect community of interest between the Negro and his white brother."[82]

These themes are also present in a report issued by a committee of ministers that the AME Church appointed to study the exodus movements in 1878. The committee, under the leadership of Bishop Benjamin T. Tanner, reminded members of the denomination that Liberia was the "offspring" of "American prejudice and American slavery." The committee's statement also recalled the fact that dividing the black community had always been the main goal of the ACS (and other white emigrationists). "Perhaps no one will deny," the Tanner Committee wrote, "that the first practical object which the slaveholder hoped to reach by Liberian emigration was the getting rid of that troublesome element described as 'free negroes, mulattoes, and persons of color,' and thus to render their pet institution more secure."[83]

The Tanner committee did recognize, however, that the end of slavery put the emigration issue in a new frame for many black Americans. It also stated that it saw a clear distinction between the programs initiated by the ACS in the antebellum period and the "organic movements" that were "springing up voluntarily" among black southerners. At the same time, the committee expressed concerns about whether the grassroots exodus movements were "safely organized and prudently managed" enough to "meet all [their] promises." In the final analysis, these concerns led the committee to "express its unqualified disapprobation of any organized effort to expatriate" black Americans "from the country dear to [them] by every memory of [their lives]."[84] In short, the Tanner committee recommended to the AME Church that it not endorse the exodus movements because the committee feared that they would fail and have a detrimental effect on the black masses. Thus, the opposition of the black elite to emigration was primarily an expression of paternalism and not a repudiation of linked fate.

Content analysis of the editorials and letters on the exodus movements that appeared in the *Christian Recorder* between 1875 and 1885 substantiates this claim. The paper, published by the AME Church, is an excellent source for gauging black elite views on emigrationism during this period for two reasons. First, the *Christian Recorder* was the most widely circulated black-controlled newspaper during the Counter-Reconstruction period. As a result, black leaders frequently opined in its pages in hopes of reaching a mass audience. Second, despite the fact that most of the leadership of the AME Church opposed the exodus movements, they instructed the editor of the *Christian Recorder* to maintain an open editorial policy with regard to the emigration issue. Moreover, the paper even announced this policy in a front-page editorial on April 18, 1878.[85]

The *Christian Recorder* ran fifty-seven editorials and letters from correspondents on the exodus movements between 1875 and 1885. Eight of these items took a neutral position on the exodus movements; in other words, the authors of these pieces spent an equal amount of space discussing the benefits and downsides of repatriation in Liberia. Eighteen of the items took a positive stance on the exodus movements and emigration to Liberia. The remaining thirty-one pieces expressed decidedly negative views of emigration.

Figure 1.2 graphs the results of a content analysis of these thirty-one negative items, focusing on the predominant frames that black leaders used when condemning the exodus movements. As shown, only two of the items cited negative effects on the Republican coalition as the primary reason for opposing the exodus movements; three of the items cited deep concerns that the exodus movements were defrauding freed blacks as the primary source of opposition to these movements. The second most prevalent frame, with seventeen appearances in these thirty-one negative editorials and letters, was that the leaders of the exodus movements and the ACS were misleading downtrodden blacks about conditions in Liberia, in other words that conditions in Liberia were generally worse than the Counter-Reconstruction South. The most prevalent frame, with twenty-two appearances, was that black Americans had a birthright to equal citizenship in the United States and that it was their duty, in light of what their slave ancestors had suffered in previous generations, to remain in the United States and to defend this right at all costs.

This analysis again demonstrates that black leaders opposed the exodus movements more out of paternalism than out of a desire to protect its own prerogatives in the postbellum period. In other words, black leaders assumed that they knew what was best for the black masses, and they remained determined to protect their "ignorant" brethren from the follies of emigrationism at all costs.

Several refugee crises that sprang up in northern port cities between 1877 and 1880 only served to reinforce this attitude. These crises resulted from would-be

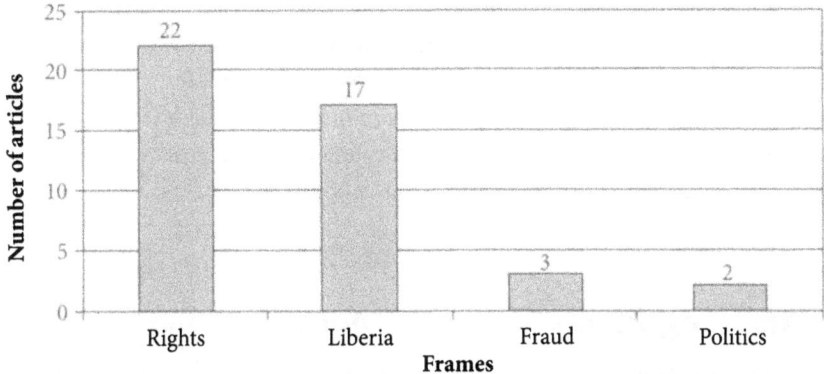

FIGURE 1.2 Negative frames of the exodus movement in the *Christian Recorder*, 1875–1885; numbers of editorials and letters.
Source: *Christian Recorder*

black emigrants streaming to northern ports without sufficient funds to pay for either their immediate passage to Liberia or accommodations as they tried to obtain these funds.[86] On March 26, 1880, for example, one hundred black Arkansans arrived in New York City; their intent was to gain the assistance of the ACS with booking passage to Liberia.[87] Of course, because the ACS had not invited these exodusters to New York and lacked advance knowledge of their arrival, there was no one from the organization on hand to provide them with assistance when they arrived in the city.[88] Undaunted, these "dusty, travel-worn, and scantily-clad refugees," to use the words of the *New York Times*, took up residence at the Young Men's Colored Christian Association.[89]

Within a few days of their arrival, however, the group had exhausted all of its funds for paid accommodations. Fortunately, the refugees' story had been so widely reported in the New York press that the local black community became aware of their plight and began to organize relief efforts.[90] Reverend Henry Highland Garnett, who had been an ardent opponent of emigrationism in the 1850s and 1860s, led these relief organizations through his Shiloh Colored Presbyterian Church.[91]

Although the relief committee raised enough aid to feed, clothe, and house the refugees, it was never able to provide for the group beyond a subsistence level. For example, two weeks into their odyssey in New York, most of the one hundred refugees remained housed in the tiny basement of Garnett's church.[92] These poor living conditions quickly gave rise to diseases such as measles and pneumonia among the refugees. By the end of their first month in New York, four members of the Arkansas group had died of these illnesses.[93] Despite the fact that the ACS raised enough capital to send the entire party to Liberia within two months of their arrival in New York, which made this effort one of the most successful ACS campaigns of the period, the hardships that the group faced, and not its eventual repatriation, continued to resonate in the black counterpublic.[94]

These stories, along with narratives about the hardships that the freed blacks faced once they arrived in Liberia, fanned the flames of the paternalistic approach of the black elite to the emigration issue in the postbellum period.

Rethinking James Milton Turner's Diplomacy

There is no evidence that President Grant was privy to the Delany-Douglass debate over patronage. He did, however, finally appoint a black man, James Milton Turner, to the diplomatic post in Liberia in March 1871.[95] Moreover, Grant's decision to give the post to Turner, who had been instrumental in organizing the black vote in his native Missouri, shows that he was indeed making connections between black electoral clout and the distribution of spoils.

Turner's tenure as U.S. minister to Liberia has figured prominently in the interdisciplinary literature on the black elite's engagement with African affairs in the nineteenth century.[96] Historians have largely viewed Turner's term as U.S. minister as a failure because his vehement opposition to the exodus movements created tensions between him and the Liberian people.[97] Moreover, Turner's anti-emigration activism has also led some historians to portray him as the quintessential example of how members of the black elite allowed their own interests to stifle the burgeoning transnationalism of downtrodden blacks.[98]

The documentary record certainly supports the first proposition. Indeed, even Turner's own dispatches to the Department of State make it clear that the rift between him and the Liberian people over emigration limited his ability to function in Monrovia. On March 30, 1872, for example, Turner wrote to Secretary of State Hamilton Fish that his views had made him the victim of "gross personal indignities" on the part of both "officials and others" in Liberia.[99] Although Turner was able to redeem himself somewhat in the eyes of the Liberians by mediating a war between the Americo-Liberians and the indigenous Grebo people in 1875,[100] the outbreak of Liberia Fever in the United States later in that same year quickly soured this détente by thrusting his anti-emigrationist views to the forefront of the Liberian media.[101]

The animosity that the Americo-Liberians exhibited toward Turner deeply distressed him for two reasons. First, as the first black American diplomat to Africa, he felt enormous pressure to serve the interests of both his nation and race. Second, his race consciousness led him to take a genuine interest in the development of Liberia. Turner candidly gave voice to these concerns in a dispatch to Secretary Fish:

> I am fully aware and highly appreciative of the importance of the position taken by the Administration in the presence of our entire country in elevating one like myself to a position of great responsibility, trust, and confidence. I have therefore made it my highest acme to be in every sense true to the interests of the Government of our own country. Meantime I am frank to confess that I have desire to be of service to this immature State which is composed of men with whom I am identified by blood and race.[102]

Because the U.S. government during this period had no position on black emigration to Liberia and the Americo-Liberians actively encouraged the exodus movements, modifying his position to smooth out relations with the government in Monrovia would have certainly guaranteed his ability to achieve both of these ends. Throughout his five years in Liberia, however, Turner refused to soften his anti-emigrationist views to mollify the Americo-Liberians.[103] Previous studies have turned up some evidence that Turner was somewhat blinded by his status as a member of the black elite. Indeed, some of his correspondence on the subject of emigration demonstrates that he possessed an overly optimistic view of the United States during the Reconstruction. "Now that such signal changes have occurred in the United States with reference to the conditions of this class of persons [the freed blacks]," Turner wrote to Hamilton Fish on May 25, 1872, "the wisdom of continuing such a policy [emigration] is thought by many at least to be questionable."[104] Although it was clear that the Counter-Reconstruction was already limiting the life chances of downtrodden southern blacks when he penned this letter in 1872, Turner's background as the leader of a successful biracial coalition in Missouri (one of only two states to avoid the Counter-Reconstruction pattern) made it hard for him to see these realities.

Because Turner garnered his appointment by demonstrating his ability to "control" the black vote in Missouri,[105] it is certainly reasonable to hypothesize (as Painter does in her work) that he also opposed emigration because he wanted to keep downtrodden blacks in the South, where their potential votes would continue to bolster the patronage demands of the black elite. There is, however, no real documentary evidence to support this interpretation. Indeed, Turner's substantial correspondences with Frederick Douglass, Bishop Benjamin T. Tanner, Blanche K. Bruce, and a host of other black Republicans during their efforts to cure Liberia Fever never touch on the subject of patronage.

Most of Turner's writings do exhibit the same paternalistic vision of the relationship of the black elite to rank-and-file blacks that grew out of the free black community's first anti-emigration protests. Indeed, Turner's statements about emigration between 1872 and 1877 reveal that he believed that the grassroots exodus movements in the postbellum South were nothing more than a scheme propagated by the ACS to defraud the most "ignorant" classes of blacks out of their U.S. citizenship rights.[106] Turner also accused the government in Monrovia of working in league with the ACS to spread misinformation about the conditions that emigrants would face on their arrival in Liberia.[107] Indeed, Turner asserted that none of the migrants that he had observed in Monrovia would have left the "relative comfort" of their "homes" in the United States if they had had a realistic impression of what they would face in Liberia.[108]

Although Turner had a well-developed ideological position against emigration, the documentary record suggests that this was not just an editorialized statement. On the contrary, Turner often recorded in his dispatches to the Department of State the hardships that black American immigrants who made their way to Liberia faced on their arrival.[109] A recent analysis by Kenneth Barnes, a historian, suggests that the kinds of hardships that Turner wrote about led to incredibly high mortality rates among new arrivals in Liberia.[110]

The letters written by would-be black emigrants to the ACS during Turner's tenure in Monrovia also seem to support his claims. The results from a content analysis conducted on a random sample of 360 of the more than 2,000 letters that freed blacks wrote to the ACS seeking assistance with emigration to Liberia between 1870 and 1900[111] reveals that transnationalism was a motivation for only a tiny minority of the correspondents. Indeed, only 43 (or 12 percent) of the letters frame the would-be emigrants' desire to go to Liberia primarily as a function of affective ties to the continent of Africa. By contrast, 266 (or 74 percent) of the letters frame the correspondents' motivation as a desire to escape the hardships of the Counter-Reconstruction; moreover, 164 (or 62 percent) of the 266 letters also use terms like *homeland* and *nativity* to refer to the United States.

Although this finding does not justify the paternalism that Turner demonstrated toward low-status blacks, it does reorient our understanding of his efforts to undermine the exodus movements. In short, Turner failed in his role as minister to Liberia not because he was interested in preserving the prerogatives of his own class of black Americans but because of his sense that he was duty bound to protect the freed blacks.

Of course, the Americo-Liberians were never able to see anything positive in Turner's tenure. On the contrary, after the ACS published some of his dispatches in the Liberian newspapers, the "indignities" that he described to Secretary of

State Hamilton Fish throughout the first three years of his term only multiplied. Moreover, the U.S. legation in Monrovia became a constant target of vandalism and mob actions. Ultimately, these acts convinced Turner that he could no longer effectively serve the interests of his government in Liberia, so he expressed his desire for a recall to the United States.[112] One month later, James Milton Turner set sail for the United States from the port of Monrovia disappointed with his tenure but convinced that he had done his best for his nation and the "ignorant" classes among his race who were struggling on the home front.[113]

Dissident Voices

James Milton Turner's unwavering insistence that the black lower class not give up their U.S. citizenship for life in Liberia was rooted in his observations of the hardships that new immigrants faced in Monrovia. Although the majority of the members of the black elite shared Turner's commitment to protecting the rights of the downtrodden members of their community, the realities of the Counter-Reconstruction led many of them to take a more sympathetic stance to the exodus movements. In other words, some members of the black elite found the hardships that freed blacks faced in the United States so troubling that it mollified their staunch opposition to emigration.

One prominent example of this trend was Frederick Douglass. As we have seen, Douglass had been a hard-line opponent of emigrationism since he came to prominence in abolitionist circles in the 1840s. In 1855, for example, he described Liberia as a land of "plagues and poisons" that was at the center of a colonizationist plot to "expatriate" black Americans.[114] By 1878, however, Douglass was so ambivalent about the conditions facing freed blacks in the South that he was comfortable recommending John H. Smyth, a fervent emigrationist, to President Rutherford B. Hayes for the post of minister resident in Liberia.[115]

A few notable black leaders even became advocates for the exodus movements during the Counter-Reconstruction. It is not surprising that Martin Robinson Delany was one of the first and most committed of these dissident voices. Delany, who was one of the first blacks admitted to Harvard Medical School, had demonstrated a willingness to challenge the consensus within the black elite against emigration to Africa as early as the 1850s.[116] In 1852, Delany, who began his brilliant career in abolitionist politics as a staunch opponent of all variants of emigrationism, published a pro-emigration treatise entitled *The Condition, Elevation, Emigration, and Destiny of the Colored People of the United States*. Delany's central proposition in this book was that free blacks should be more open to emigration in the wake of the Compromise of 1850, which contained a provision that compelled northern law enforcement officials to help southerners track down fugitive slaves.

One of the most interesting dimensions of Delany's argument in *The Condition, Elevation, Emigration, and Destiny of the Colored People* is his pronounced preference for a destination in Canada or Latin America over Liberia.[117] Delany's preference for these locales over Africa was rooted in his deep disdain for the relationship that the Liberian government maintained with its patrons at the ACS. Although Delany had been something of a maverick on emigrationism throughout his career, he joined his cohorts in the black elite in their near universal condemnations of the ACS.[118] Moreover, he believed that Liberia would never be a truly independent nation as long as it was in league with the ACS. Indeed, Delany dismissed the newly independent republic as a "*burlesque* on a government" and "a pitiful dependency on the American Colonizationists."[119]

In the aftermath of the Kansas-Nebraska Act, which strengthened the federal fugitive slave law, Delany became convinced that neither Canada nor Latin America was far enough away from the United States to guarantee the safety and stability of any future black settlement.[120] In August 1858, he took his case for African emigration to the tiny cadre of his fellow black dissidents on the issue, who had convened annual meetings under the banner of the National Emigration Convention since 1855.[121] As the historical record shows, Delany, who had served as president of this organization since its inception, had no trouble convincing his fellow emigrationists that the future of the race was in Africa.[122] Armed with both his vision of establishing a new independent black nation in the Niger delta and the hopes of his colleagues in the National Emigration Convention, Delany set sail for West Africa on May 24, 1859.[123]

Delany did successfully negotiate a treaty with the king of the Egba that would have allowed the "African race in America" the "right and privilege of settling in common" with his people.[124] By the time Delany made his way back to the United States in 1860, however, the British government, which feared that a black American colony in Yorubaland would interfere with its plans for exploiting the region, had convinced the king to renege on the treaty.[125] The Civil War broke out just as Delany scrambled to make a new treaty with indigenous peoples. Encouraged by the possibility that blacks might know freedom in the United States in the aftermath of the war, Delany shelved his plan to return to Africa and joined the Union Army.

Delany was one of the most prominent black leaders to sign on to work as a field agent for the Freedmen's Bureau after the war.[126] He began his work among the newly freed communities of South Carolina very optimistic about the possibilities that Reconstruction offered black Americans.[127] It did not take long, however, for him to have a number of experiences in the New South that raised fresh questions in his mind about the future of blacks in the United States. Like many of the black elite who went to work in the Freedmen's Bureau and Reconstruction governments, Delany frequently encountered racist attitudes among his white counterparts in these institutions. These frustrations compounded Delany's disappointment with Grant's decision to pass him over for the diplomatic post in Liberia.

Delany's concerns about the racially exclusive nature of the Republican patronage network paled in comparison to his consternation about the declining environment that freed blacks faced in the 1870s. Indeed, Delany was one of the first black leaders of national standing to express concerns about the refusals of the federal government to stem the rising tide of violence against freed blacks in the South. Delany's worst fears were realized when the Republican-controlled Senate in the 44th Congress signed on to the Hayes-Tilden Compromise. Crestfallen, Delany came to see independent emigration projects to Liberia as the best chance for black Americans to achieve their dreams of freedom. In fall 1877, Delany joined with three activists from the South Carolina Piedmont region and organized the Liberian Exodus Joint Stock Steamship Company.[128]

Black South Carolinians reacted enthusiastically to Delany's new venture. Indeed, by some estimates as many as 30,000 families expressed an interest in obtaining passage to Liberia on one of the company ships.[129] Moreover, within six months of its formation, the Liberian Exodus Joint Stock Steamship Company had raised enough money to purchase a ship, the *Azor*, to transport emigrants to Monrovia.[130] In April 1878, the *Azor* set sail from Charleston with 206 would-be Liberians.[131] When the *Azor* returned to South Carolina a few months later, undercapitalization, opposition from local black leaders, and negative reports on the conditions in Liberia from the first wave of emigrants had ruined the company.[132] The demise of the Liberian Exodus Joint Stock Steamship Company spelled the end of Delany's career as an activist on the emigration issue. It also marked the last time in the nineteenth century that a black-led effort actually repatriated freed blacks to Africa.

As the aging Delany moved toward retirement, Henry McNeal Turner, a bishop of the AME Church in Georgia, emerged as the leading black advocate of emigration to Africa. Turner was born to free black parents in Newberry County, South Carolina, in 1834.[133] In his twenties, Turner became an ordained minister in the AME Church.[134] During his tenure on the ministerial staff of a church in Washington, D.C., Turner attracted the attention of many prominent white Republicans for his fiery speeches in support of the Union war effort. When Lincoln finally integrated the armed forces in 1863, Turner accepted an appointment as the first black chaplain in the history of the U.S. military.[135]

After the war, Turner pursued a career in electoral politics. His abilities and national reputation vaulted him into the state legislature of his adopted state of Georgia.[136] When a conservative coalition of Democratic and Republican legislators voted to expel black members, Turner led the campaign for federal intervention in the matter.[137] Although this campaign was successful, the progress of Counter-Reconstruction during the 1870 legislative session so frustrated Turner that he resigned his seat to become postmaster of Macon, Georgia. And Turner encountered so much resistance from the white citizens of Macon that he resigned this federal post after just two weeks in the job.[138] Now completely discouraged with the civil service, Turner returned full time to the work of building the AME organization in the South.

Turner had developed a sympathetic perspective on emigration during an encounter with the Liberian commissioners who toured Washington, D.C., at the height of the Civil War.[139] It was not until he began his pastoral work among the freed blacks in Georgia, however, that Turner became a full-fledged proponent of emigration to Liberia. Like Delany, Turner read the violence perpetrated against freed blacks during the Counter-Reconstruction as a sign that white Americans would never share the republic with blacks. "There is no doubt in my mind that we have ultimately to *return* to Africa than there is in the existence of God; and the sooner we begin to recognize the fact and prepare for it, the better it will be for us as a people," Turner repeatedly told AME congregations throughout the South during the Counter-Reconstruction.[140]

Turner stands out among the dissident voices of the postbellum period because he was willing to work with anyone and everyone who advocated that downtrodden members of the black community go to Africa for a new start. He lent his formidable talents as an orator to Delany's campaign for recruits for the Liberian Exodus Joint Stock Steamship Company.[141] Turner was also involved with the ACS during this period. In 1875, for example, Turner accepted the title of honorary vice president from the leadership of the ACS. Turner officially joined the ACS board of directors and began to direct its recruitment efforts among blacks in 1890.[142]

Bishop Turner's rationale for working with the ACS grew out of his experiences with the Liberian Exodus Joint Stock Steamship Company. In his view, the demise of the company demonstrated the necessity of securing funds from the federal government to provide passage for the vast number of black southerners who claimed that they wanted to try a new life in Liberia. Of course, this was a logical step for any true believer in the promises of "Liberia's offerings" for black Americans. Turner soon learned, however, that the tolerance that his fellow members of the black elite demonstrated for projects such as the Liberian Exodus Joint Stock Steamship Company at the height of the Counter-Reconstruction did not signal a sea change in their attitudes toward either the ACS or government policies aimed at stimulating emigration to Liberia.

The Butler Bill and the Death Knell Of Emigrationism

The leaders of the ACS had hoped that bringing Bishop Turner into their ranks would mollify critics of the organization among the black elite. But, as the historical record makes clear, Turner's involvement with the group generated the opposite effect. Indeed, when news of Turner's work with the ACS became public, the pages of the black newspapers erupted with venomous attacks against him.[143]

Many of these attacks against Bishop Turner's views on emigration took place in the pages of the *Christian Recorder*, the weekly newspaper of the AME Church, which, because of the rapid growth of the denomination in the postbellum South, was the most widely read black periodical in the nation after 1875. A survey of the articles that appeared in the *Christian Recorder* during this period reveals that the black elite saw Turner's cooperation with the ACS as an abrogation of his responsibility to protect the interests of lower-class blacks. Professor John H. Sampson, for example, urged the readers of the newspaper to remember that emigrationism had always been the tool of those who sought to "de-Americanize" blacks. So, Professor Sampson argued, Turner's support for the philosophy must mean that he had joined the ranks of the "greatest traitors" to the black race. In closing, Sampson defended black Americans' "inalienable right to remain" in the United States and to "expect the highest possibilities" from their "native land."[144]

The paternalistic attitudes of the black elite were also on full display in many of these anti-Turner articles that ran in the *Christian Recorder*. In a series of editorials that ran in the paper in the late 1880s, Bishop Benjamin Tanner, a prominent AME cleric who had worked among freed blacks in Maryland, challenged Turner's argument that the majority of freed blacks wanted to go to Liberia. When Turner responded to some of these charges with his own editorials, Tanner wrote a piece that tried to bolster his position, arguing that only the opinions of literate blacks should be counted in the debate over emigration.[145]

The opposition of his fellow members of the black elite did not discourage Turner. On the contrary, he joined the ACS and the Liberian government in lobbying the Congress to pass a bill that Senator Matthew Butler (D-S.C.) introduced in 1890, calling for the federal government to provide financial assistance to blacks who wanted to go to Liberia. The Bourbon Democrats had traditionally opposed emigration for the simple fact that a mass exodus of black laborers would undermine the crop-lien (or sharecropping) system that kept them in their positions of power and privilege in the New South. This situation changed dramatically after the federal elections of 1888.

In 1884, the Republicans lost control of the White House for the first time in the postbellum period. This was a direct result of the Counter-Reconstruction regimes' suppressing black voting rights, and it jolted Republican leaders to the recognition that the terms of the Hayes-Tilden Compromise weakened their position significantly in close contests. To complicate matters further for the Republicans, black leaders, whom they had ignored for more than a decade, and President Grover Cleveland, a northern Democrat, began to flirt with the possibility of forming an alliance.[146] It was in this context that the Republicans decided to abandon their laissez-faire approach to the South when Benjamin Harrison recaptured the White House for the party in 1888.

Harrison's inaugural address gave the nation an idea of the course that the Republican Party intended to pursue with regard to black civil rights. After urging white southerners to "make the black man their efficient and safe ally" in building the New South, Harrison made it clear that his administration would abandon Hayes's "let alone policy" in the region.[147] Shortly after Harrison's speech, the Republican-controlled 51st Congress moved to consider legislation enforcing the Fifteenth Amendment in the South.[148]

The reaction of southern whites to these moves was swift and defiant. Democrats waved the bloody shirt in both chambers of Congress by repeatedly denouncing the federal elections measures as "force bills" akin to the Reconstruction amendments. It was in this context that Senator Butler introduced his emigration bill.[149] Like the Republican legislators who passed the bills providing for the colonization of blacks in Africa during the Civil War, Butler hoped that his legislative efforts would preserve both the sectional peace and white rule in the South by solving America's "Negro problem."

Given the composition of the Congress, Butler knew that he faced an uphill battle in bringing his bill to the floor of the Senate for a vote. However, he hoped that a strong show of support for the bill from his Democratic colleagues and from southern blacks would indicate to the Republicans that both races favored separation for their "mutual progress."[150] By speaking out for the bill in both the black and white presses and by providing Senator Butler with the statements of poor southern blacks who wanted to emigrate, Bishop Turner certainly did his part to move the bill through Congress.[151]

Of course, the black elite vehemently opposed Butler's legislation.[152] But, in the final analysis, it was misgivings among Butler's partisans in the Senate that doomed the bill. As the debate over the bill played out in the press, most Democratic senators came to see the measure as a losing proposition for their region for two reasons. First, as their fathers and grandfathers had understood, federal funding for the would-be emigrants would undermine their illegitimate aristocracy and labor system. Second, agreeing to help blacks leave the South would be tantamount to surrender in the sectional conflict between the two parties.[153] Thus, the majority of Butler's colleagues ultimately chose direct confrontation with the Republicans over his emigration bill.[154] Without solid support from his own party, Butler's bill died in the Senate Foreign Relations Committee without ever coming to a vote.

Because private efforts could not provide passage for the vast number of southern blacks who wanted to go to Liberia, Butler's inability to bring his bill on to the Senate floor for a vote was a death knell for the emigration movement in the United States. Despite this fact, Bishop Turner and his friends at the ACS and in the Liberian government continued to preach the gospel of emigration to downtrodden southern blacks.[155] Although Turner's target audience understood what the demise of the Butler bill meant for their chances of actually going to Africa, the hardships of life under southern regimes that were now emboldened by the Republicans' decision to renege on their promises to enforce the Fifteenth Amendment continued to give him credibility with many southern blacks.[156]

At the same time, it is important to note that continued support for emigration among the black masses was also a function of limited options. For Frederick Douglass, James Milton Turner, Bishop Benjamin T. Tanner, and the rest of the old guard black leaders who had led the charge against emigrationism in the nineteenth century, the fight over the Butler bill was a last act in their long crusade to protect downtrodden blacks from giving up their rights on the home front. The retirement of these leaders meant that the traditional position of the black elite vis-à-vis emigration was underrepresented in the black counterpublic during the years immediately following the debate over the Butler bill.

Of course, there is no evidence that the black elite would have done any better in winning the hearts and minds of these men and women that they wanted so desperately to protect from Liberia Fever than they had in the period prior to the debate over the Butler bill. After all, the gruesome violence of the second wave of the Counter-Reconstruction in the South after the Democrats won the federal elections of 1892 undermined the ability of the black elite to counsel patience with the political process.[157] What we do know is that scores of blacks joined the internal exodus movements focused on Kansas and that many more continued to write to the ACS about Liberia during this period.[158]

Although passage to either Kansas or Liberia never came for most, a new black leader did emerge to fill the vacuum created as the old lions of the nineteenth century retreated from public life. In 1895, Booker T. Washington, the founder of the Tuskegee Institute, urged black Americans to abandon both emigrationsim and their demands for social and political equality in his Atlanta Compromise speech.[159] Although Washington's speech did nothing more than announce the complete surrender to the harsh realities of the Counter-Reconstruction that most black southerners had already been forced to accept in their personal lives, the acclaim that he garnered from whites after the speech made him the most powerful and revered figure in black America.[160] By embracing Washington as their spokesperson, the black community finally reached a consensus on the emigration issue that bridged the class divide of the postbellum period. As I illustrate in the next chapter, much of the hostility that Marcus Garvey encountered from the generation of radical black leaders who supplanted Washington in the early second decade of the twentieth century was rooted in the fact that his Universal Negro Improvement Association (UNIA) program threatened to rupture this long-sought détente on the issue.

• • •

The behavior of the black elite in the U.S. foreign policymaking arena has never held more significance for black America's domestic struggle for equality than between 1816 and 1890. This is because the federal government frequently embraced policies (promoted by the ACS) that encouraged black emigration to Liberia as a means of reconstituting the United States as an all-white republic. For the most part, the black elite largely rejected association with the continent during this period and worked hard to block policies that sought to stimulate the growth of Liberia to defend their rights and prerogatives on the home front.

There were also rare instances in which the black elite worked to assist the development of Liberia. The conventional wisdom within the interdisciplinary literature on black engagement in the U.S. foreign policymaking arena suggests that the ideational commitments of the black elite derived from transnationalism trumped their concerns about their citizenship status in America during these periods; however, my analyses of archival materials undermine this assertion. Indeed, my central finding is that members of the black elite entered the foreign policymaking arena in support of Liberia only when they calculated that doing so would shift the national discourse about the capacity of the black race for U.S. citizenship.

When we examine the implications of the hard line taken by the black elite on the grassroots exodus movements that emerged during the Counter-Reconstruction for the dominant paradigm on black representation, we see that the members of the black elite behaved in a manner consistent with Michael Dawson's theory of linked fate when seeking to undermine these movements. Their paternalistic attitudes toward rank-and-file blacks, however, generated a set of outcomes that prevented a sizable minority of southern blacks from pursuing a strategy that they believed would improve their life chances. This finding bolsters recent cautionary tales about the nature of linked fate that have appeared in the fields of black politics and social history.

"HIS FAILURE WILL BE THEIRS"
Why the Black Elite Resisted Garveyism and Embraced Ethiopia

> Where I have thought Marcus Garvey to be right, I have said so.... In this Klu Klux Klan attitude, he is just about the wrongest [*sic*] black man that has even tried to lead American Negroes anywhere.
>
> —William Pickens, open letter to Marcus Garvey, July 24, 1922

> Marcus Garvey is either a crook or a liar.... People now are fighting for the erection of democracies not empires. The Negroes don't want to be the victims of black despotism anymore than white despotism.
>
> —A. Philip Randolph, speech on Garveyism before the Friends of Negro Freedom, August 25, 1922

On July 16, 1920, Marcus Mosiah Garvey sat perched in his office in Liberty Hall, the Harlem-based headquarters of his Universal Negro Improvement Association (UNIA), drafting letters. The focal point of his correspondence that day was to invite members of the black elite to attend the UNIA International Conference, which was to take place in Madison Square Garden later that month. W. E. B. Du Bois, one of the founders of the NAACP and the principal architect of the Pan-African Congress Movement, was at the top of Garvey's invitation list.

Garvey's letter to Du Bois asked him to attend the proceedings as a candidate for election to the post of "leader of the American Negro People."[1] (Du Bois and the rest of the black world would learn one month later that the UNIA had already reserved the office of provisional president of Africa for Garvey.) According to the historical record, Du Bois wrote back to Garvey and emphatically declined both the invitation to the conference and Garvey's offer to nominate him to any of his fabricated offices. Du Bois did request, however, that Garvey send him information about the convention for publication in the NAACP's *Crisis* magazine.[2]

After Du Bois rejected his invitation, Garvey scrambled to find a presumptive leader for black Americans among other notable members of the black elite. When all the established black leadership rebuffed his advances,[3] Garvey and the UNIA elected James W. H. Eason, a minister who was little known outside his native Philadelphia, to the post from the floor of the convention. These events typify the gulf that existed between Garvey and the U.S. black elite by the end of the period that Wilson Jeremiah Moses calls the "Golden Age of Black Nationalism."[4]

This dynamic has been a central issue in the historiography of the U.S. black experience since at least the 1950s.[5] The literature revolves around the question: Why did the U.S. black elite reject Garveyism, the most successful mass movement with Pan-African goals, at a time when they exhibited such a strong ideational commitment to transnationalism? Most of the literature on this subject points to an enduring theme in the study of the black elite—the clash of personalities.[6] In other words, most studies suggest that the personal animus between Garvey and leading figures in the black American elite made cooperation impossible.[7] A subtle variation on this argument often appears in the neo-Marxist historiography of Pan-Africanism. These largely pro-Garvey studies portray the UNIA head as a populist who tried to forge ties with the black elite in the United States but found himself rebuffed at every turn because the latter were jealous of his popularity among rank-and-file black Americans.[8]

In this chapter, I present a strong challenge to this notion that the tensions between Garvey and the black elite boiled down to a clash of personalities. I demonstrate that the opposition of black leaders to the Garvey movement was a function of their representational imperative, derived from their sense of linked fate with downtrodden blacks. They judged Garvey's program to be a threat to the interests of the black masses for two reasons. First, his emphasis on repatriation to Africa revived the specter of the late-nineteenth-century emigration movements at a time when the New Negro elite saw opportunities for rank-and-file blacks on the political horizon. Second, the black elite feared that Garvey's support for segregation (like Booker T. Washington's politics of accommodation) provided legitimacy to the white supremacist cause in the South. These causal inferences emerge from both my reexamination of the historical record and new archival research.

The Age of New Negro Pan-Africanism

Members of the black elite had never been as unified about the connection of their community to Africa as they were between 1895 and 1930. Before this time, both the ACS and the grassroots exodusters had always found one or two notable allies among the black elite. As we have seen in chapter 1, both Bishop Henry McNeal Turner and Martin Delany, two of the most prominent black leaders of the Reconstruction era, supported Senator Matthew Butler's 1890 bill calling on the federal government to provide assistance to blacks who wanted to repatriate to Africa.[9]

As black members of the Democratic Party, both Turner and Delany were, undeniably, far outside the mainstream by then. The vast majority of black leaders actively campaigned against the Butler bill, and when the bill was defeated in committee in the Republican-controlled 51st Congress, it represented a rare political victory for the black community in the Nadir period.[10] But the fact of the matter is that the black elite won this day only because their interests converged with the majority of the Republican senators (and a few Democrats too), who continued to see the labor of black Americans as essential to capitalist development in the South.[11]

In light of this fact, it is fitting that Booker T. Washington—whose meteoric rise to prominence in national politics was pushed by this same constellation of interests[12]—proclaimed the death of emigrationism in his infamous 1895 Atlanta Exposition address. "To those of my race who depend on bettering their condition in a foreign land," Washington told the (predominantly white) crowd at the Cotton States and International Exposition, "I would say cast down your bucket where you are—cast it down in making friends in every manly way of the people of all races by whom we are surrounded."[13] Thus, Washington, like the vast majority of black leaders in the nineteenth century, saw facing the social and economic hardships that the United States doled out to blacks as preferable to repatriation in Africa.

Washington's staunch repudiation of emigrationism is not the only similarity between him and the men and women from whom he claimed the mantle of leadership in the black community in 1895. On the contrary, Washington's engagement with Liberia in the first decade of the twentieth century shows that he, too, believed that preserving the independence of the only black republic in the world was a crucially important act in the global theater that was black–white relations in the period. Between 1907 and 1910, Washington emerged as a strong advocate for the Republic of Liberia before both the Theodore Roosevelt and William Taft administrations.[14] In 1909, for example, Washington used his influence with the Taft administration to secure the government of Liberia a loan for the sum of $1.5 million.[15]

At the same time that Washington was using his influence with the Roosevelt and Taft administrations to help preserve the sovereignty of Liberia, he was also engaged in partnerships with colonial powers that sought to spread his model of industrial education and accommodation among indigenous Africans. Indeed, after a speaking tour in Europe, Washington was deluged with letters from leading European colonial powers beseeching his help in training their "native populations" for second-class citizenship.[16] Washington, who was a firm believer in the inferiority of African civilizations, eagerly accepted these opportunities to test his theories abroad.[17]

Even before Washington's efforts on behalf of the Liberians, other members of the black elite were pushing for a more expansive notion of black America's relationship with Africa at the Pan-African Congress of 1900. Henry Sylvester Williams, the West Indian activist, and W. E. B. Du Bois convened the conference in London.[18] The organizers invited Booker T. Washington to attend the proceedings, but he was too busy with activities on the home front to cross the Atlantic to confer with the then-unknown Williams and Du Bois.[19]

It is hard to say how Washington would have viewed the proceedings had he chosen to make the trip. What we do know is that the "Address to the Nations of the World," the main public statement of the conference, which Du Bois authored, contained at least some of the conservative language of social Darwinism that Washington had made the primary mantle of his approach to helping the Europeans with their colonial projects in Africa.[20]

Washington would have almost certainly rejected the remainder of the document because it evinced a radicalism that foreshadowed the rise of the New Negro on the world stage. "[W]e the men and women of Africa, in world congress assembled," Du Bois wrote, "do now solemnly appeal; let not mere colour or race be a feature of distinction drawn between white and black men, regardless of worth or ability."[21] More important, the document made an explicit link between the racism that motivated abuses against black Americans and the forces that drove Europeans to "scramble" for Africa after the Vienna Conference of 1885.[22] This element of the New Negro's Pan-Africanism made a fundamental break with the transnationalism of their forebears, who largely believed (along with the Europeans) that Africa beyond Liberia and Ethiopia was a wasteland ripe for their evangelizing and civilizing missions.[23]

In terms of promoting social and political change in the world system, the London Pan-African Conference was not a success. The European powers completely ignored the "Address to the Nations of the World." The delegates responded to this silence with a pledge of further activism. Indeed, the official report released by the conference announced plans to form a permanent Pan-African Association, comprising a headquarters in London and eleven branch offices around the globe, to lobby the great powers on black issues. The document also stated the delegates' intention to reconvene every two years to gauge the progress of their efforts.[24]

Du Bois's outstanding contributions to the conference made him an obvious choice for the post of vice president of the new Pan-African Association. His duties in this new role were to inaugurate an American branch of the association and lay plans for the 1902 gathering, which was supposed to take place in the United States.[25] Nevertheless, "There is no evidence," writes Clarence Contee, "to show that Du Bois made a substantial effort between 1900 and 1905 to develop a permanent Pan-African Association branch organization in the United States or to prepare for a meeting in 1902."[26]

Historians have not judged Du Bois very harshly for his failure to achieve these goals for three reasons. First, the entire movement stalled because of a lack of funds.[27] Second, it is clear that Du Bois was so heavily engaged in the campaign to topple Booker T. Washington's Tuskegee machine between 1900 and 1912 that he had little time for any other organizing efforts.[28] Third, once he and the other New Negro radicals had toppled the tyranny of "King Booker," as they mockingly referred to Washington in their internal communications, Du Bois reemerged as the driving force behind the resurgent Pan-African Conference movements between 1919 and 1930.[29]

It was Du Bois, for example, who urged the fledgling NAACP to issue a call for delegates to attend a Pan-African Congress in Paris in 1919.[30] His intention was to use the conference, which was to coincide with negotiations over the Versailles Treaty, to exert pressure on the great powers to extend the rights of self-determination to the African colonies. In Du Bois's view, the integration of independent African nations into the new world order that Versailles would establish was a crucial first step to winning more freedoms for blacks living under white supremacist regimes in the diaspora.[31]

The U.S. and French governments must have seen at least some legitimacy in the case that the Pan-African Congress hoped to lay before the world community in Paris; the documentary record clearly indicates that both powers worked to quash the Pan-African Congress through administrative back channels. The Woodrow Wilson administration, for example, prevented most of the Americans slated to attend the conference from obtaining passports.[32] Moreover, the French government denied entry to or deported many of the delegates who did make it to Paris.[33] The deportations ceased only when Blaise Diagne, the highest-ranking African in the French government and a member of Georges Clemenceau's war cabinet, interceded on behalf of the conference.[34]

In the end, fifty-seven delegates from more than fifteen colonies, territories, and nations attended the conference. Although the proceedings were lively and well attended;[35] the conference fell far short of its primary objective of influencing the behavior of the Allied powers.[36] Indeed, even with a powerful insider like Diagne in their corner, the delegates could not get an audience with any of the Allied governments. Moreover, it is clear that only small newspapers paid attention to the proceedings of the Pan-African Congress.[37]

Still, the 1919 gathering was a success in terms of its impact on Africans and blacks living in the diaspora. Before the 1919 conference, the black elite in the United States had consistently demonstrated ambivalent feelings toward Africans and European colonialism on the continent.[38] After the conference, the notion that black Americans should work with Africans and other blacks living in the diaspora through the global system took root in the black community.³⁹

The Rise of the Universal Negro Improvement Association

Born in Jamaica in 1887 into what Tony Martin calls "a peasant environment," Marcus Mosiah Garvey received the standard education for someone of his station under the British colonial system.⁴⁰ At fourteen, Garvey interrupted his formal education because of financial difficulties in his family and took an apprenticeship with a local printer.⁴¹ By the time Garvey reached the age of twenty, he was a master printer and foreman at a Kingston printing firm.⁴² When a strike broke out among the laborers at his firm, a sympathetic Garvey left the ranks of management to help organize the picketers.⁴³ Although, by all accounts, Garvey was an excellent leader, the work stoppage failed to gain concessions from the plant managers, who simply replaced the strikers with lower-cost foreign laborers. Whereas the other printers were able to either return to their jobs or to find work elsewhere after the strike, their young leader was "branded a troublemaker" and completely blacklisted by the major printing firms in Jamaica.⁴⁴ Ironically, this turn of events inspired Garvey to take on the ventures that would convince him that his destiny was in "race leadership."⁴⁵

Garvey's experience with the strike, which he viewed in racial terms, convinced him that only coordinated action by Jamaican blacks would lead whites to give them a better deal. Believing that he could best help to bring this coordination about through journalistic work, Garvey founded two journals in Jamaica between 1910 and 1912.⁴⁶ When both of these enterprises failed, the young rabble-rouser decided to seek further education in England. All of Garvey's biographers agree that time he spent in London was transformative.⁴⁷ Robert H. Brisbane, one of the first scholars to write about Garvey, describes his time in London:

> In [London] the young provincial West Indian...met the members of other darker races who also had their grievances against the Caucasian. These men—followers of Ghandi, Mustapha Kemal Pasha, Dr. Sun Yat Sen, Saad Zaghlul, and Ibn Saud—had definite, clear cut programs to follow. Garvey heard such slogans as "India for the Indians" and "Asia for the Asians." He became interested in the condition of the African Negro as a result of discussions with the followers of Chilembwe of Nyasaland and Kimbangu of the Congo. As a result of these experiences, Garvey's vision broadened perceptibly.⁴⁸

It was also in London where Garvey first became exposed to the ideas of his early role model, Booker T. Washington. Although, as Tony Martin and Colin Grant have demonstrated, Garvey was exposed to the writings of many black thinkers during his time working as a journalist in London, it is clear from his own testimony that Washington's autobiography had a profound effect on him.[49] "I read *Up from Slavery* by Booker T. Washington and then my doom—if I may call it that—of being a race leader dawned upon me," Garvey once confided to his wife and future biographer, Amy Jacques Garvey.[50] Imbibed with this new sense of his life mission, Garvey abandoned his journalism career in London to return to Jamaica and start his career as a full-time "race leader."[51]

Believing that he needed an organizational foundation to implement his vision of black uplift, Garvey founded the Universal Negro Improvement Association and African Communities Imperial League (UNIA) in Kingston in 1914.[52] Although the UNIA manifesto spoke of such Pan-African themes as rehabilitating the race through a universal confraternity, the early program of the organization was, as E. David Cronon has pointed out, more Bookerite than radical.[53] Unfortunately for Garvey, black Jamaicans were not ready for him to lead either a Jamaican Tuskegee or a confraternity promoting radical action on the island. Indeed, Garvey's organization was stunted by his inability to make inroads with middle-class blacks and marred by Garvey's financial improprieties during its one year of operations in Kingston.[54] Ignoring his own foibles, Garvey chalked up his difficulties in his homeland to the fact that "[n]obody wanted to be a Negro."[55]

Refusing to abandon his dream of uniting the black peoples of the world for their mutual progress, Garvey decided to seek fresher fields in the United States.[56] After an inauspicious start on the thriving (and highly competitive) Harlem speakers' circuit, Garvey began to find his stride in his adopted homeland.[57] By the close of 1917, Garvey was successfully recruiting members to his reconstituted UNIA.[58] Two years later, Garvey reported that his UNIA consisted of over thirty branches with 2 million members.[59] By 1920, Garvey was at the head of a complex organization that consisted of a newspaper, several corporations, and a steamship line.[60]

It is clear that Garvey benefited greatly from the fact that he had arrived in the United States in the middle of the realignment of the black rank-and-file from Washington's Tuskegee machine to the radical reformers of the NAACP. Although the black masses supported NAACP efforts to push legal reforms at home and abroad, the failure of the organization to articulate a message helping them to cope with the psychological hardships of daily life under Jim Crow during this period left the people hungry for the type of pro-black self-help messages that Garvey bandied about the black counterpublic. "The profound disillusionment felt by Negroes at the end of the war," writes Cronon, "had much to do with their widespread acceptance of a new and alien leader with an extreme program of racial nationalism."[61]

Most scholars assume that the conflicts that erupted between Garvey (and his followers) and other black advocacy organizations during the height of his movement were a function of their trying to wrest this mantle of leadership from him. On the contrary, my analysis of archival materials demonstrates that these conflicts were rooted in the paternalistic desires of the black elite to protect the masses and the broader civil rights movement from Garvey's malfeasance.

Beyond the Clash of Personalities Thesis

Garvey's relationship with the black elite has been the subject of numerous studies. The consensus is that Garvey and his rivals—W. E. B. Du Bois, A. Philip Randolph, and Kelly Miller—missed a crucial opportunity to advance the black struggle for civil rights in the United States and black equality on the world stage by allowing their personalities to divide them.[62] This literature also tends to stress the similarities between the Pan-African ideals espoused by Garvey and Du Bois. Nevertheless, the historical record does not bear out these claims.[63]

It is easy to understand why previous researchers have put so much emphasis on the personalities of Garvey and the leading figures of the black elite who shared the counterpublic with him between 1916 and 1940. Indeed, even a cursory examination of the documentary records of the UNIA reveals that Garvey saw himself as the victim of continual slights and attacks from the mainstream black elite. Moreover, it is clear that Garvey placed Du Bois, whom he had something of a fixation on, at the center of this movement to defeat the UNIA.[64] It is also true that Du Bois and other members of the black elite did occasionally launch *ad hominem* attacks against Garvey. In 1923, for example, Du Bois described Garvey as "[a] little, fat black man, ugly, but with intelligent eyes and a big head."[65] This comment, however, which Du Bois penned in the middle of Garvey's trial for perpetuating mail fraud against the black community, was particularly out of character for the NAACP activist.

In general, the historical record does not bear out Garvey's claims that he was constantly under assault by the black elite after his arrival in Harlem. On the contrary, a few notable members of the black elite held out high hopes for Garvey's UNIA in the early phase of its development. For example, A. Philip Randolph, who emerged as one of Garvey's harshest critics after 1919, was instrumental in helping the West Indian immigrant gain a foothold in the thriving Harlem network of activists and politicians.[66] In addition, the vast majority of the black elite seemed to be completely uninterested in Garvey or the UNIA during the early years of operation of the organization. Indeed, the records of the NAACP contain no mention of him or his UNIA until 1918.

Moreover, the first record of contact between Garvey and Du Bois appears in Garvey's papers. On April 30, 1915, Garvey wrote to Du Bois to protest an NAACP operative's praising the government of his native Jamaica for progress in race relations.[67] There is no evidence that Du Bois ever received this letter.

Almost one year later, Garvey, who was now working from New York, wrote to Du Bois to ask him to moderate his first public lecture in the United States.[68] Du Bois's secretary returned a form letter to Garvey telling him that her employer was not available on the date of interest.[69] Given that Garvey had yet to make a name for himself in either the United States or his native Jamaica, it is clear that these early dismissive contacts were more a function of his lack of stature than any animus that Du Bois had for the UNIA leader.

The first real notice that Du Bois took of the Garvey movement came in the months after the 1919 Pan-African Congress. On March 27, 1919, Garvey's *Negro World* newspaper ran an editorial that charged that Du Bois had worked to "sabotage" the lobbying efforts of the UNIA emissary to the Versailles Peace Conference.[70] Given the wide circulation of the *Negro World*, Du Bois had to respond to the charges or risk losing credibility with the masses. "The truth was," Du Bois wrote in the December 1920 issue of the *Crisis*, "that Mr. Du Bois never saw or heard of [Garvey's] 'High Commissioner'...and would have been delighted to welcome and co-operate with any colored fellow-worker."[71]

Even after this incident, Du Bois continued to show great restraint when making public statements about Garvey and the UNIA. His treatment of the UNIA 1920 International Convention, the same one that he refused to attend as a nominee for the office of "leader of the American Negro people," is illustrative of his temperate approach to the Garvey movement. In the midst of the convention, Du Bois commented to Charles Mowbray White, a journalist, that the success of the event was borne of the "frustrations" of black servicemen who returned from Europe to find that their "valiant campaigns for democracy" abroad did little to help them in their own communities. Du Bois also told White that he believed that the UNIA movement was likely to "collapse in a short time." In the event that the movement did continue to grow, however, Du Bois pledged that he would not "raise a hand to stop it."[72] Although not exactly a ringing endorsement of Garveyism, these comments make it clear that Du Bois did not see himself as engaged in a turf war with Garvey over the affections of the black rank-and-file.

Black leaders demonstrated an even greater commitment to speaking about the Garvey movement in dispassionate tones in their correspondences with constituents. Between 1919 and 1921, figures such as Du Bois, James Weldon Johnson, and William Pickens were deluged with letters from black citizens who were interested in divining the purity of Garvey's motives and whether his movement had a credible chance of accomplishing his lofty goals. On September 25, 1920, for example, E. G. Woodford of Seattle, Washington, wrote to James Weldon Johnson with hopes of securing accurate information about the "Back-to-Africa Movement" recently "organized by a Mr. Marcus Garvey in New York City."[73] Despite the fact that the leaders of the NAACP were already becoming concerned about the trajectory of the UNIA, a staff member responded promptly, reporting to Mr. Woodford that "Marcus Garvey's address is 56 West 125th Street, New York City."[74]

At the height of Garvey's popularity in 1920 and early 1921, the more traditional civil rights organizations sometimes found themselves in correspondence with black citizens who wrote to express their enthusiasm about the UNIA. Charles Beasley of Ketchikan, Alaska, wrote to the organization to express his sentiment that "Marcus Garvey has done more than any Negro of [the] day to put a lime light on the colored race."[75] On that same day, Walter White, then serving as the assistant field secretary of the organization, wrote back to Mr. Beasley, "We have no quarrel with you if you feel that Marcus Garvey is doing more than any other Negro today for the colored man."[76] This spirit of equanimity demonstrated by the members of the black elite when talking and writing about Garvey and the UNIA from 1918 until the middle of 1921 undermines the view that they worked against the UNIA from its inception.

The measured approach that characterized the response of the black leadership to Garveyism between 1918 and 1921 provides a stark contrast to the way that the black press portrayed the UNIA movement. Indeed, when we chart the levels of positive, neutral, and negative coverage of the Garvey movement in four of the largest U.S. black newspapers between 1918 and 1923 (figure 2.1), we find that the view of Garvey in the black press was overwhelmingly negative. Moreover, by 1922, the year that the government indicted Garvey on charges of mail fraud, negative items in the black press about the provisional president of Africa outnumbered positive items by a ratio of eight to one.

As this negative commentary and coverage began to fill the pages of the black press, Du Bois and other black leaders began to speak out more forcefully against Garvey and his followers in the UNIA.[77] Indeed, just one month after his interview with White, Du Bois began to express some real concerns about the Garvey movement in the *Crisis*. In particular, Du Bois warned that Garvey's espousal of the virtues of black separatism and limited emigration to Africa was sending the wrong message to the U.S. power structure.[78] In the September 1920 issue of the *Crisis*, for example, Du Bois urged Garvey and his mostly "West Indian" followers to beware of violating the political norms of the "12 million black men of America."[79]

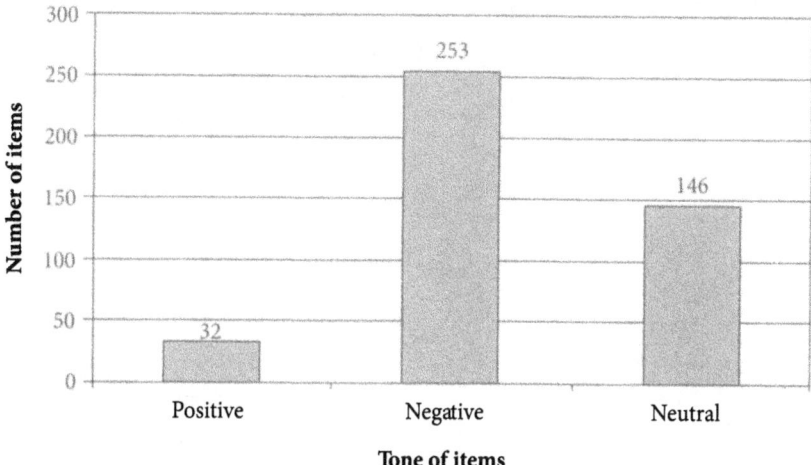

FIGURE 2.1 The Garvey movement in the black press, 1918–1923; numbers of articles, editorials, and letters.
Sources: *Atlanta Daily World; Chicago Defender; New York Amsterdam News; Pittsburgh Courier*

Some scholars have suggested that Du Bois's essay was more propaganda than a dispassionate analysis of the Garvey movement; in other words, Du Bois tried to minimize the importance of the UNIA by portraying it as a movement dominated by foreign-born blacks. A quantitative content analysis of black print sources between 1916 and 1928, however, shows that Du Bois was certainly not alone in thinking that Afro-Caribbean immigrants were the backbone of the UNIA. The first two columns in figure 2.2, which summarizes the results of the content analysis, focus on the sixty editorials and letters that appeared in four leading black newspapers in this period and addressed the ethnic composition of the Garvey movement. The analysis shows that 53 of the items (88 percent) represented in these two columns framed the UNIA as a movement with a largely foreign-born membership base. By contrast, only 7 items (12 percent) in this sample saw the UNIA as a movement comprising mostly native-born blacks. Moreover, because 35 percent of the items that contain this frame appeared in print before Du Bois published his editorial in the *Crisis*, it is clear that he was merely reproducing a well-worn interpretation of the movement.

Whereas Du Bois's essay was a not so subtle nudge for Garvey to take his cues on domestic issues from native-born blacks, other members of the black elite attacked the UNIA leader more directly. William Pickens, an officer of the NAACP, published an open letter to Garvey in the *Chicago Defender* in which he attacked Garvey for attempting to "decitizenize the American Negro" by stirring up the "foolish" ideology of emigrationism.[80] Similarly, A. Philip Randolph—the man who had helped Garvey get his start in Harlem—rebuked him in the pages

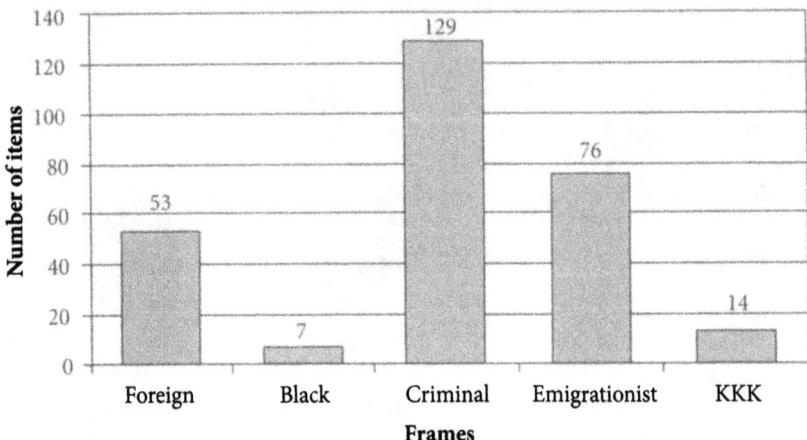

FIGURE 2.2 Black media frames of Marcus Garvey, 1916–1928. KKK, Ku Klux Klan. Sources: *Atlanta Daily World; Chicago Defender; New York Amsterdam News; Pittsburgh Courier*

of the *Messenger* for selling downtrodden blacks the "pipe dream" of a better life in Africa.[81] These responses show how deeply engrained negative sentiments toward emigrationism remained in the black elite even two generations after the end of the Civil War.

Although Du Bois was also deeply concerned about Garvey's resurrection of emigrationism in the black counterpublic, he took greater issue (at least throughout 1920) with the UNIA chief's rhetorical style and the disarray of his organization. In other words, the larger problem for Du Bois was that Garvey was becoming "bombastic, wasteful, illogical and ineffective" at precisely the moment that his movement was garnering more attention from the mainstream press.[82] Even at this point, however, Du Bois maintained (at least in public) that Garvey was "essentially an honest and sincere man with a tremendous vision, great dynamic force, stubborn determination and unselfish desire to serve."[83] At the same time, he feared that Garvey's inability to follow through on his increasingly grandiose claims would ultimately reflect poorly on the entire black community. Du Bois's remark that he was worried about the rank-and-file blacks who joined the UNIA in droves because he did not want Garvey's inevitable "failure" to become "theirs" eloquently sums up his sentiments during this period.[84]

Within two years of the publication of Du Bois's assessment in the pages of *Crisis*, both Garvey's sincerity and honesty were on trial in the black counterpublic and the federal courts. As Du Bois had predicted, Garvey's tactics and management style led him down a path of self-destruction. Although Garvey's deficiencies as a leader—particularly his tendency to delegate important financial and operational decisions to incompetent subordinates—weakened UNIA businesses across the board, the poor performance of the Black Star Line was the iceberg that ultimately sank his movement.

Garvey first floated the idea of establishing the Black Star Line to compete with the large steamship companies that traversed the Atlantic in a series of speeches at Liberty Hall in early 1919.[85] Tony Martin has argued that "Garvey was attempting to fulfill a long-felt need [in the black community]" when he established the Black Star Line; in other words, Garvey's vision was a direct response to the fact that blacks "were routinely subjected to racist practices on existing shipping lines."[86] The popular response to Garvey's announcement of the formation of the Black Star Line in black communities certainly supports Martin's interpretation.

Despite the timeliness of Garvey's idea, however, it is clear that the Black Star Line was doomed from its inception because neither Garvey nor any of the other directors of the corporation had experience in the shipping industry.[87] Because of this lack of knowledge about complex business and legal issues entailed by running such an enterprise, the group deferred to Joshua Cockburn, the man whom they had hired to captain the first vessel of the line, regarding the purchase of the first ship and most of the early business transactions of the corporation. There is no doubt that Cockburn had the credentials to captain the Black Star Line vessels. Indeed, the forty-three-year-old, who like Garvey was an Afro-Caribbean immigrant to New York, had served in the British Navy and was one of the few blacks living in the United States who was certified to captain an ocean-going steamship.[88]

The vessel that Cockburn recommended that the UNIA purchase and make the Black Star Line flagship was a thirty-year-old steamship, *SS Yarmouth*, that had been recently decommissioned from its role as a supply ship for the Allied powers during World War I.[89] Although, as some employees of the Black Star Line later recalled, the poor condition of the ship was obvious to anyone who set foot on board, Cockburn assured the directors that it was seaworthy. He also convinced them that the $165,000 asking price for the vessel was reasonable.[90]

The first snag in the development of the Black Star Line was that, despite Garvey's constant boasting about the financial successes of the UNIA business enterprises, the organization did not have the 10 percent cash deposit that the sellers required for him to take possession of the ship. Cockburn suggested that the directors resolve this problem by entering into a $2,000 per month lease agreement.[91] In Cockburn's view, leasing the ship would produce such a "psychological effect on the people" that it was bound to "boost the sale of stock" enough to raise the capital for the down payment.[92] Because the entire Garvey movement was based on this type of prospective thinking, the Black Star Line directors enthusiastically embraced Cockburn's proposal.[93] Indeed, throughout the summer of 1919, Garvey raced around the country pushing Black Star Line stock on black audiences.[94] Thanks to these engagements, the enterprise was able to accumulate enough capital to take possession of the *Yarmouth* and schedule its maiden voyage for October 31, 1919.[95]

Claude Mckay, a leading intellectual light of the Harlem Renaissance, reported in his landmark history of Harlem that a "delirious" crowd turned out to witness the *Yarmouth* sail for the first time as the flagship of the Black Star Line.[96] What the crowd did not know at the time, however, was that the *Yarmouth* would only be allowed to sail down the Hudson as far as 23rd Street because the Black Star Line had not properly worked out the transfer of insurance from the previous owners.[97] Although the insurance problem was corrected in a few days, this was only the first of the problems that the Black Star Line encountered in the field of transatlantic shipping.

Cockburn, who was drawing a princely salary of $400 per month from his captaincy, had been both a poor and dishonest agent for the Black Star Line.[98] Almost as soon as the company took control of the *Yarmouth*, it became abundantly clear that both Cockburn's valuation of the ship and estimation that it was seaworthy were false. Indeed, the Black Star Line had to spend $5,000 to repair the main boiler of the ship just to make it safe for its first scheduled run between New York City and Havana, Cuba. A Black Star Line employee later stated that the ship's condition made it clear that it was not "worth a penny over $25,000."[99]

Cockburn immediately proclaimed the boiler problem sabotage. It is possible that he might have actually believed this interpretation because he became increasingly erratic—even paranoid—about the movements of the *Yarmouth* after this incident. At the same time, the fact that Cockburn had received a kickback from the sellers for pushing the ship on the UNIA stands as clear evidence that he knew that the ship was overvalued.[100] Thus, perhaps his behavior was just an elaborate ruse to help him maintain Garvey's confidence and his lucrative position. Whatever Cockburn's intentions, he did maintain Garvey's trust in the first months of the operation of the line.

Despite the dark clouds that seemed to swirl around the venture from its inception, Garvey and the directors continued to push an aggressive plan for the Black Star Line. Indeed, even before the *Yarmouth* returned to port from its first run, Garvey negotiated an $11,000 charter with the Green River Distillery to ship its remaining supply of spirits, worth $4 million, out of the United States before the start of Prohibition. The contract showcased the inexperience of Garvey and the other managers of the Black Star Line—the fee was roughly 10 percent of what an experienced shipping company would have charged the liquor company for such a job.[101] To make matters worse, the contract that Garvey signed violated the norms of the shipping industry by promising to fully indemnify the cargo.[102]

This indemnity clause ultimately proved disastrous when the *Yarmouth* encountered a storm soon after it set sail from New York to meet the obligations of the contract. Although the storm was minor, the *Yarmouth*—which was still not in good sailing order—began to list.[103] To keep the ship from capsizing, Cockburn ordered the crew to throw five hundred bottles of whiskey overboard. In addition, an unspecified amount of the Green River Distillery shipment had been damaged due to the crew's hasty loading job.[104] To make matters worse, federal prohibition officers seized the cargo once the vessel was towed back to the port of New York; this meant that the Black Star Line failed to meet the agreed-on delivery date spelled out in the contract.[105] As a result of all these problems, the Black Star Line ended up paying damages and delay penalties to the Green River Distillery that far exceeded the $11,000 pittance that it had been promised to carry the cargo.[106]

Yet the dismal performance of the *Yarmouth* during its first major shipping operation did not dampen Garvey's belief in the enterprise. On the contrary, he announced his intentions to expand the Black Star Line fleet just one month after concluding the Green River Distillery contract.[107] Garvey did make one major change in the operation of the company—he decided to fire Cockburn.[108] But even with a new captain at the helm, the Black Star Line remained unprofitable. Indeed, the company spent every penny that it took in during its first year of operations.

Despite the fact that Garvey had lost faith in Cockburn after the Green River Distillery fiasco, he remained committed to the confidence man's business model for the Black Star Line. In other words, Garvey continued to use the excitement that swirled around his acquisition of the *Yarmouth* to prop up the worthless company stock in the black community.[109] This practice, as the more than $750,000 in revenue illustrate, was the only successful part of the Black Star Line operation. Of course, it was also a very volatile strategy because it increased the demands on the company to perform in an efficient and profitable manner. For example, there was considerable backlash among the shareholders when Garvey announced that the Black Star Line would yield no dividends for investors at the end of its first year of operations.[110]

By the middle of 1921, Garvey's credibility in the black community began to sag under the weight of complaints from disgruntled investors in the Black Star Line. Many of these investors wrote to the leaders of other black organizations seeking counsel about how best to recoup their investments. It was in this context that some black politicians and activists began to talk openly among themselves about organizing a movement to lobby the federal government to press charges against Garvey and the UNIA.[111]

The Federal Bureau of Investigation (FBI) had already been steadily building a case against Garvey since 1919. The government's efforts were not motivated by a desire to protect the black community from Garvey's malfeasance; on the contrary, the central aim was to suppress Garvey's tendency to stir up the masses in large black population centers. J. Edgar Hoover, who led a campaign to undermine the entire movement for black civil rights when he took over the FBI in the 1950s, actually got his start in the agency by signaling to his superiors that Garvey was a "dangerous alien" who they should prosecute as soon as he gave them the opportunity by violating a federal law.[112]

The federal government, which integrated the FBI to infiltrate the UNIA, did not have to wait long for Garvey to provide them with enough fodder to press a case against him. By 1921, the entire Black Star Line was nothing more than a kiting scheme. In February of that year, Garvey announced that the company, which was now the owner of three decrepit ships that attempted to travel between New York and the Caribbean, would add a ship to its fleet that would travel to the coast of West Africa.[113] As Garvey planned yet another stock offering to raise capital for the Black Star Line, he added a new dimension to his pitch—a flier with an image of the ship that he intended to purchase. Garvey did not tell his would-be shareholders that the ship depicted on the flier, the *SS Orion*, was not yet in the possession of the company. On the contrary, he encouraged potential investors to think that the Black Star Line already owned the ship by embossing the image of the *Orion* with the name *SS Phyllis Wheatley*, which was the name he had pledged to use to christen the new ship in several speeches and in UNIA propaganda.[114]

Garvey's defenders in the historical literature have pointed out that the Black Star Line was engaged in negotiations to purchase the *Orion* at the time of the stock offering; nevertheless, the flier constituted fraud under most state and federal commerce laws.[115] Moreover, Garvey's decision to circulate the flier through the U.S. mail left him vulnerable to the very serious charge of mail fraud. And, indeed, this was the offense Garvey was charged with when he was arrested by federal agents (along with several of his subordinates) on January 12, 1922.[116]

Garvey wasted no time in rising to his own defense against the mail fraud charges in the black counterpublic. Indeed, he addressed a large rally of more than 1,000 supporters at Liberty Hall just one day after he was released from the Tombs prison on a $2,500 bond.[117] Despite the facts that the *SS Phyllis Wheatley* circulars were a complete misrepresentation of the health of the Black Star Line and that the company was in shambles due to his own gross incompetence as a manager, Garvey laid the blame for his predicament on "Negro Advancement Associations" that had paid "saboteurs" to destroy the company.[118] As Gary Grant has pointed out, Garvey clearly intended his remarks to suggest that W. E. B. Du Bois and the NAACP were to blame for the downfall of the Black Star Line.[119]

Pinning the blame on his rivals was a well-worn tactic that Garvey used quite frequently when something went wrong with one of his UNIA operations. Of course, Garvey's claim that rival black organizations were behind the woes of the Black Star Line was preposterous. Despite this, some historians have maintained that the attacks that rival black leaders launched against the Black Star Line (and against the broader Garvey movement) in the black counterpublic provided the federal government with the necessary cover to move against Garvey.[120]

This interpretation ignores three facts: (1) the plaintiffs in the government case against Garvey were members of the black rank-and-file (not the rival organizations) who had a real stake in having the court provide them with a remedy, (2) Garvey's own disgruntled employees (not the rival organizations) were the ones who first tipped off a government agency that the operations of the Black Star Line were legally suspect,[121] and (3) the architects of the government case against the Garvey movement were certainly not inclined to form alliances with any organizations whose principal aim was the advancement of black equality in the United States. At the same time, it is certainly true that many black leaders became more forthcoming about their opposition to Garveyism after Garvey was arrested for mail fraud. Du Bois, for example, reversed his early public stance on Garvey's character in a scathing editorial in the *Crisis* that labeled the UNIA leader a "demagogue."[122]

Garvey organized a nationwide speaking tour to present his side of the Black Star Line story and to raise money for a dense fund. It was on this tour that he made the tactical error that proved to be the death knell of the UNIA. Believing that the Klu Klux Klan (KKK), an organization with one of the largest memberships in the United States in the 1920s, might be able to intercede on his behalf with the U.S. government and pump much needed cash into the Black Star Line, Garvey courted the favor of Edward Young Clarke, the KKK leader.[123] In the aftermath of the Clarke meeting, Garvey's many opponents within the black elite banded together in the Garvey Must Go! campaign to urge the federal government to remain vigilant in its prosecution of Garvey for mail fraud.[124] Moreover, after the Clarke meeting, Garvey lost virtually all of his support among the U.S. black masses. Two years after this public relations fiasco, the federal government finally won its conviction against Garvey for mail fraud.

Ironically, jail time convinced Garvey that the failure of his movement was rooted in his lack of attention to the domestic issues. From his cell, Garvey instructed his remaining followers to convert the UNIA into an organization dedicated to achieving full citizenship rights and equality for blacks in the United States. In short, the man who once denounced the NAACP agenda as being "more dangerous" for black Americans than the activities of the Ku Klux Klan now shared the vision of that organization. Unfortunately for Garvey (and his followers), he was now saddled with such negative associations in the black counterpublic that there was no chance for his vision of a UNIA refocused on the domestic civil rights struggle in the United States ever coming to fruition. Indeed, as figure 2.2 illustrations, 129 (46 percent) of the items that appeared about Garvey in the four leading black newspapers between 1916 and 1928 framed him as a criminal. Seventy-six (27 percent) of the items framed Garvey as a nineteenth-century–style emigrationist who wanted black Americans to give up their citizenship rights in the United States. Finally, 14 items (5 percent of the coverage) framed Garvey as an agent of the Ku Klux Klan.

Pan-Africanism versus Black Imperialism

In 1955, Ben F. Rogers published an article in the *Journal of Negro History* entitled "William E.B. Du Bois, Marcus Garvey, and Pan-Africa." This article is a seminal paper in the development of the clash-of-personalities thesis. In it, Rogers makes two central claims: (1) that both Du Bois and Garvey believed that "uniting all the Negroes of the world into one great organization" was the best way to advance the race and (2) that the two men allowed a "bitter" rivalry to prevent them from cooperating in achieving this common vision.[125] But, as we have seen in the previous section, Du Bois and the other black leaders who opposed Garvey's movement acted primarily out of a sense of linked fate with rank-and-file blacks, not out of personal animosity; in other words, the black elite opposed Garveyism because they saw the UNIA leader's program as a threat to the masses. In this section, I show that this same dynamic was at work when the black elite confronted Garveyism in the external context. Moreover, contrary to the position taken by Rogers and a number of other scholars, most black leaders saw a world of difference between the Pan-Africanism espoused by figures such as W. E. B. Du Bois and the vision of black world unity promoted by Garvey.

It is easy to see why some historians have argued that Du Bois and Garvey had similar visions of Pan-Africanism. This is so because throughout 1919 and the first few months of 1920, the UNIA's engagement with issues in African affairs was essentially a boiled-down version of the Pan-African Congress movement. By the close of 1920, however, the same bombast and unsteadiness that undermined Garvey on the home front began to manifest itself in his statements about colonialism, issues in African affairs, and U.S. foreign policy.

The first UNIA foray into international affairs was an attempt to influence the behavior of the great powers at the Versailles Peace Conference. Indeed, like the delegates to the Second Pan-African Congress, Garvey saw the gathering as a prime opportunity to articulate the grievances of the black world to the dominant power structure. In December 1918, Garvey announced in the pages of the *Negro World* that he intended to dispatch an envoy to the conference to lobby the great powers to make "Africa for the Africans."[126] Garvey's decision to appoint Eliezer Cadet the UNIA high commissioner to the Versailles conference further illustrates his penchant for assigning important roles to people completely unqualified to fill them.

Cadet was a twenty-one-year-old Haitian immigrant. Shortly after he arrived in his adopted home of West Virginia, he became an avid reader of the *Negro World* and eventually joined the local UNIA branch.[127] Cadet came to Garvey's attention after he wrote a passionate letter to the *Negro World* condemning the U.S. military occupation of Haiti.[128] Beyond this editorial letter, Cadet's only qualification for such a high-level mission was that he was fluent in French.[129]

Not surprisingly, the inexperienced Cadet, lacking accreditation from the French bureaucracy to attend the closed sessions of the conference, had no more success in influencing (or even contacting) the representatives of the great powers than did his rivals at the Pan-African Congress.[130] During his brief time in Garvey's inner circle, Cadet obviously had imbibed the central lesson that UNIA leaders should never let the truth intrude on the movement because the reports that he wired back to New York were pure fiction. In his first cable back to UNIA headquarters, which Garvey read to a gathering of the faithful, Cadet wrote that he had already hand-delivered the demands of the organization to French Prime Minister Georges Clemenceau.[131]

We know from contemporaneous accounts that Cadet found it impossible to get access to Clemenceau or any of the major players at Versailles. Moreover, Cadet also found himself rebuffed by C. D. B. King, the Liberian secretary of state and president-elect, and the only delegate to the conference who represented a functioning black republic. Henry Worley, an U.S.-appointed financial advisor who accompanied King to most of the sessions at Versailles, recorded in his journal that the president-elect scolded Cadet in their brief encounter because he was displeased with some of the outlandish statements that he had read in the *Negro World*.[132]

Perhaps it was Cadet's recognition that there would be other records of his time in Paris than his own that prompted his next move. On March 22, 1919, Cadet wired UNIA headquarters to report that W. E. B. Du Bois was now sabotaging his efforts in Paris by speaking out against articles chronicling the horrors of lynchings in the United States that he had circulated to the French press.[133] It is hard to know how seriously Garvey, who now routinely blamed just about every setback that the UNIA movement experienced on sabotage perpetrated by Du

Bois and the NAACP, took Cadet's charges. What we do know is that on receiving the cable he immediately convened a mass meeting at the Mother Zion AME Church in Harlem, where he denounced Du Bois a "race traitor" for interfering with his envoy's mission.[134] Garvey also sent a telegram "repudiating" Du Bois's efforts to sabotage Cadet to the French press.[135]

Du Bois responded to Cadet's charges against him in the pages of the *Crisis* magazine. "The truth," Du Bois wrote in defense of himself, "was that Mr. Du Bois never saw or heard of [Garvey's] 'High Commissioner,' never denied his nor anyone's statements of the wretched American conditions, did everything possible to arouse rather than quiet the French press and would have been delighted to welcome and co-operate with any colored fellow-worker."[136] As Elliot Skinner has pointed out, the historical record clearly supports Du Bois's interpretation of events.[137]

Cadet's poor showing in France did not alter Garvey's belief that the UNIA could make an impact on the international system. On the contrary, the UNIA chief decided to pursue further diplomatic operations on Cadet's return to the United States. During the 1920 UNIA convention, for example, Garvey announced his plans to send a commission to the League of Nations to establish formal relations between the international organization and the UNIA. In May 1922, this commission, under the leadership of George Marke, an Oxford-trained UNIA official from Sierra Leone, traveled to Geneva, Switzerland, to deliver a petition from the UNIA to Sir Eric Drummond, the League's secretary-general.[138]

The petition articulately spelled out a number of grievances that the black world held as a result of exploitation at the hands of the great powers and other European nations. It also demanded that the League should give the UNIA control over the colonies that Germany had been forced to cede to the League as part of the Treaty of Versailles.[139] From the perspective of the UNIA, handing over these mandate territories to the organization would be an important first step toward redress and racial reconciliation.

Although the Marke delegation did not meet with Drummond, they did present their petition to the head of the Mandate Section of the League. Moreover, as the historical record indicates, the secretary-general did eventually pass the petition on to the full membership of the League. But, because the great powers remained committed to holding on to their colonial possessions in Africa and Asia, it is not at all surprising that the UNIA petition and all subsequent overtures made by the organization to the League were patently ignored by the Secretariat.[140]

The actions of the Marke delegation in Geneva illustrate the crucial difference between Garvey's vision of black world unity and that put forward by Du Bois and the Pan-African Congress movement. The First Pan-African Congress that took place in London in 1900 was flawed because none of the delegates was from Africa. As a result, the delegates to the gathering have been (justly) criticized for making the essentialist claim that their skin color enabled them to represent the interests of the continent. The push among the conveners of the Second Pan-African Congress to include African voices among the delegates was a direct response to this problem. But by petitioning for control of the German mandates without consulting even one inhabitant of these territories, the UNIA went far beyond the essentialist fallacy that marred the first Pan-African Congress. In short, the UNIA was advocating replacing European imperialism with imperialism in the name of racial advancement—a position that fueled much of the opposition that Garvey encountered from black leaders in the U.S. foreign policymaking arena and on the global stage.

We see this dynamic at work very clearly in the narrative of the UNIA efforts to establish a UNIA settlement in the Republic of Liberia. At the same conference where he divulged his plans to send the Marke delegation to the League of Nations, Garvey also announced that he hoped to secure a base in Liberia.[141] Although he had not yet entered into formal negotiations for such a base, Garvey was confident that his relationship with Gabriel Moore Johnson, whom he bestowed with the title leader of the African people during the conference proceedings, would pave the way to such talks. Johnson was both the mayor of Monrovia (the Liberian capital city) and the father-in-law of Charles D. B. King (the Liberian president), so it is easy to see why Garvey believed he was the right man to help him curry favor with the Liberian government. On January 18, 1921, Garvey wrote to Johnson asking him to use his "good offices" with President King to help the UNIA secure 5,000 acres of land in Liberia.[142]

This display of political ingenuity not withstanding, Garvey remained the erratic man that Du Bois had described in his 1920 *Crisis* editorial. For example, in the same week that he secured Johnson's support, Garvey undermined his new ally's ability to work on his behalf by announcing that he was dispatching men from the UNIA to Liberia to facilitate the "conquest" of Africa.[143] Garvey's opponents in the U.S. black elite seized on this statement as evidence that the UNIA head, who had taken to calling himself the "Provisional President of Africa," was committed to destabilizing Liberia. W. E. B. Du Bois, the man whom Garvey's envoy had falsely accused of sabotaging his efforts during the Versailles conference, led the charge against the UNIA. "[W]ithout arms, money, effective organization or a base of operations," Du Bois wrote in an editorial in the *Crisis*, "Mr. Garvey talks of 'Conquest'...and of himself becoming a black Napoleon!"[144] A. Philip Randolph's response to Garvey's speech was even more direct. "Negro exploiters and tyrants," Randolph wrote of Garvey's plans in the *Messenger*, "are as bad as white ones."[145]

The majority of editorialists and letter writers who commented on Garvey's engagement with Africa in the leading black newspapers also saw the UNIA head's stance toward Liberia (and toward the rest of Africa) as imperialistic. Indeed, a full 56 percent of the 108 items focused on UNIA activities in Africa that appeared in the four black newspapers with the largest circulation between 1918 and 1923 described Garvey as an imperialist. And according to the historical record, the leaders of the Republic of Liberia concurred with this interpretation of the Garvey movement.

Garvey's statement, made at a crucial stage in the relations between the United States and Liberia, could not have been uttered at a worse time. In March 1921, almost two months after Garvey's statement about conquering Africa, a diplomatic delegation from Liberia, led by President King, arrived in the United States to attempt to extract yet another financial lifeline from the U.S. government. The loan negotiations had started under the Wilson administration's postwar program of economic revival for small nations trying to consolidate their democratic institutions. By the time the United States and Liberia really got into the thick of negotiations over the loan, however, Americans were exhibiting signs of revitalized isolationist tendencies. The Republicans capitalized on this sentiment in the election of 1920, and they quickly went to work dismantling the last remnants of Wilson's foreign policy, including the loan.

Unlike the other nations trying to maintain aid flows from the United States to their coffers, however, Liberia had always maintained a special relationship with the United States.[146] Because these historical connections were generated primarily to make an impact on the structure of race relations within the United States, it is not at all surprising that the nature of racial politics in 1920 helped save the loan to Liberia from the Senate Foreign Relation Committee chopping block. Although Republican Party members were eager to dismantle Wilson's legacy, they were just as eager to consolidate their most recent round of success at the polls. One way that President Warren Harding proposed to do this was by reestablishing a positive relationship with black Americans. Like all previous Republican presidents, however, Harding was willing to reach out to blacks only on issue areas that would not cost him white supporters. Thus, the twenty-ninth president, who had been elected on a staunchly isolationist platform, sought to use the foreign policymaking arena to achieve these two competing ends. Liberia represented a win-win situation for the new president. Already garnering praise for returning to the practice of making black appointments in the civil service, particularly to foreign policy posts dealing with the black world, Harding knew that a well-timed gesture in support of Liberia would continue to strike a stark contrast to his thoroughly racist Democratic predecessor.

In this new, more open environment in the foreign affairs arena, mainstream black politicians were given a tremendous amount of access to the Liberian delegation when they arrived in Washington, D.C., to close the negotiations on the loan agreement.[147] Because the great majority of these men viewed Garveyism as a distinct threat, it is not surprising that their closeness to President King of Liberia had a deleterious effect on Garvey's negotiations with the Liberian government for land within its territory. On June 8, 1921, during the height of congressional action on the Liberian loan, President King published an open letter in the pages of Du Bois's *Crisis* in which he denounced Garvey's plan to make his nation a "center of aggression or conspiracy against other sovereign states."[148] On the heels of this statement, all negotiations between the Liberian legislature and the UNIA delegation headed by the mayor of Monrovia ceased;[149] moreover, during their two months in the United States, King and his diplomatic team forged a strong working relationship with W. E. B. Du Bois and the NAACP.[150]

King's cooperation with the NAACP and repudiation of Garvey demonstrate that the Liberian government, at least, drew a sharp distinction between the Pan-Africanism of the New Negro and Garveyism. This provides a serious challenge to the view that there was a fundamental basis for cooperation between the two camps in the U.S. foreign policymaking arena.

Psalm 48:31

After the European "scramble for Africa" in 1885 and 1886, Liberia and Ethiopia were the only two independent nations on the African continent. The Americo-Liberians faced constant threats to Liberian sovereignty from the colonial powers that shared their borders, and the U.S. black elite remained consistently engaged in the business of helping Liberians to preserve their independence in the late nineteenth and twentieth centuries. Despite the depth of these ties between the black elite and Liberia, it was Ethiopia that played the leading role in the most important event in the history of black America's connection with Africa prior to World War II.

Two critical events placed Ethiopia over Liberia in the consciousness of the black elite in the 1930s. The first was a report issued in 1930 by Charles S. Johnson, a leading black sociologist, which revealed that the Americo-Liberians were driving the indigenous peoples of Liberia into forced labor for multinational corporations.[151] Given that most of the New Negro elite members were just one generation removed from the peonage of sharecropping, it is not surprising that they reacted to this news with outrage. In the wake of Johnson's report, there was a significant cooling in relations between Liberia and black leaders in the United States.

Despite the importance of the Liberian labor scandal in reorienting the foreign policy goals of the civil rights establishment, it was the attempt by Benito Mussolini, the Italian dictator, to conquer Ethiopia, the only independent nation in Africa that black Americans still felt was worthy of their affections, that made Ethiopia the top priority of the black elite in the U.S. foreign policymaking arena. It is also important to note that the black masses pushed their leaders to act in the U.S. foreign policymaking arena by making the preservation of Ethiopian independence an issue in domestic politics. This hypermobilization around the issue on the home front shows that many of Garvey's lessons about their bonds of kinship with Africa remained salient for the black masses even though his own movement had ended in disgrace.

But, despite Garvey's importance in laying the groundwork for many of the grassroots activists who would take center stage during black America's response to the Italian-Ethiopian War, he was not the first person to make the black masses aware of the special status of Ethiopia in the community of nations. On the contrary, it was Emperor Menelik II of Ethiopia who had first reached across the Atlantic to communicate a message of kinship to black Americans when his kingdom came under assault by the forces of King Umberto during the first Italian-Ethiopian War (1895–1896). Moreover, after his armies had repelled the Italian forces, Menelik, believing that modernization was the best way to protect Ethiopian sovereignty, encouraged skilled blacks from the diaspora to settle in Ethiopia and serve in his court.[152]

Emperor Haile Selassie continued his predecessor's practice of reaching out to blacks in the diaspora when he ascended to the throne in 1918.[153] In 1927, for example, he dispatched Azaj Workneh Martin, the Ethiopian ambassador to the United Kingdom, on a mission to the United States to renew diplomatic ties with the government and recruit skilled black Americans for the service of the kingdom. Although Martin received a warm reception from the black community in New York and Washington, D.C., his efforts were unsuccessful in terms of producing a migration flow.[154] In light of these warm relations between the Ethiopian government and black Americans, it is not at all surprising that the second attempt by Italy to conquer the east African kingdom in 1935 "stoked deep passions," to borrow the historian Robert Weisbord's words, in the black masses.[155]

What is surprising is the level of grassroots mobilization that took place in response to the conflict. Indeed, even though many blacks believed that Selassie's government was guaranteed a victory by the messianic prophecy at the heart of Psalm 48:31, which reads, "Princes shall come out of Africa: Ethiopia shall stretch forth her hands to God," black population centers erupted in mass demonstrations in support of the Ethiopian cause.[156] In addition, as it became clearer that Ethiopia faced an uphill fight against Mussolini's modernized Italian army, many blacks began to inquire about how they could volunteer for service in the Ethiopian army. "We earnestly pledge to you our support and assistance in every way possible for the cause of Ethiopia, our mother land, that we will dye [sic] if necessary for her protection to which we are interested," wrote a group of black men from Philadelphia to the emperor.[157] Even more impressive than black men pledging to fight in a far-off land they had never set eyes on is the fact that, in the pinch of the Great Depression, thousands of black Americans demonstrated their solidarity with Ethiopia by contributing their extremely hard-earned dollars to fund-raising drives in support of Ethiopia.[158] Many historians of this period rightly see remnants of Garveyism in the willingness of black Americans to make these sacrifices.[159]

The Ethiopian government was pleased with these demonstrations, but it did not want to encourage black Americans to do anything to violate the laws of the United States. Because President Franklin Roosevelt had ordered Secretary of State Cordell Hull to declare strict neutrality in the conflict just a few hours after learning that Italian planes were bombing Adowa on October 5, 1935, there was no doubt that U.S. citizens' enlisting in the Ethiopian army would be a violation of federal law.[160] In this context, the Ethiopian government began to view its kith and kin in the U.S. black community more as a political ally in the fight to get the Roosevelt administration to reverse its stance than as a source of fighting men.[161] Apparently this tactic worked because the leading civil rights organizations in the United States, the NAACP and the Urban League, undertook a lobbying campaign to get the United States to sanction Italy.[162]

But the fact that the Ethiopian government and the mainstream civil rights organizations of the U.S. black community had all turned away from the idea of black Americans entering the war as combatants did little to discourage rank-and-file blacks from continuing to advocate the idea themselves. The idea was also kept alive by a number of populist organizations.[163] Most of these groups were led by entrepreneurial activists associated with the same Harlem tradition of soapbox oratory that had brought Marcus Garvey to prominence in the second decade of the twentieth century. Like Garvey, many of the most popular of these figures were West Indian immigrants; moreover, many of these speakers had initiated their careers as political agitators in the Garvey movement of the 1920s.[164] Joseph Harris describes how the UNIA movement served as a training ground for some of the most prominent grassroots organizers who operated in black neighborhoods during the Italian-Ethiopian conflict:

> Most of the street speakers...were blacks from the Caribbean affiliated with the Garvey movement. The principal speakers were James Thornhill, of the Universal Negro Improvement Association; William Jordan, of the Ethiopian Pacifist Movement; Ira Kemp of the African Patriotic League; Reggie Thomas, of a local branch of the International Labor Defense; and Charles Romney, of the American Civil Rights Association.

The [FBI] report called Sufi Abdul Hamid, of the International Black League, a "decidedly interesting" speaker who dressed like an Arab and was a "linguist" commanding "about six languages." Samuel Daniels was described as founder and spokesman of the Pan-African Reconstruction Association (PARA), the "largest and most active of the new organizations."[165]

Hamid and Daniels seem to have been the most successful recruiters on this list of organizers. Through his leadership positions in the African Legion and International Black League organizations, Hamid was able to convince at least several hundred black men to join his volunteer rolls. Even after similar groups had abandoned the notion of enlisting black volunteers to remain in compliance with U.S. neutrality laws, Hamid openly defied the Justice Department warnings and continued his program. Hamid repeatedly claimed to have a legion of more than 3,000 troops training for service in Ethiopia at a military base in upstate New York. The lack of veracity of this statement is easy to assess given that he never produced any evidence of such a camp and Hamid had a well-known penchant for making untruthful statements. On a recruitment trip to Goldsboro, North Carolina, for example, Hamid told his black audience that it was he who dispatched Hubert Julian, a black U.S. pilot who had received a great deal of print in the black press, to take charge of the Imperial Air Force; clearly, because Malaku Bayen initially recruited Julian in 1930 to train pilots in Ethiopia, Hamid's claim was completely false. The most striking thing about Hamid (beyond his tendency to bend the truth) was that he openly encouraged black Americans to renounce their citizenship to fight for Ethiopia.[166]

Daniels, too, had a penchant for hyperbole. Throughout the conflict, he claimed that his PARA organization maintained a membership of no fewer than 4,000 black Americans who were ready to lay down their lives to preserve the Makonnen dynasty. Although it has proven impossible to verify these claims, we do know that his Harlem recruitment fairs were attended by thousands of blacks claiming to be eager to "knock out Mussolini" like "Joe Louis had [done to] Carnera."[167]

Although Daniels also used fiery rhetoric during recruitment drives, his portrayal of the Italian-Ethiopian War as the perfect opportunity for the black man to enact the tenets of Garveyism was what really set the PARA apart from other organizations operating in Harlem. Indeed, Daniels repeatedly told his black audiences that he hoped that they would stay in Ethiopia after the war to help not only rebuild the country after the expulsion of Italian forces but to launch a new black industrial empire geared toward liberating the entire black world.[168] Although such statements were in line with those made by high-ranking Ethiopian officials about the need of their country for skilled black immigrants to help them rebuild after the war, there is no evidence that Daniels had any contact with the imperial government about any land grant that would facilitate this immigration.[169]

Neither Hamid nor Daniels ever sent any of their "recruits" to fight in Ethiopia. Despite the fact that their fiery rhetoric drew thousands of black Americans to their rallies in Harlem, obviously very few blacks were willing to give up their U.S. citizenship or risk imprisonment by violating the neutrality laws; indeed, even Hamid and Daniels themselves never went so far. Still, like Garvey, their Harlem pageants provided the black masses with forums for expressing their frustrations with the limitations they faced in the United States.

The street-level encounters that occurred between blacks and Italian Americans in the New York area serve as prime examples of this frustration. At first, the recruitment pageants of the Harlem soapbox speakers worked as an escape valve for the psychological pressures felt by the black community, although their ability to serve these needs in the black community was significantly reduced by the Roosevelt administration's neutrality proclamation. Although it is now clear that that neutrality was based more on the strength of isolationist values that permeated mainstream U.S. culture than on racism,[170] given the history of black Americans, it is easy to see why many found the soapbox orators' claims of U.S. complicity to be completely plausible. Describing the rise of these sentiments in the black community, one historian writes:

> New York's rabid race patriots concluded that U.S. government opposition to the volunteer movement was calculated to serve the interests of Italian imperialism rather than those of American neutrality.... Many Harlemites tended to agree with the reported observation of Robert L. Ephraim, president of the Negro World Alliance of Chicago, that Washington's stand against the volunteer effort and its refusal to act against Mussolini could only be taken as an indication that the white races of the world were lining up against the black.[171]

Black Americans were frustrated with the entire structure of the global race system. And Italian Americans living and working in and around the black community became the focal point of their rage.

The most important aspect of the deteriorating relations between black and Italian Americans was its effect on economic relationships between the two groups. That many Italian American (and other white-owned) businesses flourished in the black sections of New York prior to the war had always been a sore point for black Americans because they were denied equal access to the white-owned lending institutions that made small business ownership possible. As the war progressed, racial entrepreneurs such as Daniels and Hamid mobilized black New Yorkers around this traditional grievance, encouraging boycotts and vandalism of Italian American businesses.[172] In the end, the boycott movement was the most successful aspect of the wave of activism that swept over black communities in response to the Italian-Ethiopian War. The number of white-owned businesses in Harlem declined, and those that remained were forced to adopt much more cordial relationships with their black customers than they had maintained before the war.

But the mass movements in support of Ethiopia had no effect on the outcome of the conflict. On May 2, 1936, just five months after Mussolini's warplanes first buzzed Adowa, the Ethiopian imperial army was in full retreat and Emperor Selassie was forced to flee to London. Although the mainstream civil rights groups continued to extend moral support to Emperor Selassie as he sought redress from the League of Nations, U.S. black communities, deeply distraught by the outcome of the war, for the most part returned to the challenge of trying to overcome the closed opportunity structures that they faced at home.[173] Ten years later, as the nation emerged from World War II, black Americans would again find that the status of Africa (and U.S. policies on the continent) was intertwined with their core ideas about navigating these structures on the home front.

· · ·

In this chapter, I present a strong challenge to the notion that the tensions between Garvey and the black elite boiled down to a clash of personalities. Instead, opposition to the Garvey movement among the black elite was a function of their representational imperative derived from a sense of linked fate with downtrodden blacks; in short, the black elite judged Garvey's program to be a threat to the interests of the black masses.

The black elite saw Garvey's improprieties and managerial incompetence as a threat to downtrodden blacks. In other words, the black elite feared that Garvey was, as A. Philip Randolph charged, "a crook and a liar" more than a black leader. In addition, Garvey's emphasis on repatriation to Africa revived the specter of the late-nineteenth-century emigration movements. The black elite also feared that Garvey's support for segregation (like Booker T. Washington's politics of accommodation) provided legitimacy to the white supremacist cause in the South.

Even though the UNIA collapsed under Garvey, the best of his ideals continued to reverberate throughout black communities into the middle of the twentieth century. Indeed, it is clear that Garvey's central message—that the diaspora needed to mobilize to gain a stake in Africa—was partly responsible for the outpouring of affection that blacks demonstrated toward Ethiopia during the second Italian-Ethiopian conflict.

Moreover, as I discuss in the next chapter, even mainstream civil rights organizations such as the NAACP became divided about whether they should try to mobilize rank-and-file blacks against European colonialism as Garvey had attempted to do or should remain committed to their more legalistic strategies. Ironically, W. E. B. Du Bois, Garvey's principal opponent in the black intelligentsia, would lead the call for change in the 1940s and 1950s.

3

PROTECTING "FERTILE FIELDS"
The NAACP and Africa during the Cold War

> **While we are not satisfied with conditions faced by our people in this country, the communist doctrine is not the way out. The right use of the ballot is the way out. This is our country, and the only country we know.**
>
> —Rep. Oscar De Priest (R-Ill.), speech in Cleveland, Ohio, January 8, 1932

> **If I were Stalin, I would advertise the statements of the Byrd's and the Tuck's as propaganda for Communism. Their disloyalty is dangerously close to treason.**
>
> —Walter White, speech in Richmond, Virginia, April 10, 1948

On June 6, 1946, an interracial crowd of more than 15,000 gathered in Madison Square Garden in New York City.[1] The attendees congregated at the behest of the Council on African Affairs (CAA) to demonstrate to the Truman administration and the fledgling United Nations the depth of support within U.S. civil society for policies that would hasten decolonization in Africa. The rally, which Hollis Lynch reports was the "most successful mass public meeting" of the organization, gave the leaders of the CAA hope that their eight years of toiling to raise the consciousness of the U.S. public about the evils of colonialism were finally beginning to bear fruit.[2]

The Madison Square Garden meeting also emboldened the tiny organization to reinvigorate its long-standing lobbying efforts at the U.S. Department of State and United Nations Plaza. The CAA earned a major victory on this front when it convinced both the Truman administration and the Trusteeship Council of the United Nations to oppose the attempt of Jan Smuts, the head of the white-minority regime in South Africa, to annex Southwest Africa.[3] In the wake of this triumph, the CAA executive committee decided to expand the membership of the organization from thirty-six to seventy-two.[4]

The CAA had much less success in and after 1947 than it did in its banner year of 1946. This was because the national security regime that the Truman administration put in place after 1945 to wage the Cold War began to calcify during this period.[5] The first sign of this reality came when Secretary of Labor Lewis B. Schwellenbach told the press that he had urged President Truman to declare the American Communist Party (Communist Party–USA, CP-USA) an illegal organization.⁶ Five months after the article ran, Tom Clark, the attorney general of the United States, circulated a list of organizations that the Justice Department was placing under scrutiny for having "totalitarian, fascist, communist, or subversive elements" within their ranks. Given the long CAA record of cooperation with the CP-USA, and the fact that Paul Robeson, chairperson of the CAA executive committee, was an avowed Marxist, it is not at all surprising that the organization ended up on this now-infamous list.⁷

The CAA quickly entered a downward spiral after Clark placed the organization on his watch list. The two principal figures in the CAA, Robeson and Max Yergan, who had founded the organization on his return from missionary work in South Africa in 1938, grew divided over strategy in this new era of repression. Having recently extolled the virtues of "Soviet Democracy," Robeson, who was one of the two avowed Marxists in the organization at this point, refused to bend his principles to the increasingly repressive political climate.⁸ For Yergan, cooperation with communists or any other group was meaningful only as long as it advanced the broader goals of the CAA. Thus, he advocated distancing the organization from the CP-USA and falling in line with the domestic loyalty program of the Truman administration, which was the primary means for persecuted groups to barter their way off Clark's list.⁹ After waging a dramatic legal battle for control of the CAA (and its property) throughout 1948, Yergan, and the six members of the group that joined his lawsuit, finally conceded defeat and withdrew from the organization.¹⁰

After the 1948 rupture, the CAA entered a phase of rapid decline. The membership of the organization declined almost as rapidly in 1949 as it had expanded two years earlier. Defiantly vowing to push the organization forward, Robeson embarked on a barnstorming campaign to raise the membership to its previous level. Despite his status as an international celebrity and his impossible promises that the CAA executive committee would keep the identities of new members confidential, Robeson could not boost the sagging membership.¹¹ Moreover, the fact that the vast majority of mainstream black organizations fell in line with Truman's loyalty program to curry favor with the administration on the home front only further compounded the problems of the CAA.

The CAA did win one notable new member in this period. W. E. B. Du Bois, a principal architect of both the Pan-African Congress Movement and the NAACP, joined the organization in 1948. On first glance, we might think that having such a venerable member of the black vanguard join the fold would have a positive impact on the CAA. By 1948, however, Du Bois, whom the NAACP board of directors voted to expel for criticizing the Truman doctrine in September 1948, was just as much a pariah in the black community as were the leaders of the CAA.¹²

Despite the courageous, or perhaps foolhardy, efforts of Robeson, Du Bois, and the eight others who tried to keep the organization afloat, the CAA could not sustain itself in the face of constant persecution from the federal government. Thus, on June 14, 1955, with only six members in attendance, the CAA voted itself out of existence.[13]

The historiography of black elite engagement with U.S. foreign policy toward Africa during the Cold War displays almost as many complexities as the period. There is broad agreement among historians that most mainstream civil rights groups distanced themselves from the CAA in the late 1940s because they were afraid that recalcitrance would damage their efforts on the home front.[14] This view dovetails nicely with the strategic behavior model of black elite behavior in the U.S. foreign policymaking arena that I have developed throughout this book.

Although there is consensus among historians about the nature of black elite behavior during the rise of the Cold War, there remains a robust debate about the ramifications of this shift to the right. Some historians believe that these strategic moves helped civil rights organizations remain viable through the Cold War period and ultimately ratcheted up the pressure on the Truman, Dwight Eisenhower, and John F. Kennedy administrations to promote reforms in the domestic and external environments.[15] Other scholars assert, building on W. E. B. Du Bois's parting shots at the leaders of the NAACP, that the "provincialism" evinced by most civil rights groups during the Truman years undermined the struggle for black equality in the global context and on the home front.[16]

Indeed, scholars in this latter camp assert that during this period the black elite all but abandoned the commitment to anticolonialism that they had demonstrated throughout World War II. They also argue that the marked decline in NAACP membership that coincided with the embrace by the organization of the Truman doctrine stands as evidence that the black masses wanted their leaders to take a less provincial approach.[17] In short, these scholars argue that there was an ideological rupture between black leaders and the masses over the elite pursuit of a strategic course in the U.S. foreign policymaking arena.

I test these claims in this chapter using archival materials and newspaper accounts to reconstruct discourse about the NAACP approach to both issues in African affairs and the Truman doctrine between 1945 and 1957. My central finding is that the assessments of NAACP performance in the U.S. foreign policymaking arena that appear in black newspapers and the archival record are generally positive. Although not a perfect measure of black public opinion, this finding illustrates the potential for leaders of the NAACP (and the other civil rights organizations) to frame their actions as consistent with the demands of their constituents. That the same analysis shows that Truman was a very popular figure in the black community because of his stands on domestic civil rights issues further enriches our understanding of the political context in which the NAACP was operating during the Cold War.

My analysis also shows that the break of the NAACP with the CAA and its shift to an anticommunist stance during the rise of the Cold War shocked very few of their constituents. This is so because the leaders of the organization had charted a course that was both pragmatic about Pan-Africanism and vehemently anticommunist for most of the thirty years prior to World War II. The political discourse on these issues that took place in the black counterpublic during this period often shared these orientations. Finally, I show that the anticommunism of the NAACP actually advanced the struggle of the organization against colonialism during the early Cold War.

Toward a Pragmatic Pan-Africanism

Du Bois was by no means surprised when the NAACP board of directors voted to oust him for inflammatory remarks about the foreign policies of the Truman administration.[18] After all, he had maintained tense relationships with the other central figures in the organization for two decades.[19] Like the conflict that led Du Bois and the NAACP to divorce in 1948, disagreements over the role of the organization on the world stage had been the source of these tensions.

Du Bois had actually left the NAACP once before. In 1934, Du Bois resigned his post as editor of the *Crisis* to take a position at Atlanta University because he was frustrated that the NAACP would not commit any more of its financial resources to the Pan-African congresses.[20] Two years later, Du Bois accused the NAACP leaders of a "race provincialism" that "objected to any mingling or attempt to mingle the problems of Africa with the problems of the Untied States."[21]

As his early writings on the Garvey movement illustrate, Du Bois was typically a fair-minded commentator when writing about conflicts with other activists engaged in the struggle for black equality. In this instance, however, he clearly missed the mark. Indeed, as the historical record shows, the NAACP had a long history of engagement with Africa. And Du Bois certainly knew this to be the case; after all, he was the one who had first convinced the NAACP board of directors to take an interest in the continent.

In 1919, Du Bois sent a "Memorandum on the Future of Africa" to the NAACP board of directors.[22] The document urged the NAACP to see a link between decolonization in Africa and black freedom in the United States.[23] It also issued a call for the organization to take the lead in reviving the moribund Pan-African Congress movement that Du Bois and a handful of other intellectuals from the diaspora had initiated in 1900 with a conference in London (see chap. 2).[24] The board of directors agreed with Du Bois that the organization should put "the freedom of Africa" at the "forefront of its program" and voted overwhelmingly to fund a second Pan-African Congress in 1918. They also authorized Du Bois to lead a delegation from the congress in Paris to lobby the delegates to the Versailles Peace Conference on behalf of Africa and the diaspora.[25]

Despite the fact that Du Bois had organized the conference hastily, fifty-seven delegates from fifteen countries and colonies attended the Second Pan-African Congress. The delegates passed a number of resolutions calling for the great powers to end racial discrimination and colonial rule.[26] Although the delegates forwarded their resolutions to the representatives of the great powers convened at Versailles, there is no evidence that the delegates discussed them during the proceedings. Moreover, the mainstream press completely ignored the congress.[27]

Even though the Pan-African Congress yielded no tangible gains for the organization, the NAACP's board of directors continued to support the movement. Indeed, the organization footed the bill for two more gatherings in 1921 and 1923.[28] But as the postwar economy began to grind toward the Great Depression, the NAACP began to take a more conservative stance on foreign affairs activism. In 1925, for example, citing financial strains, the NAACP declined Du Bois's request to fund the Fourth Pan-African Congress, which was to take place in New York.[29] Surprisingly, there is no evidence that Du Bois took umbrage at the new pragmatic approach of the NAACP in 1925. Instead, it was a fight for control of the *Crisis* magazine that was the major flashpoint between Du Bois and the NAACP board of directors between 1926 and his first resignation from the organization.[30]

Du Bois began to lose faith in the NAACP approach to foreign affairs during the start of the second Italian-Ethiopian War in 1934. In his view, the slow-footed response of the organization had allowed new groups like the CAA to take the lead in channeling black Americans' rage about the invasion by Italy toward constructive ends. In Du Bois's view, the NAACP had missed this crucial opportunity because the directors' race provincialism prevented them from seeing it. Years later, Du Bois wrote in his autobiography that his frustration with the NAACP during this period was a function of the fact that the organization "shrank back to its narrowest program: to make Negroes American citizens" in the aftermath of World War I.[31]

Recent scholarship in black studies and social history has largely vindicated Du Bois's claims that the NAACP was slow to address the Italian-Ethiopian War and largely stayed aloof from the mass actions that characterized the first black responses in New York, Chicago, and other large urban areas.[32] These same works have also provided something of a defense for the NAACP actions during the crisis. As several scholars have pointed out, for example, the NAACP board of directors, fearing that early action would run afoul of official U.S. policy, wanted to wait until they knew their range of options under the law.[33] Moreover, the U.S. having recently come out of a war in which European ethnic groups were often accused of disloyalty when they carved out positions supporting their homelands before the government had a chance to set its own policies makes the trepidation of the NAACP about moving too quickly during the Italian-Ethiopian War is easy to understand.[34]

Once Roosevelt declared that the United States would remain neutral in the conflict, the NAACP did press the administration within the parameters of this framework. On March 20, 1935, for example, Walter White cabled Secretary of State Cordell Hull to ask him to assert to the League of Nations that the NAACP and the people of the United States have "a real interest" in preserving Ethiopian independence.[35] White also wrote to the Soviet ambassador at the League of Nations to urge him to make good on the claims of his government that it was interested in defending the rights of the powerless before the community of nations.[36] When the NAACP's board of directors saw that these communications were making no impact on the behavior of the U.S. government and the League of Nations, they instructed Walter White to organize a delegation of distinguished black Americans to engage in personal diplomacy with President Roosevelt and Secretary Hull.[37] White even reached out to W. E. B. Du Bois to join this proposed delegation.[38] Du Bois, who by this time had already decided to withdraw from the NAACP, refused to serve.[39]

White had no better luck recruiting any of the other notable members of the black elite that the NAACP believed would have the ability to sway the Roosevelt administration.[40] Some of these leaders were already participating in other activities aimed at trying to shape the U.S. government response to the war. For the most part, however, the individuals that White targeted reported that they were either opposed to sending a delegation to the government or simply too busy with the work of their own groups to join a last-minute campaign organized by the NAACP.[41]

With no visible contributions to the burgeoning Pan-African social movement that was sweeping the black communities, the NAACP began to draw criticism from correspondents to the black press.[42] Always deeply concerned about the relation of the organization with the black masses, the NAACP board of directors moved swiftly to bring the organization in line with the demands of its constituents. On October 19, 1935, the board instructed Walter White to announce that the NAACP would "take part wherever possible in demonstrations against the Italian war in Ethiopia."[43]

The NAACP used a pragmatic strategy between 1919 and 1936 that sought to strengthen the position of the organization vis-à-vis both the government and its constituents to guide its engagements with the continent of Africa. During the Italian-Ethiopian War, the NAACP learned that balancing between these two forces was fraught with challenges. But, in the final analysis, the NAACP pursued a course that reflected the demands of their constituents.

For Du Bois, the fact that the NAACP had followed public opinion instead of attempting to mobilize it was a sign of the weakness of the organization. Du Bois and the NAACP mended fences later during World War II, only to part ways again at the beginning of the Red Scare in 1948. When Du Bois parted ways with the organization after World War II, he assumed that public opinion in the black community resembled the opinion it had held during the Italian-Ethiopian War. But this was not the case; on the contrary, by the time Du Bois parted ways with the NAACP for the second time, it was already clear that the NAACP was moving at precisely the pace on Africa and other issues in the global context that the black community wanted. We can see this by reconstructing black public opinion through analyses of media content and constituent mail sent to the NAACP's national headquarters between 1945 and 1955.

The Black Counterpublic and the Truman Doctrine

According to some historians, the NAACP paid a heavy price in terms of both membership and black public opinion for supporting the muscular domestic loyalty program of the Truman administration during the Cold War.[44] This conclusion grows in part from impressionistic analyses of black print media and correspondence directed toward the NAACP during the height of the Red Scare that questioned its support for the government. But my quantitative and qualitative analyses of these archival records provide a strong challenge to many of the findings presented in this literature. Indeed, the more systematic content analyses demonstrate that the NAACP did not fall out of favor with black editorialists or their constituents for supporting the Truman doctrine and framing their opposition to colonialism in terms of the broader U.S. Cold War aims. On the contrary, it is clear that the black community overwhelmingly supported President Truman's efforts to contain communism and viewed the NAACP's alliance with his administration as a boon to both the black community and to Africa.

According to most of the studies of the impact of the Cold War on black elite engagement with Africa, the break of the NAACP from communist-tinged organizations after the imposition of the Truman doctrine represented a departure from long-standing norms of openness and collaboration that had reigned in the black counterpublic in the early decades of the twentieth century. It is easy to understand the basis of this conclusion. The period between 1936 and 1946, the decade on which previous studies have drawn for their impressionistic analyses of black print culture, represented a high-water mark in cooperation between mainstream civil rights groups and communists in the black community. But an examination of both the historical record and the content of black newspapers in the decade before 1936 reveals that this period between the Italian-Ethiopian War and the close of World War II was actually an exceptional time in the black counterpublic.

Historians who have criticized the NAACP leadership for breaking off its working relationships with activists and organizations that maintained communist ties have largely portrayed these moves as a cynical response to the rise of the Truman doctrine. Although there is no doubt that the NAACP leaders worried a great deal about avoiding the kind of persecution that figures such as Paul Robeson experienced during the Red Scare period in U.S. history, this is only one part of the story. Indeed, most of the current scholarship that criticizes the anticommunist stance of the NAACP during the Cold War ignores the depth of anticommunism that had persisted in the organization from its inception in the first decade of the twentieth century. In this section, I review this history with an eye to providing greater context for the responses of the organization to the rise of Truman's national security apparatus.

The NAACP was born in 1909 through the collaboration between black intellectuals and white philanthropists eager to move the nation beyond the conservative approach to racial advancement advocated by Booker T. Washington.[45] The organization immediately set to work battling all forms of discrimination against black Americans through both legal and political means. Although the leaders of the NAACP charted a much more radical course toward black liberation than did their chief rivals in Washington's Tuskegee machine, they agreed with the Bookerites that black freedom would come through liberal reforms and not revolutionary actions. "The NAACP," Manfred Berg writes, "expected racial change to result from political reforms."[46]

The NAACP had been working peacefully to achieve these reforms for almost a decade when the Bolsheviks demonstrated to the world how rapidly social and political change could come through revolution in October 1917. Not surprisingly, the success of the Bolsheviks raised the profile of communism and prompted a great deal of soul searching on the part of marginalized groups around the world. It was in this context that 128 dissident members of the American Socialist Party gathered in Chicago on September 27, 1919, to discuss the prospects of forming a party that espoused communist ideology. By the conclusion of their meetings, the delegates to the convention, who were mostly foreign-born immigrants from Europe, had established the Communist Party–USA (CP-USA). Like the Bolsheviks who had inspired their conversion to communism, the delegates hammered out a platform for their new party that espoused international revolution to place workers at the head of both the government and economy of the United States.47

News of the founding of the party did not make a big splash in the black community. Indeed, none of the four leading black newspapers (*the Atlanta Daily World, Chicago Defender, New York Amsterdam News,* and *Pittsburgh Courier*) carried a story about the convention or the founding of the CP-USA. There were several reasons why the rise of the CP-USA did not garner much attention in the black counterpublic: (1) these papers had also reported only sparingly on the Bolshevik Revolution, (2) the central players in the rise of the CP-USA were a fringe element that the Associated Negro Press probably deemed unworthy of much attention, and (3) the one thing that most members of the black elite knew about communists was that they saw black oppression in America as epiphenomenal of capitalism and not as a color caste system.

For anyone with a basic knowledge of race relations in the United States, let alone firsthand experience living under the crushing oppression of Jim Crow, the communists' frame of the black condition demonstrated a fundamental misunderstanding of the conditions that most blacks faced on the ground. Moreover, the incredibly condescending tone that communists often took when speaking and writing about black inequality created an instant wedge between their movement and the black community.48 Consider, for example, the tone taken by the CP-USA magazine, *Worker's Council,* when it editorialized against the horrific race riot that took place in Tulsa, Oklahoma, in 1921. Although, as Earl Ofari Hutchinson has noted, the editors of the magazine sympathized with the plight of the black victims of the riot, they completely undercut the force of their support by suggesting that the only resolution for such matters was for blacks to stop being "ignorant" of their rights and gain the "self-confidence" to organize as workers.49

But by 1922 several factors prompted the CP-USA to shift its position on the black struggle for equality in the United States. First, the onset of the Great Migration in 1916 resulted in the movement of 7 million blacks from the Deep South to the industrial centers in the North, Mid-West, and West. By 1920, the second year of the existence of the CP-USA, the first wave of these migrants had already begun to make their presence felt on the factory, shop, and plant floors that the communists saw as fertile fields for their recruitment efforts. Indeed, a Department of Labor study conducted in 1920 showed that the percentage of blacks working in industrial settings had increased by 150 percent over the previous decade.[50] It did not take the CP-USA long to realize that it needed to demonstrate greater sensitivity to the special plight of black Americans if it was to successfully bring this burgeoning segment of the industrial workforce into its ranks.

Second, the CP-USA also came to believe that the racial strife that plagued many U.S. labor and trade unions provided it with a unique opportunity to make inroads with black workers.[51] It is easy to see why they came to this conclusion. After all, mainstream labor had an appalling record in terms of integrating the skilled trades.[52] Moreover, the newly industrialized black labor force had only begun to challenge these racist exclusions in earnest at the 1919 American Federation of Labor (AFL) convention.

In that year, twenty-three black delegates attended the convention with a mandate from their fellow black workers to press the oldest U.S. federation of labor unions to enact five resolutions to address racism within the movement.[53] The black delegates' chief concern was the fact that the AFL allowed local affiliates to write clauses into their charters that barred blacks (and other people of color) from membership.[54] Another paramount concern was that even locals that did not have these "lily white" clauses often refused to recruit black workers. Thus, the delegates asked the convention to pass resolutions opposing both these practices. At the same time, the black delegates—perhaps anticipating the opposition they would face from their white counterparts—asked the AFL to grant charters to all black unions and form an alliance with the International Union of Organized Colored Labor.[55]

The AFL Executive Council worked very hard behind the scenes to ensure that most of the black delegates' demands would not come to the convention floor for a vote.[56] Indeed, the council killed four of the five resolutions as soon as it had the opportunity to act on them. The council did recommend, however, that the AFL undertake special efforts to organize black workers all over the country. Although the convention ultimately passed this resolution, the fact that it had no teeth signaled to the locals that it was just a symbolic gesture.[57] Thus, the majority of the locals that had exclusionary practices before the convention maintained them in its aftermath.[58]

The final factor compelling the CP-USA to modify its position on race was external pressure from the Soviet Union. As several scholars have pointed out, Lenin viewed incorporating people of color into the worldwide communist movement as an essential step in the process of overthrowing both imperialism and capitalism.[59] After this announcement, the CP-USA came under enormous pressure to, in the words of Theodore Draper, labor historian, "break out of their narrow ethnic shell."[60] Moreover, the Soviets urged their American comrades to give special attention to recruiting black Americans, whom they deemed the most exploited segment of the proletariat in the United States.[61]

Within two years of Moscow's issuing this directive, the CP-USA went on record at its 1922 convention with a resolution that acknowledged that blacks were "oppressed more ruthlessly" than their white counterparts in the U.S. proletariat.[62] The delegates also passed a resolution that promised to help blacks fight for economic and political equality.[63] These statements certainly generated a small buzz in the black community. Indeed, it was in the wake of these resolutions that black newspapers began to cover the activities of the CP-USA. Moreover, editorial opinions among the leading black newspapers generally welcomed the new perspective of the party on the black experience in the United States. The *New York Amsterdam News*, for example, commended the CP-USA for agreeing to "support the Negroes in their struggle for liberation."[64]

Some notable black activists and intellectuals exhibited a greater interest in learning more about Marxism and the CP-USA after its shift to a more color-conscious position on reforming the United States. For example, Cyril Briggs, the founder of the African Blood Brotherhood (ABB) and a strident critic of Marcus Garvey, became an avowed Marxist and member of the CP-USA during this period.[65] The most prominent member of the black establishment to shift his viewpoint on Marxism and the CP-USA in the 1920s, however, was Claude McKay.

McKay, who is widely remembered for his indelible contributions to the literary canon of the Harlem Renaissance, had been a strong critic of communism and the CP-USA between 1918 and 1924. In 1924, Mckay, who was also a prolific editorialist for several black newspapers between 1920 and 1940, accepted an invitation from the leaders of the Soviet Union to attend the Fourth World Congress of the Communist International on a fact-finding tour. Before he left for the Soviet Union, the skeptical McKay told a reporter for the *Baltimore Afro-American* that Marxists had no framework for understanding the plight of black Americans.[66]

The Soviets had invited McKay with hopes that he would, if treated well, write a glowing account of the nation and the racial tolerance of its citizens. According to McKay's account of the trip, which appeared in the *Crisis* magazine, the Soviet leaders gave him a first-class tour of the most important institutions modern Russia. He also recounted that Russians of all stations in life treated him as a "symbol of the great American Negro group."[67] Although the first-class treatment that he received from Soviet leaders made an impression on him, it was the statement on U.S. race relations that Gregori Zinoviev, the chairman of the Communist International, released to the Soviet press in honor of his visit that swayed him. Foreshadowing the strategy that the CP-USA would soon employ in its recruitment efforts, Zinoviev acknowledged the special hardships faced by blacks in the United States. McKay was so impressed with Soviet Russia that he declared it a land without racism when he returned to the United States.[68]

Even with ringing endorsements from figures such as Briggs and McKay, CP-USA recruitment efforts in the black community continued to lag well behind the expectations set by the Communist International in Moscow. In 1921, W. E. B. Du Bois had predicted that the CP-USA would never make gains among blacks because of the racism exuded by the "white proletariat" in the United States. "We are the victims of [the white proletariat's] physical oppression, social ostracism, economic exclusion and personal hatred," Du Bois wrote in an editorial in the *Crisis* in 1921.[69] Before it adopted the Moscow line on U.S. race relations, it is unlikely that the CP-USA would have taken Du Bois's charge very seriously. After 1922, however, the party, determined to meet its recruitment goals in the black community, began to take a long look at the racial attitudes of its members.

Later that year, the leaders of the CP-USA announced that they were undertaking a campaign to eliminate "white chauvinism" from the consciousness of its rank-and-file.[70] The party also announced that it intended to create a bloc within its ranks, the American Negro Labor Congress, for black workers to organize around their racial identity and help facilitate the eradication of white racism from the organization.[71]

Although there is no doubt that these symbolic gestures got the attention of the black community, they did not translate into large gains for the communists for several reasons. First, rank-and-file blacks had many other options for channeling their deep desires to achieve racial equality in the 1920s. Indeed, both the NAACP and the National Urban League had already been in existence for more than a decade when the CP-USA emerged on the U.S. political scene. Moreover, Marcus Garvey's UNIA movement was generating unprecedented levels of mass mobilization in the black community during this same period. It is not surprising that most blacks found these organizations and movements, with their organic ties to the community, more appealing than the CP-USA.

It is also true that these more established organizations actively worked to undermine the communists in the eyes of rank-and-file blacks. According to the historical record, most of the leaders of these organizations viewed communism as a threat to the black community during the 1920s and 1930s. The proceedings of the Negro Sanhedrin conference, which took place in Chicago, Illinois, in 1924, and the interactions between the NAACP and the International Labor Defense (ILD), an affiliate of the CP-USA, over representation of the Scottsboro Boys in the early 1930s provide prime illustrations of this dynamic.

In 1923, the NAACP and five other black organizations with national standing issued a call for the "leaders" of the black race to come together in an "All Race Assembly" and chart a path for the future of the black struggle for equality in the United States.[72] The response to the call was incredibly positive; indeed, ten other black organizations immediately signed on to join the planning committee for the conference. When the committee met in July 1923, the representatives decided that the conference would take place in Chicago, Illinois, in February 1924.[73] By evoking the Sanhedrin (the supreme court of ancient Israel), the planners intended to send the message that the delegates to the meeting would be interrogating the gravest questions related to their common goal of uplifting the race.

Thanks to the intervention of Cyril Briggs, who served as secretary of the call committee, black communists were included both on the planning committee and as delegates to the Sanhedrin conference.[74] The participation of communists at the planning meeting was largely pedestrian; indeed, a statement entered into the record by Richard Moore, an ABB member and organizer for the CP-USA, urging the committee to see the black fight for civil rights in the United States as part of a global struggle that people of color were waging for self-determination, represented the only display of Marxist thought in the minutes.[75]

But, at the Sanhedrin conference itself, the communist delegates caused a great stir with the resolutions that they brought to the floor for debate. The root cause of the first conflict to emerge between the communists and the more than two hundred other delegates who gathered in the Wendell Phillips High School auditorium in Chicago for the proceedings was a symbolic issue. The only black leader who had been barred by the conference planning committee from attending the All Race Assembly was Marcus Garvey. When the delegates from the CP-USA got wind of this, they sent a resolution to the floor that called for wiring Garvey to ask him to join the proceedings.[76] Because the vast majority of the delegates—including their patron Cyril Briggs—had just spent the past year working to rid the black community of Garveyism, they saw this resolution as an affront to their judgment. Moreover, the fact that the federal government had hauled Garvey off to prison on the mail fraud conviction that had brought down the UNIA months before the Sanhedrin made the resolution seem like nothing more than pointless grandstanding.

There was a method behind the communist delegates' seemingly mad opening salvo at the Sanhedrin. The CP-USA had held out high hopes that the UNIA would be the bridge between them and the recruitment of black workers because Garvey had invited Rose Pastor Stokes, a leading member of the CP-USA, to address the delegates to the UNIA second annual convention in 1922. Thus, they probably meant to signal to Garvey and his supporters that they still hoped to form an alliance. After all, no one knew whether Garvey would be able to rebuild his movement at that point.

What the communist delegates did not realize, however, was that an abiding skepticism about communism is about the only thing that Garvey had in common with most of the other delegates to the Sanhedrin. Indeed, as the documentary record shows, following Stokes's speech at the UNIA convention Garvey immediately had taken the floor and announced that the comments should not lead anyone to "misinterpret us [the UNIA] as Soviets."[77] Moreover, Garvey frequently had denounced communism in both his subsequent speeches and articles in the *Negro World*.[78]

The Garvey resolution did not win the communist delegates any friends among the other attendees to the Sanhedrin. Undaunted by the icy reaction of the delegates to their first resolution, the black communists introduced a barrage of foreign and domestic policy proposals aimed at pushing the Sanhedrin to adopt the positions favored by the Soviet Union and the CP-USA. On the foreign affairs side, the communist delegates called on the Sanhedrin to recognize the Soviet Union.[79] This idea was a nonstarter for the convention for several reasons. Paramount among these was that not even the U.S. government under Woodrow Wilson had moved to recognize the Bolshevik government. Because one of the stated aims of the Sanhedrin was to advance the position of blacks by gaining more influence with the U.S. government, there was no way that the delegates were going to risk alienating the executive branch by moving first on this issue.

The resolutions that the CP-USA members submitted on domestic issues were a mixed bag. On the one hand, the black communists were far ahead of their time by proposing that the Sanhedrin press the federal and state governments to pass a constitutional amendment that would make interracial marriage legal throughout the United States. On the other hand, the communists undercut their own work at the Sanhedrin by pushing ideas that were either completely unrealistic or simply off the radar screen of most of the other attendees. The CP-USA delegates' call for the Sanhedrin to press the U.S. government to nationalize the railroads stands as a prime example of a proposal that languished because it satisfied both of these conditions.[80]

Despite the communist delegates' erratic behavior, the Sanhedrin did engage in serious debate about their main policy proposal—a resolution censuring the AFL for allowing its locals to maintain discriminatory practices against blacks.[81] As we have seen, addressing racism within the AFL had long been a high priority for the NAACP and many of the other mainstream civil rights organizations that sent delegates to the Sanhedrin, and this was undoubtedly the reason that the delegates gave the proposal such a thorough airing at the convention.[82]

As the debate moved forward, however, many of the delegates, led by Dean Kelly Miller of Howard University, became convinced that what the communists really wanted out of the resolution was a full-blown condemnation of the mainstream labor movement and a repudiation of capitalism.[83] The communist delegates' introduction of a corollary measure that called for the Sanhedrin, which was officially a nonpartisan organization, to forge a formal alliance with the Farmer-Labor

Party, the political arm of the CP-USA, only fueled this perception. Ultimately, the Sanhedrin rejected both of the communists' proposals and passed a resolution that simply called for the AFL and other mainstream labor organizations to welcome blacks into their ranks "on the basis of equality."[84]

When the Sanhedrin adjourned, it was clear that neither the communists nor the moderates were satisfied with their encounter in Chicago. "The Sanhedrin," Robert Minor, head of the CP-USA, wrote in summary of the reports he received from the communist delegates, "flatly and cold bloodedly rejected the proposal to organize the millions of Negro industrial workers."[85] For most moderates, the clashes with the communists had prevented them from hammering out a plan to win more concessions from organized labor. For Kelly Miller and the other delegates that took a hard line against communism during the proceedings, what transpired at the Sanhedrin was a warning sign that the CP-USA was now planning to highjack the civil rights agenda. One year after his run-in with the communists at the Sanhedrin, Miller made these concerns public in a *New York Times* editorial in which he warned blacks that embracing communism would be "fatuous suicide."[86]

One month before his editorial hit the newsstands, the communists hatched a plan that seemed to confirm Miller's worst fears. In August 1925, the CP-USA decided that it would try to forge a working relationship with the NAACP. Instead of approaching the organization directly, which it knew would probably have led to its efforts' being rebuffed, the CP-USA decided to infiltrate the NAACP through its conventions. In short, the party planned to have communists attend the conventions as delegates and "enlighten" the members of the organization about the nature of "class struggle" in the United States.[87] This strategy, like the communists' other efforts in the black community in the 1920s, failed miserably. Indeed, the only success that the CP-USA had with this strategy was when the NAACP allowed James Ford to address its 1926 convention as a delegate from the American Negro Labor Congress.[88] After this speech, no avowed communist ever addressed the organization again.

After the 1926 convention, NAACP leaders, who were already skeptical of the CP-USA, became extremely sensitive about the threat of communist infiltration. Thus, instead of fomenting cooperation between the two organizations, the covert approach of the CP-USA poisoned the well and made cooperation virtually impossible. The conflicts that ensued between the two groups as they both tried to provide defense support for the Scottsboro Boys reverberated through the black counterpublic in the 1930s.

In 1931, two destitute white women falsely accused nine black males between the ages of nine and twenty of gang-raping them on a train car. Based on the accusations of the women, the local authorities, backed by a vigilante mob, removed the black men and boys from the train and took them to jail in the town of Scottsboro, Alabama. Despite the fact that one of the women recanted her testimony, admitting that she and her traveling companion had fabricated the story to gain attention, an all-white grand jury indicted the accused anyway. Two weeks later, another all-white jury found all nine of the Scottsboro Boys guilty and sentenced all but the youngest defendant, Roy Wright, to death.

The case, which generated national headlines, became a rallying point for black Americans to protest the injustices that they routinely faced in the criminal justice system. Not surprisingly, the NAACP dispatched a team of lawyers to Scottsboro to assist the defendants, who had virtually no representation during their first trial, with their appeal.[89] When they arrived, the NAACP operatives found that the CP-USA–affiliated ILD had already beaten them to the punch.[90]

Initially, the NAACP and ILD worked in harmony together in defending the Scottsboro Boys. Indeed, William Pickens, the NAACP's national field secretary, even sent a letter to the CP-USA's *Daily Worker* newspaper praising the ILD for its early entry into the fray and urging blacks to send money to the defense fund established by the group.[91] It did not take long, however, for this alliance to break apart over ideological and tactical differences.

Although the ILD lawyers were working extremely effectively through the courts to mount a defense of the Scottsboro Boys, the CP-USA consistently claimed in its propaganda that it would be impossible for the defendants to win justice from a system created by capitalists unless the proletariat mobilized for revolution.[92] The leaders of the NAACP were mortified that the CP-USA was making such statements while the Scottsboro Boys were fighting for their lives before all-white juries and appeals courts.[93] Moreover, in the eyes of the NAACP leaders, these statements further illustrated that the CP-USA was out of touch with the realities of the black experience in the South. After all, the lynch mobs that consistently formed outside the courtrooms where the Scottsboro Boys were trying to obtain justice were made up of the proletariat, not capitalists.

The relationship between the two groups deteriorated further when the CP-USA began to pepper its propaganda materials with hostile attacks against the NAACP. Both the *Daily Worker* and *Southern Worker* ran articles that accused the liberal reformers of the NAACP of being part of a "petty-bourgeois" bent on stifling the development of the black masses through "social fascism."[94] As the conflict between the two organizations wore on, the rhetoric in the communist papers grew even more hostile. One article in the *Southern Worker*, for example, even accused the NAACP's "misleaders" of "joining the lynching mob" mentality that reigned in the environment of Scottsboro; in other words, the communists claimed that the NAACP's refusal to help the black masses see that class struggle was the key to their liberation was tantamount to wanting the Scottsboro Boys convicted.[95]

Finally, the NAACP also began to worry that the CP-USA was fleecing the black masses in the name of the Scottsboro Boys. On May 1, 1934, Walter White announced that the organization was severing all ties with the ILD. One of the major grievances that White pointed to in his statement was the communists' practice of sending black women to rallies to pose as the defendants' mothers to grease the wheels of their fund-raising efforts. White also stated that he believed that more of this money went to further CP-USA propagandizing than to the defense of the Scottsboro Boys.[96]

Some historians have suggested that White's statement was more a heated response to the unfair charges that the communists had leveled against the NAACP between 1931 and 1934 than a well-grounded accusation. But there is simply insufficient documentary evidence to adjudicate this matter. We do know, however, that the ILD legal team had the trust of many of the Scottsboro Boys and their families throughout the ordeal.[97] We also know that by 1940 the separate efforts of the ILD and an NAACP-led coalition of black civil rights groups had won either the acquittal or pardon of all nine defendants. Even in the midst of these great triumphs, the chasm between the NAACP and the CP-USA remained wide and deep throughout the 1930s.[98]

From the standpoint of NAACP leaders, steering clear of the communists became increasingly important to preserve the civil rights movement between 1938 and 1941 (the attack on Pearl Harbor). This was largely because of the pressures that the House Un-American Activities Committee (HUAC) put on civil rights groups to demonstrate that they did not have ties to communist organizations. The House of Representatives formed the HUAC in 1934 to investigate the impact of Nazi and other fascist propaganda on U.S. citizens. Between 1934 and 1937, the HUAC, which was chaired in this period by Representative John H. McCormack (D-Ill.) and Representative Samuel Dickstein (D-N.Y.), remained narrowly focused on ascertaining how deeply fascists had penetrated the fabric of American life.

The HUAC shifted gears dramatically when Martin Dies (D-Tex.) replaced McCormack as co-leader of the committee. Whereas McCormack and Dickstein had focused primarily on the behavior of German immigrants living in ethnic enclaves within large cities, Dies pushed the committee to broaden its scope to examine the extent to which communists had captured the New Deal. Dies, who (like many southern Democrats) was already worried that the New Deal was expanding federal power in a way that would undermine southerners' ability to keep blacks in their subordinate position, became concerned that agencies such as the National Labor Relations Board, Federal Theater, and the Writers' Project were providing communists with staging grounds for their recruitment efforts.[99]

The HUAC (or Dies Committee, as both members of Congress and the press began to call the body in this period) held a series of hearings that targeted elected officials in the Democratic Party who had drawn the electoral support of communists in recent elections or had demonstrated a willingness to work with popular front organizations.[100] Frank Murphy, the governor of Michigan and a close associate of President Roosevelt, was the most prominent politician to gain the scrutiny of the HUAC when he refused to use the weight of his office to crush a sit-down strike at a General Motors production plant.[101] In the wake of the investigation, which did not turn up any evidence that he was cooperating with communists, Murphy lost his reelection bid handily to his Republican rival.

Although the decision of the Dies Committee to target such a powerful figure as Governor Murphy made national headlines, it did not seem to have much of a chilling effect on civil society.[102] On the contrary, most of the stories that reported on the hearings in the leading U.S. newspapers saw the incident as merely a power struggle between President Roosevelt and Dies over the New Deal.[103] Black newspapers generally agreed with this frame.[104] At the same time, the editorial staff at the *Chicago Defender* did see the HUAC's willingness to go after Murphy as an ominous sign for black Americans. In short, the editors feared that Dies, who was no friend to the black struggle for civil rights, would use his tactic against Murphy to undermine black institutions and organizations. [105]

In this warning, the *Defender* editorial was not particularly prescient. After all, the Dies Committee was already targeting Howard University President Mordecai Wyatt Johnson for exposing Howard students to lectures about communism and other radical ideas.[106] Moreover, Oscar De Priest (R-Ill.), the first black person to win election to Congress in the twentieth century, had warned the black community that southern Democrats were going to use this tactic to try to undermine the black advancements made since the beginning of the decade.[107] There is some evidence that the NAACP and other black organizations paid considerable attention to De Priest's warnings, so they were ready for the prospect of facing the Dies Committee. In the end, these challenges never manifested themselves before World War II. The infamous Hitler-Stalin Pact of 1939 immediately made the CP-USA such a pariah in U.S. civil society that any trumped-up charges of collaboration made by the Dies Committee would not have stuck to most groups.

A content analysis of articles, editorials, and letters published in the four black newspapers with largest circulations between 1926 and 1936 (the same four as in 1919) reveals that these negative attitudes were widespread in the black counterpublic. These papers published 541 pieces that focused directly on the issue of the relationship between the black community and the communists or on views on communism during this period. Of this sample, 248 items (46 percent) contain negative tones about communism or communist activities in the black community. Only 103 items (19 percent) exhibit a positive tone about communism. The remaining 190 items (35 percent) are articles that report on the activities of the communists in neutral tones. These results make it clear that the opinions of black Americans who editorialized in and corresponded with the four major black newspapers during the interwar period were decidedly anticommunist.

The overwhelming majority of the 103 articles that contain positive appraisals of communism and communists (73 percent) frame the ideology as inherently antiracist. Consider, for example, R. J. Burgess's letter to the editor of the *Chicago Defender* on July 1, 1933. Mr. Burgess urged his fellow readers of the paper to go to Russia because "the Negro element can more easily fit in there than in this land of sainted bigots and thinly veneered barbarians who appreciate us only when we are in our places, wherever that may be."[108] The remaining items that contain a positive tone frame communism as a system that is more likely to bring blacks and whites into economic parity.

The frame that 248 items with a negative tone use most frequently (32 percent) characterize communism as dictatorial. The second most widely used frame (28 percent) in this category describes communism as an inherently evil ideology. Twenty-three percent of the pieces in the negative category contain a frame that portrays communists as insincere about their ostensible commitment to racial equality, and 15 percent of the negative items find fault with communism because it is an atheistic or godless ideology.

Most of the items with a negative tone also urge the power structure in the United States to eliminate Jim Crow to prevent the communists from making inroads in black communities. On March 21, 1931, for example, the *Pittsburgh Courier* carried excerpts of a speech that Marian V. Cuthbert, the recently retired dean of women at Talladega College, delivered before the Missionary Society of the First Presbyterian Church of Brooklyn and entitled "Treat Negro as Equal or Make Him a Radical." Cuthbert's argument was that blacks were being "forced into radicalism because [white America] was not Christian enough to permit them to earn the same living as the white man."[109] Similarly, Walter White wrote in a piece that was widely circulated in the black press that the "drastic revision of the almost chronic American indifference to the Negro's plight" was the "one effective and intelligent way in which to counteract communist efforts proselytizing among American Negroes."[110] Thus, the argument that came to dominate the approach of the civil rights establishment to Africa in the wake of the Truman doctrine was really just an extension of the frame it had used in domestic politics in the interwar period.

Understanding the depth of anticommunist feeling in the black counterpublic in the period before Word War II gives us traction on the debate about the behavior of the NAACP and other mainstream civil rights groups during the Cold War. The consensus view in the literature holds that the NAACP was out of step with its constituents when it embraced the Truman doctrine. The problem with this perspective is that the content of black newspapers between 1944 and 1955 does not support it. On the contrary, quantitative analyses of editorials, letters, and articles published in the four largest black newspapers during this period reveal that both the Truman administration and its approach to managing the Cold War had broad support in the black community.

The four leading papers published 315 items that focused exclusively on the Truman doctrine and President Truman's policies for managing the Cold War between 1944 and 1955. Of the items in this sample, 79 (25 percent) are news articles that report on the actions of the Truman administration with a neutral tone. The remaining 237 items contain either positive or negative tones about the administration or its policies—193 items (61 percent) positive and only 44 items (14 percent) negative. In light of these findings, it is easy to understand why the NAACP saw fit to stay in line with the Truman administration's approach to fighting the Cold War.

A content analysis of these same sources also shows that the NAACP remained very popular with black editorialists and correspondents during this period. Between 1944 and 1955, the four major black newspapers published fifty-eight items that focused on the role of the NAACP in foreign affairs during the Cold War. Thirty-two of these items (55 percent) simply report on NAACP activities on the global stage without bias. The remaining twenty-six items (45 percent) evinced tones that reflect either positive or negative appraisals of the actions of the NAACP. The vast majority of these remaining items, twenty-four (44 percent of the total sample), evaluate the NAACP positively; only two items contain a negative tone. These findings provide a strong challenge to the view that public opinion in the black community turned against the NAACP after it endorsed the Truman doctrine.

A content analysis of items that reported on the activities of the CAA during 1944–1955 adds further credibility to my findings. During this period, the leading black newspapers published ninety items about CAA activities. Not surprisingly, most of these pieces (54 percent) are neutral reports about the efforts of the organization to shape U.S. foreign policy toward Africa and internal politics. What is surprising is that, despite the important role that the CAA played in organizing anticolonial protests in black communities during World War II, the black press published very few letters and editorials praising the organization in this period. Indeed, only thirteen items (14 percent of the total sample) contain a positive tone about the CAA. By contrast, twenty-seven items (31 percent) have a predominantly negative tone.

It is important to note that twenty-five (90 percent) of the items about the CAA that fall into the negative category appeared in the press after 1947, the year that Attorney General Tom Clark announced the Truman administration policy on subversive groups. Moreover, 80 percent items published after 1947 adopted a negative tone toward the CAA because of the links of the organization to communists.

In light of these findings, it is very hard to believe that the NAACP lost any support among rank-and-file blacks because it refused to stand with the CAA after the organization came under the intense scrutiny of the Truman administration's repressive national security regime.

Keeping Africa Safe from the Reds

As we have seen, civil rights groups and rank-and-file black Americans attempted to pin their claims for greater equality on the home front to the burgeoning confrontation of the federal government with communism in the 1930s. In other words, black Americans tried to sell Uncle Sam on the idea that ending Jim Crow policies against blacks would, as the *Chicago Defender*'s editorial board opined in 1930, "make America impregnable against foreign propaganda and anti-American invaders."[111] Of course, as several recent studies have documented, the U.S. government did not begin to weigh the value of this argument until the closing days of World War II.[112]

As tensions mounted between the United States and the Soviet Union, however, the Truman administration came to view promoting black equality as a fundamental component of checking the spread of communism on the home front. Indeed, President Truman frequently articulated this position when he came under fire from racial conservatives for using the weight of his office to upgrade the status of black Americans. On June 30, 1947, for example, Truman delivered a speech before the NAACP—becoming the first sitting president to address the group—in which he stated that the nation "could no longer afford the luxury of a leisurely attack upon prejudice and discrimination."[113] Similarly, when Truman delivered a special message to Congress that outlined his plans for promoting black civil rights, he stated that the United States "must correct the remaining imperfections in our practice of democracy" to "inspire the peoples of the world whose freedom is in jeopardy."[114] Truman backed up his pro–civil rights rhetoric when he issued Executive Order 9981, desegregating the U.S. armed forces, on July 26, 1948.[115]

Unfortunately for the black community, President Truman lacked the power to end Jim Crow in other aspects of U.S. life through unilateral action. On the contrary, the fact that separation of powers and federalism are fundamental components of the U.S. Constitution meant that other choke points in the federal government had to loosen before there could be real progress in ending Jim Crow. In the wake of Executive Order 9981, it became clear that Congress was not yet committed to the view that containing the spread of communism required equality for black Americans. Indeed, the powerful southern Democrats who controlled the reins of power in both houses of Congress slowed the pace of reform between 1949 and 1954.[116] Moreover, many of the most committed segregationists in the Congress tried to use McCarthyism to undermine the civil rights movement.[117] Of course, the NAACP and other mainstream civil rights organizations had already done such an excellent job inoculating themselves against charges of having communist ties that this tactic never bore much fruit for the radical segregationists.[118]

In 1954, the Warren Court's ruling in *Brown v. Board of Education of Topeka, Kansas* announced to the world that the highest U.S. court was now committed to overturning Jim Crow (at least in public education).[119] Although the unanimous opinion does not cite anticommunism as a factor in the decision of the Court to strike down the "separate but equal" doctrine, recent work by historians has demonstrated that the Cold War context was an important backdrop in the justices' internal deliberations in *Brown v. Board of Education*.[120] Mary Dudziak, a historian who pioneered the study of the Cold War dimensions of *Brown v. Board of Education*, has demonstrated that many of the justices had already talked publicly and written about how antiblack racism damaged U.S. credibility in the emerging nations of the Third World.[121] Three years later, President Eisenhower bowed to this same logic when he enforced the desegregation order of the Warren Court at Central High School in Little Rock, Arkansas.[122]

In light of how successful the civil rights establishment had been in using anticommunism as a rhetorical cudgel to advance their position on the home front between 1947 and 1954, it is not at all surprising that this became their dominant mode of talking about U.S. foreign policy in Africa during this period. Several studies have chronicled how the NAACP toned down its criticisms of U.S. allies that held colonial possessions in Africa and began to talk more about keeping the continent safe from the Reds during the Cold War.[123] Moreover, in the view of many of these scholars, this pragmatic shift ceded ground in the struggle for decolonization.[124]

But an examination of archival materials of the period challenges this interpretation. On the contrary, the NAACP remained deeply committed to pushing the U.S. government to adopt anticolonial policies during the Cold War; indeed, the NAACP actually engaged in more anticolonial activism during the Cold War than it had during the interwar period or during World War II. In other words, embracing the Truman doctrine seems to have provided the NAACP with *more* opportunities to speak out against colonialism.

According to the historical record, the NAACP initiated contacts with the U.S. government on the issue of colonialism in Africa only ten times between 1926 and 1936. Between 1936 and 1946, which most scholars regard as a golden age of anticolonial activism in the black community, the NAACP made only four overtures to press the government to pursue policies that would lead to the decolonization of Africa. But between 1947 and 1955, the height of the Cold War, the NAACP contacted the federal government twenty-one times to press for anticolonialist policies. Moreover, twelve of these twenty-one contacts (more than 57 percent) framed the demands of the NAACP in terms of the U.S. struggle to contain the spread of communism. In other words, the NAACP argument was that the Truman and Eisenhower administrations should press their European allies to decolonize the African continent because failing to do so aided the Reds in their quest for global domination.

Nevertheless, despite the robustness of their alliance with the Truman administration during the early Cold War, there is no evidence that the NAACP efforts on behalf of Africa made an impact on U.S. foreign policy toward the colonial powers. Indeed, as the historical record makes clear, the U.S. government remained averse to confronting its allies to push the pace of decolonization on the continent well into the 1960s.[125]

As we have noted, there is a consensus in the historical literature that the NAACP support for the Truman administration loyalty program ceded ground in the struggle for decolonization in Africa. Penny Von Eschen argues that anticolonial voices in the black press in general were also a "casualty" of this period. She builds her case for this interpretation on the fact that there was a "sharp drop in the circulation" of these papers in the early years of the Cold War.[126] In Von Eschen's view, this decline in circulation was a result of the newspapers' having lost credibility with their readers, who remained committed to an anticolonialist view of the world, by reducing the amount of content that focused on colonial issues.[127]

Although there is no disputing that the circulation of these papers declined in the postwar period, a quantitative analysis of the content of the four black newspapers with the largest circulation between 1936 and 1955 suggests that a reduction in content related to colonialism was not the source of this decline. The black press published 314 articles about colonialism in Africa between 1936 and 1946. The efforts of the NAACP to push the U.S. government to pursue anticolonial policies featured in 104 (33 percent) of these news items. From 1946 to 1955, the black press published 556 articles focusing on decolonization in Africa. NAACP anticolonial activism took center stage in 288 (52 percent) of these items. The press content on anticolonism clearly did not decrease.

Positive Externalities

For most critics of the NAACP within the literature, the inability of the organization to bring about shifts in U.S. policy stands as evidence that its conservative approach was flawed. To the contrary, further analysis demonstrates that the NAACP strategy generated positive externalities that kept anticolonialism a vibrant force in the black counterpublic and paved the way for new gains in the domestic environment.

The anticommunist stance taken by the NAACP (and other mainstream civil rights groups) during the Cold War also facilitated the formation of ties with anticolonial elements within the U.S. government. The critics of the NAACP's approach in the literature tend to write about the executive branch during the Cold War using the theoretical assumptions of the classic principal-agent model of bureaucratic control, which suggests that bureaucratic agents in the Department of State and other agencies were passive implementers of their principal's strategic initiatives in the Cold War.[128] The upshot of this model is that, if a president takes a soft stand on colonialism in Africa, then his or her subordinates will follow this course in areas where they have bureaucratic discretion.

The problem with this assumption is that a number of important works in the social sciences began to chip away at the principal-agent model of the bureaucracy in the middle of the twentieth century. Indeed, the more recent conventional wisdom within political science holds that bureaucrats have their own preferences and attempt to act on them.[129] Moreover, Daniel P. Carpenter, a political scientist, has shown that bureaucrats often behave in very entrepreneurial ways to mobilize allies within other branches of government and within civil society to gain a degree of "bureaucratic autonomy" from the directives issued by their superiors in the executive branch.[130]

We find an example of this in the interaction of the "Big Six" civil rights organizations and the Kennedy administration. The American Negro Leadership Conference on Africa (ANLCA), which sought to forge the NAACP and the five other Big Six civil rights organizations into a common voice on U.S. foreign policy toward Africa, grew up in large part in response to the efforts of G. Mennen Williams, a subcabinet official, to push beyond the Kennedy administration's conservative policies in Africa. In 1961, President Kennedy appointed Williams to the post of assistant secretary of state for African affairs. On first glance, this appointment was highly unusual for two reasons. First, Williams, who made his way to Foggy Bottom in the wake of twelve years in the governor's mansion in Michigan, was a man with a national reputation, who had even been a contender for the 1960 Democratic Party's presidential nomination.[131] Second, unlike his predecessor, William Roundtree, who had quietly made his way to the top of the Bureau of African Affairs through the diplomatic corps, Williams had no experience in foreign affairs.[132] Nevertheless, these were precisely the traits that Kennedy was looking for in the person to implement his New Frontier foreign policies in Africa.

Throughout his campaign for the White House in 1960, Kennedy had roundly criticized the Eisenhower administration for not doing more to reach out to the leaders of the emerging nations in Africa. In his view, the United States had lost crucial ground to the Soviets, who were actively courting these new regimes, by not pushing their European allies to accelerate the pace of decolonization.[133] Because his opponent in the 1960 campaign, Vice President Richard M. Nixon, shared this position, Kennedy assumed that the Eisenhower administration approach to Africa was rooted in the conservatism of the Europeanists who dominated the ranks of the Department of State. By appointing Williams, a man who could speak with credibility directly to the American people about his agenda in Africa, Kennedy hoped to bring a new balance of power to the Department of State.[134]

Williams wasted little time in rising to the challenge that Kennedy placed before him. Indeed, within months of his appointment, Williams had already won his first internal skirmish with the Europeanists over the administration approach to the issues of decolonization and communist containment in Africa.[135] By fall 1961, Williams was so confident about the transformations he was helping to initiate at the Department of State that he felt comfortable telling an audience in Boston, Massachusetts, that U.S. aid "should not be given [to the African nations] solely with the idea that it will stop African countries from dealing with the Communists."[136]

Williams's efforts were then undermined by President Kennedy's decision to run U.S. foreign policy directly from the White House in the wake of what he saw as the botched handling of the Berlin Crisis by the Department of State.[137] The leaders of the National Security Council and the Executive Committee, the institutions that became prominent after Kennedy lost confidence in the Department of State, saw alliances with Europe as the most valuable strategic asset of the United States.[138] Indeed, almost immediately this new power bloc sent signals to the Africa Bureau that the administration was abandoning the New Frontier approach in Africa.[139] After this shift, Williams fought to regain Kennedy's ear through more aggressive modes of entrepreneurial behavior.

Williams worked diligently to build allies in civil society that could help him achieve his goals throughout 1962. The Public Advisory Council on Africa (PACA) was the first significant product of this new strategy. The group was made up of the tiny but vibrant constituency of left-leaning academics, trade unionists, and clergy that Williams had inherited when he took over the Bureau of African Affairs.[140] Its central task was to help the Bureau of African

Affairs devise new ways to push the administration to revitalize the New Frontier in Africa.[141]

One member of the PACA, George Houser, founder and executive director of the advocacy group the American Committee on Africa (ACOA), argued that the group should try to mobilize an electoral threat to push the administration to adopt progressive policies in Africa.[142] Houser, who had come to work in African affairs through his experiences in the integrated movements for racial justice that took root in U.S. seminaries in the 1940s, had been working with the heads of most black organizations through the ACOA structure since 1956.[143] In the aftermath of the PACA meetings, Houser used statements that Williams and his staff had made in the off-the-record meetings to bolster his ongoing efforts to convince the Big Six civil rights groups that they should "organize and vocalize the position of the Negro community on the question of American policy toward Africa."[144]

On July 26, 1962, the executive officers of five of the Big Six demonstrated exactly how enthusiastic they were by announcing their intention to convene the ANLCA before the close of the year.[145] The conference took place at the Columbia University Arden House in Harriman, New York, November 24–26, 1962. Dorothy Height, who was one of the five conveners of the conference, has revealed that the Bureau of African Affairs helped to get the ANLCA off the ground.[146]

Perhaps this is why the proceedings unfolded as if Williams had scripted the entire event to provide him with rhetorical ammunition for his campaign for bureaucratic autonomy. The delegates, who came from more than one hundred black organizations, passed resolutions that called for the ANLCA to join international efforts to convince the Kennedy administration to impose sanctions on the white-minority regime in South Africa.[147] At the same time, the delegates paved the way for an effective lobbying effort by ensuring that the resolutions did not contain language that directly attacked Kennedy or the North Atlantic Treaty Organization (NATO) allies. "All phraseology that might have involved the United States government in any unpleasantness with its European allies," the *New York Times* observed, "was rejected [by the delegates] as politically unsound and of no practical value to the purposes of the conference."[148] The delegates also pledged to seek a meeting with President Kennedy to "make [their] views available to the government."[149]

Williams moved quickly to collaborate with the ANLCA and to use its Arden House resolutions to strengthen his position within the administration. On December 1, 1962, he wrote to the ANLCA Call Committee members to "wish them increasing success" in their attempt to shape "America's role in foreign affairs."[150] Two days later, Williams forwarded a copy of the Arden House resolutions to Dean Rusk along with a memorandum that urged him to encourage Kennedy to hold a meeting with the ANLCA Executive Committee.[151]

In March 1963, the executive directors of the Big Six organizations met with Kennedy in the Oval Office to press their case that the administration should push harder against colonialism to combat communism in Africa.[152] One month later, Williams worked to help the ANLCA substantiate the claims that they had laid before Kennedy about the burgeoning interest of the black community in U.S. foreign policy toward Africa by commissioning a survey research project on the subject.[153] Unfortunately, the alliance between the ANLCA and Williams did not result in a shift in U.S. foreign policy. It did pave the way, however, for subsequent lobbying efforts on the part of the black community; in June 1963, Dean Rusk, at the behest of Williams and his staff, went on record with comments that suggested that he supported the ANLCA's efforts to shape U.S. foreign policy toward Africa.[154]

・・・

The literature analyzing black elite engagement with U.S. foreign policy toward Africa focuses primarily on the activities of mainstream civil rights groups between 1935 and 1957. According to most of these studies, these organizations entered the foreign policymaking arena on behalf of Africa during the interwar period as part of a strategy to build a global movement against racism and colonialism. The literature also maintains that the rise of the Cold War forced these organizations to set aside their political commitments derived from transnationalism to avoid persecution from the national security state of the Truman administration. My findings challenge both these assumptions. Indeed, the case study of the NAACP demonstrates that the leaders of the organization (along with most other mainstream civil rights groups) had always seen their anticolonial agitation as an extension of their politics in the domestic arena. As a result, the shift of the organization to an anticommunist anticolonialism after 1947 was well in line with its behavior before World War II. Most important, the NAACP was able to use this frame as a cudgel to push the Truman, Eisenhower, and Kennedy administrations on the issue of colonialism in Africa.

Finally, there is evidence that government bureaucrats within the Kennedy administration invited the NAACP and the other Big Six organizations into the policy formulation process to gain a greater degree of autonomy within the executive branch. This finding provides a strong challenge to the view that all bureaucrats within the national security state viewed black elite activism on behalf of Africa with antipathy. It also demonstrates the importance of the NAACP's remaining a viable organization during the Red Scare period. In other words, although it is certainly regrettable that groups such as the CAA were persecuted out of existence between 1947 and 1952, there would have been no black community organizations for government bureaucrats to partner with had the NAACP failed to reframe its anticolonialism as anticommunism.

4

"THE TIME FOR FREEDOM HAS COME"
Black Leadership in the Age of Decolonization

> **The liberation struggle in Africa has been the greatest single international influence on American Negro students. Frequently I hear them say that if their African brothers can break the bonds of colonialism, surely the American Negro can break Jim Crow.**
> —Martin Luther King Jr., "The Time for Freedom Has Come," *New York Times Magazine*, 1961

> **I thank the NAACP for giving me a chance to fight back. Were it not for the NAACP, I might have been a Mau Mau or a Black Muslim, and I thank God for the National Association for the Advancement of Colored People.**
> —Lucien H. Holman, President of Illinois NAACP, speech delivered before the Fifty-Fourth Annual Convention, July 3, 1963

On February 17, 1961, Ralph Johnson Bunche addressed the delegations of the member states to the United Nations General Assembly. Although Bunche, who became the first black person to win the Nobel Prize for Peace in 1950 for his role as a mediator between Israel and the Arab states on behalf of the UN, had addressed the General Assembly many times before, this was undoubtedly one of the most difficult speeches that he had to make in his career.[1] This was so because Bunche, who was then serving in the capacity of undersecretary for special political affairs, took to the floor to apologize for the conduct of eighty-five black Americans who had disrupted an emergency session of the UN Security Council a day earlier.

The meeting had been called by Dag Hammarskjöld, the secretary-general of the United Nations, to discuss the rising tensions in the Congo in the wake of the murder of Patrice Lumumba, its democratically elected president, at the hands of a rival faction of the Congolese elite backed by Belgium, the former colonial ruler of the Congo.[2] The protesters were part of a tiny yet global community of people so moved by Lumumba's murder and outraged by the role played by Belgium that they felt compelled to engage in protest activities.[3]

Unlike the protests that took place without major incidents in the capitals of Europe, Africa, and Asia, the UN demonstration did not go as planned. On the contrary, the protest ended in a brawl between the demonstrators and UN security forces that left more than two dozen people, including some of the guards, with injuries.⁴ The protesters, who counted James Lawson, a protégé of Dr. Martin Luther King Jr., among their ranks, claimed that they had been merely standing in silent protest during a speech by the U.S. Ambassador Adlai Stevenson when the UN security forces set on them. Lawson also acknowledged that, despite their training in nonviolent tactics, a few of the protesters in the group had retaliated with violence.⁵

In the aftermath of the initial confrontation, the UN removed all visitors from the building and, for the first time in the sixteen-year history of the organization, suspended its meetings for the rest of the day. Later in the day, roughly two hundred (mostly black) protesters marched along 42nd Street to demonstrate against both the actions of the Western powers during the Congo Crisis and the UN security guards earlier in the day. Although the protesters were marching peacefully and silently toward the UN, police officers, citing their lack of a permit, ordered them to halt. When they refused to comply with this order, the authorities called in mounted police officers to disperse the marchers. Despite the fact that no further demonstrations emerged from the community, the UN secretary-general took the precautionary measure of closing the UN campus for the next two days. Moreover, when the building reopened on February 19, 1961, visitors now found a beefed-up security detail that included officers from the New York Police Department.⁶

The reports of the incident that ran in the mainstream media presented a narrative in which the UN was under siege from violent black revolutionaries. The *New York Times* reported that the "mostly American Negro" protesters had "set off the most violent demonstration inside United Nations headquarters in the world organization's history."⁷ The United Press International (UPI) alleged that the protesters, who appear in the period photographs wearing business suits, entered the Security Council chamber like a street gang to attack the UN guards with their "fists and chains."⁸ The *Washington Post* dedicated most of its coverage to the New York Police Commissioner's charge that "Black Moslems" and "Black Nationalists" were the "two general categories of Negro groups" behind the riots.⁹

The mainstream press reports also warned that the protests were part of a communist insurgency. Despite the fact that a black communist at the scene of the riot told their reporters that the other protesters had barred him from participating because of his views, the *New York Times*, in an editorial entitled "Hoodlums," concluded that the protest was "in keeping with what Communists and their dupes have been doing in widely separated parts of the world."¹⁰ Similarly, the *Washington Post* reported that the State Department believed that the events in New York were "Communist-inspired."¹¹

Beyond being an outstanding diplomat and world leader, Bunche was also a "race man." The first black American to earn a PhD in political science from Harvard University, Bunche had devoted much of his early career as an academic to studying U.S. race relations.[12] Moreover, throughout his career Bunche was a member (and frequently a leader) in a number of organizations dedicated to uplifting the black race in the United States. In light of the fact that he held these commitments, there is no doubt that Bunche was exhibiting the traditional paternalism of the black elite when he took to the floor of the General Assembly on his own accord to reassure the delegates that the protesters were "misled" and "did not represent the thinking and conduct of the American Negro."[13]

Although Bunche's apology fit into the standard narrative of the black elite's traditional defense of the civil rights movement from both the excesses of the lower classes and the Reds, the response to the speech in the black community was anything but standard. To be sure, several black elected officials, especially those serving on the local level in New York City, praised Bunche's move and stepped up to condemn the protests in their own words.[14] Roy Wilkins, remaining true to the centrist path that the NAACP had charted for decades, tried to convey support for the protestors while simultaneously co-signing Bunche's point that they "did not represent the sentiment of tactics or the American Negroes."[15] Bunche also received strong support from the editorial boards of two of the four most widely circulated black newspapers.[16] For example, Percival L. Prattis, the executive editor of the *Pittsburgh Courier*, chastised the participants in the "violent demonstration" for "embarrassing their country" before the world community.[17]

Other commentators broke ranks with the Bunche statement. James L. Hicks, a columnist with the *New York Amsterdam News*, chided Bunche and other black leaders for rushing to condemn the demonstrators. "I certainly do not agree with Dr. Bunche," Hicks wrote in his "Another Angle" column on February 25, 1961, "that this [protest] was something that he had to go apologizing to white people for on behalf of Negroes."[18] Hicks's criticism of Bunche was not just about domestic racial politics. On the contrary, his main point was that the protest action by black Americans was "warranted" because of the grave nature of the Congo Crisis. Hicks closed the piece by suggesting that either Bunche get busy protesting the injustices that were being perpetrated against blacks in Africa or "stay on the sunny side of the street with whites."[19]

Hicks's column received a torrent of positive commentary from the readers of the *Amsterdam News*. Warren Hall of Wyandanch, New York, for example, joined Hicks in condemning the "professional apologists" who make "the dubious claim of representing the views of the average American Negro."[20] Similarly, Grace Johnson wrote to tell Hicks that his column "said exactly what I felt when I heard of the gentlemen making apologies."[21] One final example came from D. Parker, who wrote in to tell Hicks that his column was "a masterpiece in guiding correct thinking and a contribution to the liberation of the Negro's mind."[22]

James Meriwether has argued that these responses were emblematic of a "rising tide of domestic militancy and interest in broader pan-African ties."[23] There is no doubt that Meriwether's statement provides an accurate summation of the times. In this chapter, I identify the sources of these ideational commitments. Of course, other scholars have devoted intellectual attention to this important question. As it now stands, the consensus view among historians is that two factors were particularly important in fomenting this third wave of Pan-Africanism among the black masses: generational change and a shift in the way that black Americans conceptualized Africa.

Generational change is the factor that scholars cite most frequently to explain the growing solidarity of the black masses with Africa in the 1960s. This argument holds that figures such as Malcolm X and the young lions in groups such as the Student Nonviolent Coordinating Committee (SNCC) and the Black Panther Party spread this new militancy throughout the black community.[24] There is no doubt that the rise of these more leftist figures played an important role in pushing the line that black Americans and Africa were inextricably linked in struggle against domination by whites in the 1960s. It is a mistake, however, to conclude that they were the primary source of this third wave of Pan-Africanism to sweep across the black community. As the UN riots demonstrate, the black masses had been revising their notions of their relationship to the continent even before these figures took center stage in the black counterpublic.

The second factor that scholars point to is a positive shift in the way that black Americans conceptualized the continent of Africa and its people. In other words, in the late 1950s and 1960s, black Americans finally shook off all of their old pejorative views about Africa as a Dark Continent. In this new context, it was easier for black Americans to see Africans struggling against colonialism as kith and kin in a global fight against white supremacy. The problem with this argument is that it tramples on the importance of the two earlier narratives we have discussed—the Italian-Ethiopian conflict and the Liberian Labor Crisis—in which the black community embraced Africans as equals worthy of respect and sympathy.

In this chapter, I demonstrate that the entire context of black politics shifted in response to decolonization movements that swept across Africa beginning in the 1950s. The intense attention that the black press devoted to these nationalist movements in Africa was the primary vehicle through which this shift occurred, fomenting a sense of black American identification with the continent. The press also provided a venue for both the black masses and members of the elite to respond to these events. One of the central aims of this chapter is to reconstruct public opinion in the black community through quantitative analyses of these statements.

As in previous chapters, my goal is to determine whether the black masses and the elite shared a similar vision of issues in U.S. foreign policy toward Africa and how much the elite deferred to the masses in trying to serve its interests. Both the black elite and the masses rewrote their prevailing notions of black authenticity in response to the decolonization movements in Africa. This new black authenticity emerged from the realization that Africa was no longer just a Dark Continent ripe for their missions; instead, it was a place to look for models to challenge white supremacy in the United States. As a result of this transformation, black Americans now saw their collective fate as linked with the new nations in Africa.

Although both black elite and rank-and-file members of the community generally agreed about the terms of this new authenticity, the paternalistic notion among the elite that they were in control of the civil rights movement did sometimes lead to disconnects—such as the riots and Bunche's subsequent apology at the UN—between these two segments of the community. These occasional breaks, however, were far less frequent than scholars suggest was the case. Indeed, for the most part, there was widespread agreement in the black community that independence movements in Africa were inspiring models for the domestic movement by the close of 1960, which the United Nations declared the Year of Africa to celebrate decolonization on the continent.

The Authenticity Blues

Stanley Crouch, social critic, has written extensively on black authenticity. For Crouch, the central dilemma of black authenticity revolves around the chasm that has arisen between blacks, like himself, who have made it into the American mainstream and those who have not. Moreover, in Crouch's view, blacks in the former category often suffer from a type of blues because the majority of both black and white Americans tend to define the cultural and social productions of downtrodden blacks as authentic.[25]

As we have seen, class tensions have often figured prominently in the history of black Americans' engagement with issues in U.S. foreign policy toward Africa. For the most part, however, the authenticity blues that black leaders who tried to shape U.S. foreign policy toward Africa during the interwar period had been most worried about revolved around their connection to Africa. In other words, black leaders fretted over how much they could and should speak for Africa in the U.S. foreign policymaking arena. The internal debate that took place in 1945 between W. E. B. Du Bois and leading members of the NAACP about sponsorship of the Fifth Pan-African Congress provides an excellent example of this dilemma.

The NAACP board of directors had extricated itself from the business of sponsoring Du Bois's Pan-African congresses after the 1927 gathering because the conferences did not yield enough dividends for the organization in the domestic environment. In 1945, Du Bois believed that the time was ripe for him to push the organization to revisit its stance toward his movement. Du Bois's viewpoint grew out of the fact that the NAACP had exhibited a burgeoning commitment to anticolonial politics during World War II. In April 1945, for example, the NAACP convened a conference with the leaders of other black organizations (including the CAA) to discuss ways in which black civil rights organizations could help those living under the yoke of European colonization to advance toward freedom.[26]

On April 6, 1945, more than fifty people gathered in Harlem for the conference. The delegates, who came from Barbados, Burma, Gold Coast Colony, Guiana, India, Indonesia, Jamaica, Nigeria, Puerto Rico, and Uganda, all agreed that they should press the great powers to make decolonization a priority in the new world order that was emerging in the wake of World War II.[27] The conferees voted unanimously in support of a resolution to send a delegation to the upcoming San Francisco Conference on the United Nations Organization to convey this sentiment to world leaders and demand representation in the new body.[28]

There is no evidence that a delegation of attendees of the NAACP conference on colonialism ever made it to San Francisco. The NAACP did send Walter White, Mary McLeod Bethune, and Du Bois to San Francisco to lobby for an agenda that was virtually identical to the one the delegates had agreed on in New York. But, despite their best efforts, the NAACP delegation did not achieve any of its goals in San Francisco. On the contrary, the colonial powers and the American delegation under Secretary of State Edward Stettinius Jr. made it clear that the language of self-determination in the UN Charter did not apply to the citizens of the subject territories.[29]

Even though the NAACP delegation failed to influence the proceedings at the San Francisco Conference, Du Bois came away from the experience with a renewed sense of optimism about the organization that he had helped to found in 1909. Indeed, Du Bois saw the decision of NAACP leaders to commit resources to the conference as a sign that they had finally shed the parochialism for which he had pilloried the organization in the black press in the 1930s.[30] Moreover, the time in San Francisco provided Du Bois and Walter White with the opportunity to thaw the chill that had existed in their personal relations since Du Bois had resigned from the NAACP in 1936.[31] It was in this context that Du Bois decided to try to get the NAACP to sign back on to the Pan-African Congress movement.

Du Bois's plan called for holding the Pan-African Congress—the fifth since 1900—six months after the defeat of the Axis Powers.[32] Du Bois, hoping to head off competition from a group of activists from the Caribbean and West Africa under the leadership of George Padmore, asked the NAACP to commit resources so that black Americans would not lose their leadership position in the movement. "If we do not lead the way," Du Bois wrote in a report on the Pan-African Congress movement to the NAACP board of directors, "there is nothing to hinder them [the Caribbean and West African activists] from forming a Pan-African movement of their own without the participation and guidance of American Negroes."[33]

Du Bois's arguments obviously moved the NAACP directors because they appointed a committee to examine the possibilities of both sponsoring and hosting the conference.[34] On July 12, 1945, the committee, chaired by Louis Wright and comprising Ralph Bunche, Elmer Carter, Russell Davenport, W. E. B. Du Bois, William Hastie, Rayford Logan, Arthur Spingarn, Channing Tobias, Roy Wilkins, and Walter White, gathered to discuss the key issues entailed in taking on the responsibilities of holding a new Pan-African Congress.[35] Although Du Bois had hoped that the meeting would focus purely on logistics, according to the documentary record substantive differences quickly emerged among several members of the committee.

The first point of disagreement was over the name of the conference. Obviously, Du Bois wanted to call the conference the Fifth Pan-African Congress to retain the continuity of the movement that he had started with Henry Sylvester Williams nearly half a century earlier. But a subset of committee members, led by Rayford Logan, Howard University historian, wanted to call the gathering Dependent Peoples' Conference to signal that the delegates would speak to colonial issues beyond the experiences of Africans and blacks living in the diaspora. Many other committee members expressed concerns about how much hosting the conference would cost and whether delegates from Europe and Africa would be able to get passage to the United States given the constraints that the war was placing on the shipping industry. When the members of the committee were unable to resolve all of their differences about these important issues, they decided to adjourn and leave the planning in the hands of a subcommittee consisting of Du Bois, Bunche, Hastie, and Tobias.[36]

It was at the meeting of this subcommittee that Du Bois's hopes that the NAACP would host the Fifth Pan-African Congress went up in smoke. Apparently, during the five days between the first committee meeting and their gathering, both Hastie and Bunche had developed strong objections to the Pan-African Congress model. In their view, Pan-Africanism, with its emphasis on racial solidarity over social class or subject status, was both passé and morally dubious.[37]

And it was the Hastie-Bunche line that the leaders of the NAACP ultimately embraced.[38] Although there was vague talk of hosting a Conference on Colonial Problems at an NAACP board meeting later in the year, the organization never set aside the resources to bring such a plan to fruition.

The NAACP board of directors did vote, however, to send Du Bois as its representative to the Pan-African Congress that Padmore and his associates had organized in Manchester, England.[39] For Du Bois, who never really understood how the NAACP could reject Pan-Africanism, this was a bitter pill to swallow. Indeed, although he dutifully attended the proceedings in Manchester on behalf of the NAACP, his correspondence from the period shows that he suffered from a bad case of the authenticity blues. "The NAACP has taken no stand nor laid down any program with regard to Africa," a frustrated Du Bois wrote to White on his return from the conference. "Individually, I have done what I could," he continued, "but I have neither the funds nor authority to accomplish much."[40]

As we have seen, Du Bois and the NAACP parted ways in the late 1940s because of the stance of the organization on the Truman doctrine; it is important to note that Du Bois's frustration with his colleagues' refusal to privilege Africa in their anticolonial activism provided part of the backdrop for this later decision to quit the NAACP and join the CAA. Du Bois was substantially ahead of his time in advocating the position that the relationship between black Americans and Africa was special. Indeed, both the black press and the masses vindicated and embraced Du Bois's vision of Pan-Africanism in the next decade. Moreover, in response to this shift in political context, even his old foils at the NAACP had to alter their positions to remain effective representatives of their constituents on the home front.

Writing Revolutions in Africa

The independent black press played a crucial role in shaping and aggregating black public opinion on U.S. foreign policy issues related to Africa. As discussed in chapter 3, most of the black editorialists and correspondents that published in these newspapers at the height of the Cold War attempted to achieve a balance between portraying the black community (and Africans) as loyal foot soldiers in the confrontation of the West with communism and speaking out against the evils of colonialism in Africa.

Racial identity was also a dominant theme in stories about Africa in the middle of the twentieth century. Of course, this will not come as a surprise to anyone who is familiar with the literature on the rise of globalism among black Americans during and immediately following World War II.[41] Most of these studies conclude that the treatment by the black press of world affairs—particularly colonial issues—evinced a shift in which the black community came to see itself as one among many peoples of color struggling against white domination. In short, much of this scholarship advances the notion that the self-conception of the U.S. black community—as gauged by the stories that ran in black-controlled newspapers—moved away from the narrow Pan-Africanism of Garvey or Du Bois toward the people-of-color model advanced by Hastie and Bunche.

James Meriwether's groundbreaking study of black America's engagement with modern Africa between 1935 and 1961 challenges this theory. He does not deny that black Americans embraced to some extent a people-of-color model in the post–World War II period, but at the same time, Meriwether argues that the continent of Africa held special significance for black Americans within this model. In short, he asserts that the anticolonial struggles that emerged on the African continent in the middle of twentieth century pushed black Americans to embrace both modern Africa and their own "Africanity" in new ways. To substantiate his claim, Meriwether relies on impressionistic examinations of black print sources and archival materials.

Although I concur with Meriwether's baseline hypothesis, there are, nevertheless, stark differences between our accounts. For example, in Meriwether's view, black Americans developed their new self-identity and awareness of Africa quite gradually in the period between 1935 and 1961. Moreover, he contends that the process was sometimes a painful and that conflicts between members of the black elite and the masses often emerged as they worked to shake off their ambivalent feelings about their ancestral heritage in Africa.[42] Although there is no doubt that these dynamics were part of the process through which black Americans remade themselves by embracing modern Africa, the evidence shows that the shift in authenticity occurred much more smoothly than Meriwether suggests. Indeed, my quantitative content analyses of the depiction of three major events in African history by the black press between 1935 and 1960 shows that the black counterpublic had fully embraced Africa well before Meriwether indicates.

This is an important point for several reasons. First, it allows us to adjudicate the debate that Du Bois and the Hastie-Bunche faction engaged in over black authenticity in the 1940s. If the ultimate goal of black leaders is to represent the interests of their constituents in the domestic environment, then we can show that Du Bois's vision of a Pan-African Congress in which race was still front and center would have come closer to achieving this end.

Second, the findings of my content analyses help us adjust the historiography of Pan-Africanism. As discussed, most scholars see the rise of the third wave of Pan-Africanism as a function of the generational shift that occurred in the civil rights movement in the wake of a decade of decolonization.[43] Under this view, these younger activists spread Pan-Africanism through the community by preaching that African independence movements were important referents for the struggle on the home front, in much the way that Marcus Garvey fomented second-wave Pan-Africanism in the 1920s. Although several studies have challenged this conclusion by pointing to the behavior of the civil rights establishment in the U.S. foreign policymaking arena, the link between this behavior and the representational environment on the home front has not yet been thoroughly explored. My analysis fills this gap in the literature by showing that mainstream black leaders had to act because their constituents were demanding a more expansive notion of blackness that incorporated ties to the realities of modern Africa.

The content analyses presented here reconstruct the visions of Africa held by the black community before and during the high point of African decolonization. The focus is on gauging editorial and public opinion about four historical events that had a major impact on black America's identification with the African continent—the Defiance Campaign in South Africa (1951), the Mau Mau uprising in Kenya (1952), the emergence of Ghana from colonial rule (1957), and the Congo Crisis (1961). The analyses gauge the tone of the articles, editorials, and correspondence that appeared during 1935–1960 and generate measures of affinity with and disassociation from the continent that are implicit within each item. For each analysis, I first provide a brief sketch of the event to give the reader a richer sense of the context in which these media accounts emerged. Although the emergence of Ghana as an independent nation-state occurred after both the Defiance Campaign in South Africa and the Mau Mau uprising in Kenya, I deal first with this event before moving on to treat the other cases in chronological order because of the singular importance of Ghana as the first independent nation to emerge from the white supremacist world order that the European powers created at the Berlin Conference of 1884–1885.

On March 6, 1957, the British colony Gold Coast morphed into the independent nation of Ghana. Despite the fact that black Americans were deeply engaged in their own struggles for domestic equality in the late 1950s, the black community took considerable notice of the independence celebrations in Ghana. According to both the Hastie-Bunche line on Pan-Africanism and the consensus within the literature on black engagement with world affairs, this enthusiastic response of the black community was more a function of its commitment to anticolonialism than to Pan-Africanism. If this theory really holds water, then a content analysis comparing the black community's response to the decolonization of Ghana and other significant moments in anticolonial politics should reveal continuity in both the levels of coverage and tone.

I use the decolonization of India in 1947 as a comparison case in this analysis for several reasons. First, black Americans had long regarded India as an important colored nation whose people were fellow travelers with Africans and blacks in the diaspora in terms of their experiences of exploitation by whites and their history of resisting white supremacy.⁴⁴ Second, India was the first major nonwhite nation to gain its independence during the postwar period. Finally, many black Americans revered Mahatma Gandhi, the principal leader of the Indian resistance movement, for his strong statements against racism and his commitment to nonviolent social protest.⁴⁵ Thus, if any decolonization movements outside Africa had garnered the attention of the black press, India would be at the top of the list.

My analysis shows that the black press devoted far more attention to the emergence of Ghana as an independent nation than it did to India. Indeed, there are 352 items focusing on Ghana that appeared in the four largest black newspapers, almost double the 189 items that these papers devoted to India. It is important to note that a companion analysis of coverage in the mainstream press revealed just the opposite trend. The *New York Times*, for example, ran 963 items about decolonization in India between 1947 and 1949 and 504 items on Ghana between 1957 and 1959.

The volume of coverage is not the only difference in the way that the black press treated the independence of India and Ghana. Figure 4.1 charts a comparison of the expressions of linked fate in the positive coverage about the two countries that appeared in the black newspapers. As we can see, more items saw the future of black Americans as bound up with Ghana than with India.⁴⁶ Indeed, even though 67 percent of the items that ran in the black press about Indian independence expressed the sentiment that it was a positive development for global race relations, only 12 percent portrayed the fate of black Americans as linked to the success of India. By contrast, 54 percent of the positive items that ran in the black press about Ghana suggested that the fate of black Americans was tied to the success of the new nation. These findings suggest that black reporters and commentators saw the racial identity that they shared with the Ghanaians as a relevant factor in determining how the decolonization experience would shape their lives.

The relatively high level of expressions of linked fate that appear in the Ghanaian-independence items undermines Meriwether's claim that black print sources contained many stories revealing black Americans' tendency to embrace stereotypes about Africa as a savage continent. There is no doubt that some black Americans continued to hold on to images of Africa as a Dark Continent well into the 1960s. Coretta Scott King makes reference to this fact when writing about attending Ghanaian independence ceremonies with her husband, Dr. Martin Luther King Jr., in 1957. "We realized," King writes after they encountered the modernity of the capital of Ghana, Accra, "that we ourselves had been the victims of the propaganda that all of Africa was primitive and dirty."⁴⁷

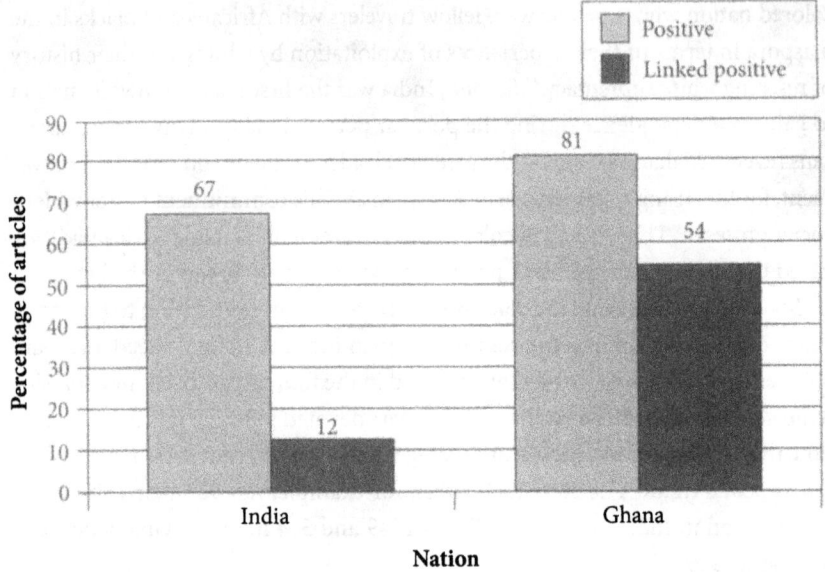

FIGURE 4.1 Percentages of positive news coverage and expressions of linked fate in positive news coverage of India and Ghana, 1947–1959
Sources: *Atlanta Daily World; Chicago Defender; New York Amsterdam News; Pittsburgh Courier*

Content analysis of the coverage devoted by the black press to the second Italian-Ethiopian War and Ghanaian independence shows that language portraying Africa as a savage continent devoid of civilization was much rarer than previous reports indicate. Only 22 percent of the more than 3,000 items about Ethiopia that ran in the black press between 1935 and 1938 contain language that evokes negative imagery of Africa. My analysis also reveals that this figure had improved dramatically by the time that the emergence of Ghana as an independent nation made headlines in the black press. Indeed, only 9 percent of the 352 items related to events in Ghana during the year it emerged as an independent nation contains such language.[48]

This does not mean, of course, that black Americans had completely abandoned the language of savagery and civilization when talking about Africa in the decade of decolonization that followed Ghanaian independence. On the contrary, these frames emerged with great frequency when black editorialists and correspondents began to write about the Mau Mau insurgency in Kenya. Before black Americans turned their gaze toward Kenya, however, another uprising on the continent took center stage in the black press.

South Africa was an important flashpoint in the global confrontation between white supremacy and black equality during the 1950s and 1960s. Like

Kenya, South Africa was a settler colony, where a tiny white minority controlled vast tracks of land and the industrial economy. Moreover, beginning in 1948, the South African government, under the leadership of Daniel Malan and his Nationalist Party, codified its traditional system of racial segregation and oppression of the black majority into apartheid laws.[49] This made South Africa one of three nations in the world where there was de jure segregation of blacks and whites. Like their counterparts in the other two nations—the United States and Rhodesia—the black citizens of South Africa constantly challenged their oppression through nonviolent social protests.

The Defiance Campaign of 1951 was the first significant, nationwide protest against apartheid in South Africa. The Defiance Campaign grew out of the 1951 convention of the African National Congress (ANC).[50] At the convention, the ANC, working in conjunction with groups representing South Asians and mixed-race peoples, decided to press the government to repeal six of the most discriminatory apartheid laws on the books. After the conference, the ANC sent a letter to Prime Minister Malan requesting that he repeal these laws or face a massive protest campaign, setting April 6, 1952, as the final deadline for compliance.[51]

Of course, Malan, who had swept into power on muscular promises to defend the Afrikaner position against all challenges, flatly rejected the ANC ultimatum. On the contrary, he promised the ANC and its allies that he would retaliate using the full force of the South African security forces. As the deadline approached, the ANC and its coalition partners began to worry that they had not properly trained enough of the protesters to prepare for the massive retaliation that Malan promised that he would unleash against the movement. In light of these concerns, the coalition announced that it was postponing the protest date to June 26, 1952.[52]

When the appointed day came, the ANC-led coalition was ready for direct action. The primary goal of the coalition protests was to defy all six laws that they had asked the Malan regime to repeal. Under the direction of Nelson Mandela, thousands of black, Asian, and mixed-race people marched into the "whites only" sections of public places in the major South African cities of Pretoria, Durban, and Johannesburg. The protesters also violated the incredibly restrictive government curfew laws.[53]

Although Malan hinted at the use of widespread violence, the government responded to the Defiance Campaign largely through police actions. By the end of the first week of the protests, the government had arrested several hundred people. Hoping to create a breakdown of governmental capacity, the coalition instructed the protesters to remain in jail rather than pay the fines for violating the segregation laws. After one month, the police had placed more than 1,500 protesters in jails throughout the country.[54] As the Malan government jailed protesters, others stepped up to take their place. For three months, the government and the ANC coalition engaged in this dance. Indeed, by the middle of October more than 5,000 protesters had taken their place in South African jails.[55]

Although there is no doubt that the Defiance Campaign created a nuisance for the Malan government, it did not generate the crisis that the coalition had hoped it would. This was because the government demonstrated as much commitment and ingenuity to finding new ways to jail the protesters as the protesters did in staging their challenges to South Africa's white supremacist laws. The Defiance Campaign ended when riots roiled the cities of East London, Elizabeth, Kimberly, and Johannesburg between October 18 and November 10, 1952. Although, the ANC-led coalition immediately disavowed responsibility and urged South Africans of color not to participate, the Malan government used the riots as a pretext for violently cracking down on the Defiance Campaign. By December, the Malan government had effectively crushed the Defiance Campaign and passed a series of tough new laws that criminalized virtually all forms of organizing and protest activity.[56]

Although the Defiance Campaign did not achieve its ultimate goals, it did have the positive effect of shining a bright light on the conditions in which nonwhites lived in South Africa and on their demands for equal citizenship. The United Nations, with its growing bloc of member nations that had just recently thrown off the yoke of colonialism, condemned the Malan government for its actions and threatened an investigation.[57] Moreover, both the mainstream and black presses in the United States reported widely on events as they transpired.

We see clear evidence that black Americans supported the Defiance Campaign and were beginning to exhibit a sense of linked fate with black South Africans in the black press coverage of these events. Of the eighty-six items on the Defiance Campaign that ran in the four leading black newspapers between 1951 and 1954, fifty-four (63 percent) had a positive tone when describing the protesters and their cause. By contrast, only 3 of the items that ran during this period had a negative tone. The remaining twenty-nine items reported on the events with a neutral tone and mostly described events on the ground as they happened.

In contrast, coverage in the black press of the Mau Mau uprising in Kenya was far less favorable. The Mau Mau uprising began on October 7, 1952, when a group of insurgents assassinated Chief Waruhiu, a prominent member of the traditional Kikuyu elite and a collaborator with the British government.[58] These insurgents, who were also of Kikuyu background, called themselves Mau Mau fighters. The movement had started in the late 1940s to organize young Kikuyu men and demand that the British colonial government reform its land tenure and immigration policies. In short, this burgeoning population wanted its fair share of land for farming and a halt to the policy of the colonial government of ceding vast tracts of productive land to white settlers from England.[59]

There is no doubt that the Kikuyu were justified in their demands. After all, from its inception, Kenya was one of the worst examples of settler colonialism on the continent. Between 1902 and the beginning of World War I, the British government simply nullified African property rights and gave land titles to any whites willing to make the trip from England.[60] As several historians have pointed out, the British government also designed this policy to force the indigenous peoples into cities, where it would be easier to control their movements and facilitate the capitalist exploitation of their labor in industrial factories.[61]

The Kikuyu had something of a reprieve from this pattern during the interwar period because the global depression after the end of World War I slowed the pace of settlers streaming into Kenya from England. Because the colonial government was extremely dependent on agricultural exports for economic growth, it encouraged the indigenous population (particularly the Kikuyu) to fill the void through squatting and tenant farming on European holdings.[62] This policy worked remarkably well as a stopgap measure during the depression and throughout World War II.

What the colonial government had not foreseen, however, was that this policy also created a renewed sense of ownership within the indigenous communities. In fact, the government believed that it would have no trouble dispossessing the indigenous Kenyans when immigration from England picked up again after the war. Part of the reason for this view is that the government believed that the traditional chiefs that it had brought into the government through their policy of indirect rule would be able to maintain social control. The problem was that the chiefs had become a symbol of the colonial government and its corrupt practices because of the huge land grants that they received for their collaboration. Indeed, when the Mau Mau movement started in the late 1940s, the chiefs were the primary targets for the violent outbursts of the insurgents.[63] Thus, it is not surprising that Chief Waruhiu was the first casualty of the 1952 insurgency.

By the middle of October, there had been so many additional attacks against the chiefs that the colonial government had to respond. On October 20, 1952, the colonial governor declared a state of emergency and arrested more than 150 Kenyans who he claimed were instrumental in fomenting the Mau Mau moveent. As part of this roundup, the colonial government arrested Jomo Kenyatta, the leader of the nationalist movement in Kenya, despite the fact that he was not a driving force behind the uprising.[64] Instead of breaking the Mau Mau insurgency, this overreach gave many indigenous Kenyans who would have never considered joining the movement a reason to fight.

Indeed, for the next four years, the incredibly underequipped Mau Mau fighters waged a guerrilla war against a force that included multiple battalions of the British army, several squadrons of the Royal Air Force, and the homegrown colonial government militia.⁶⁵ The casualty numbers speak volumes about the nature of the conflict between the insurgents and the British forces. Over these four years, the Mau Mau fighters killed 58 white settlers and 1,880 indigenous Kenyans whom they deemed to be collaborators with the government. By contrast, the colonial government forces reported killing 12,590 Mau Mau fighters.⁶⁶

The coverage of the Mau Mau in the black American press suggests that the community was more ambivalent about this movement than they had been about the Defiance Campaign in South Africa. Indeed, only 27 percent of the more than four hundred items that appeared on the Mau Mau in the four black newspapers with the largest circulation between 1952 and 1954 had a positive view of the insurgents. By contrast, 32 percent of the items were decidedly negative in their appraisal of the insurgency. The remaining coverage offered mixed assessments that tended to empathize with indigenous Kenyans but condemn the Mau Mau insurgents for turning to violence. Moreover, the black press was particularly critical of the Mau Mau fighters' attacks on other blacks.

A comparative analysis of the expressions of linked fate in the black press coverage of the Defiance Campaign and the Mau Mau also suggests that there was greater uncertainty about the latter movement in the black counterpublic. Whereas 41 percent of the items that ran in the black press on the Defiance Campaign contained an expression of linked fate, only 7 percent of the items on the Mau Mau had such content. This finding suggests that black Americans used heuristics derived from their own experiences on the home front to expand their notions of black authenticity in the 1950s.

This does not mean, however, that all the old models that black Americans developed during the postwar period to confront Africa and the rest of the world remained stable. An examination of the Congo Crisis, the fourth major event that demonstrates the burgeoning affinity of U.S. blacks with Africans, helps to drive this point home. The murder of Patrice Lumumba by his Belgian-backed rivals for power, the event that triggered the UN riots described earlier, was the grim closing chapter of a tense struggle for control of the central African nation between 1958 and 1961. The U.S. black press carved out a distinctive voice in its coverage of the crisis.

Belgium, whose record in the Congo made it the most predatory and abusive of the colonial powers, was reluctant to begin the process of decolonization, and this gave rise to the crisis. By the middle of the 1950s, both Great Britain and France had greeted the fact that the sun was setting on their empires with a realism that allowed them to forge working relationships with the indigenous elites who would form the independent governments that replaced their colonial administrations. These relationships typically allowed Britain and France to preserve lucrative economic ties to their former colonial possessions. Belgium, by contrast, greeted the demands of indigenous Congolese for independence with considerable resentment.

This is not surprising given the evolution of the relationship of Belgium with its lone colony. King Leopold II of Belgium had established a claim that the vast territory of the Congo was his personal property during the Berlin Conference of 1884–1885, at which the European powers met to forge a common understanding about how they would exploit the continent of Africa. In the wake of the conference, King Leopold leased the mineral rights and control of the Congo to several Belgian companies in return for a 50 percent share of all the wealth that they extracted from the colony.[67]

Together these companies and the Belgian military forces that provided them with security and muscle raped the Congo for the next two decades. The concession companies forced the indigenous peoples to work in the extraction of natural resources without compensation; they also frequently maimed or killed those who tried to resist or failed to meet the quotas that they established.[68] Conditions in the Congo were so bad that they attracted the attention of several reformers, including George Washington Williams, a pioneering black historian from the United States whose riveting exposés shocked and outraged the global public. It was in this context that King Leopold ceded control of his personal colony to the Belgian government in 1908.[69]

There is no doubt that conditions in the Congo improved when King Leopold handed over control of the colony to the Belgian legislature. The new colonial administration halted the forced labor practices and wanton slayings that had led to a 60 percent reduction of the population of the Congo between 1885 and 1908.[70] At the same time, the Belgian government continued to see the Congo simply as a point of capital extraction and the indigenous populations as facilitators of this process. As a result, the metropolitan government spent almost nothing on services for the colonial population. Moreover, the government intentionally limited educational opportunities for the Congolese in hopes of stifling the development of nationalist movements.[71]

Although the Belgians could limit the formal education of the indigenous people, they could do nothing to prevent them from learning the lessons of the African nationalist movements that were sweeping the continent in the 1950s from popular media sources and word of mouth. In 1956, a group of Congolese activists published a document entitled *Conscience Africaine* that advocated independence from Belgium within thirty years. This very conservative appeal for decolonization, which was widely circulated in Leopoldville, scandalized the colonial government at the time. Within two years, however, it would long for the days when the black population of the colony talked about a thirty-year timetable for independence. Between the publication of *Conscience Africaine* and the close of 1958, dozens of political parties formed to press the Belgians for an immediate withdrawal.[72] Within another two years, the Congo joined sixteen other nations in the celebration of their independence from their former colonial masters during the Year of Africa.

This quick transition shocked the Belgians, who had come to see the Congo as an idyllic experiment in civilization after the legislature took control of the colony in 1908. Patrice Lumumba's very frank assessment of the horrors of their rule on Congolese Independence Day only further cemented the Belgians' sense of loss and resentment.[73] Lumumba, who had come to power through his ability to build the only political party in the nation with multiethnic appeal, the Mouvement National Congolais (MNC), dressed down the Belgian delegation, which included King Badouin, for the "humiliating bondage" that Belgium had forced on the Congolese.[74]

Although Lumumba had an accurate read on the experiences of the Congo under Belgium, he did not have a government capable of controlling all of the centrifugal forces—many of them set in motion by Belgium—that immediately challenged his ability to hold his fledgling nation together. This became painfully obvious to Lumumba (and the world) just one month after his fiery speech. On July 5, 1960, soldiers in the Congolese Army rioted after their Belgian commander, General Emile Janssens, told them that the officer corps would remain an all-Belgian club and that they were to receive neither promotions nor more pay because of independence. A furious Lumumba hurried to the barracks, which were 90 miles outside of Leopoldville, to announce that Janssens no longer had the authority to make such decisions, that all Congolese soldiers would receive a one rank promotion and pay raise, and that the officer corps would be Africanized.[75]

Despite Lumumba's best efforts, general disorder spread throughout the Congo. On July 8, 1960, both the British and the French governments evacuated their embassies. Two days later, the Belgian government, responding to grossly exaggerated stories that ran in the press about the plight of expatriates, sent troops to reinforce its bases in the Congo. By the end of July, Belgian troops had engaged in twenty-one separate police actions throughout the Congo. The fact that he had authorized only one of these actions made Lumumba exceedingly nervous; indeed, in his view, these interventions stood as proof that Belgium continued to view itself as the legitimate government of the Congo. Moreover, the fact that Belgium had responded to the requests for intervention issued by Moise Tshombe, his chief rival and president of the mineral-rich Katanga province, reinforced Lumumba's concerns.[76]

It was at this stage that the Congo Crisis emerged as an issue in the Cold War. Dissatisfied with the support that he had received from the United Nations, Lumumba, who described the Cold War position of his MNC party as one of "positive neutrality," decided to reach out to the Soviet Union for help restoring order in the Congo. Although the Soviet Union was supportive of Lumumba's position, it was not eager to engage in a hot conflict with the West over the Congo. Thus, the Soviets joined a coalition with the Western powers and the UN to send peacekeepers to the Congo.[77]

The UN coalition did finally succeed in getting the Belgian army to stand down and leave most areas of the Congo. Katanga, which had become Lumumba's primary concern at this point because it was the most economically viable province in his young nation, was a different story; the UN-led peacekeeping forces, under the direct command of Secretary-General Dag Hammarskjöld, refused to accede to Lumumba's requests that they use force to preserve the territorial integrity of the Congo.[78] After it became clear to him that the UN would not act in this capacity, Lumumba requested that the Soviets provide him with weapons and supplies so that he could launch an invasion of Katanga. Soviet Premier Nikita Khrushchev, realizing that he now had to live up to all the lofty Soviet rhetoric about supporting the newly emerging states in Africa against the encroachments of the Western powers, did finally agree to send a limited package of military aid to Lumumba.[79]

Lumumba never launched his invasion of Katanga. Shortly after the aid package from the Soviets arrived in Leopoldville, Lumumba became embroiled in a bitter fight for control of the government with Joseph Kasavubu, his former ally. Although he successfully quashed this challenge to his authority, his overtures to the Soviets had made him a marked man in the West. While Lumumba was preoccupied solidifying his power base in the capital, the U.S. and Belgian governments recruited Joseph Mobutu, his private secretary and chief of staff of the army, to wrest power from his patron. In October 1960, Mobutu seized power and placed Lumumba under house arrest. Two months later, he transported Lumumba to the breakaway Katanga province, where Katangan and Belgian troops tortured and executed him. Not until two years later, at the behest of Mobutu, did a UN coalition lead an invasion of Katanga to restore the province to the Congo.[80]

The coverage of the Congo Crisis in the U.S. black press illustrates the transition that black Americans were undergoing vis-à-vis their relationships with modern Africa and the old Cold War coalition on the home front. Whereas the dominant theme in the coverage presented by the *New York Times* and the *Washington Post* was the possibility of the crisis leading to the communist infiltration of the Congo, the black press saw these events through the lens of black-white conflict. At the same time, it is clear that the specter of communists taking over the Congo limited the connections that blacks felt they could make to Patrice Lumumba during the crisis. Indeed, a content analysis of 439 items that appeared in the black press between 1958 and 1962 shows that the percentage of items that framed Lumumba negatively increased markedly after he invited the Soviets to intervene in the crisis. Whereas only 3 percent of the items that appeared in the black press before Lumumba courted Soviet intervention framed him negatively, 46 percent of the items that ran after he sought help from the Soviets presented negative frames of his actions.

Globalizing Black Linked Fate

Mainstream U.S. black leaders have typically used the domestic context as a heuristic for determining how to engage African issues in the U.S. foreign policymaking arena. In short, defending the home front has historically been the top priority for members of the black elite when they respond to events in Africa. Throughout most of the history of black America's contact with the African continent, black politicians and activists had the luxury of focusing on one or (at most) two issues at a time. These very limited contacts made it easy for black leaders to form a consensus around key issues: emigration, loans to Liberia, or the Italian-Ethiopian War.

This does not mean, of course, that dissenting viewpoints have been absent from the black counterpublic. On the contrary, every period has had outliers—for example, Bishop Tuner, W. E. B. Du Bois, and Paul Robeson—who provoked serious debates within the community and challenged the consensus within the black elite. It is also true that these dissident voices have typically had very little success in shifting the opinions of their fellow black leaders or shaping U.S. foreign policy toward Africa unless they had the broad support from the black masses, as in the response of the black community to the Italian-Ethiopian War.

The rapid changes that took place on the continent between 1945 and 1960 (the UN Year of Africa) shifted these dynamics in two ways. First, black leaders no longer had the luxuries of dealing with Africa one issue at a time and working to build internal consensus before presenting a unified front to their constituents, the U.S. government, and white Americans. Second, the steady diet of stories about the emerging nations gaining freedom from their colonial masters that the black press fed rank-and-file blacks heightened community identification with the continent and its peoples; in other words, the ways that the black press reported on decolonization domesticated the issues in U.S. foreign policy toward Africa as never before in the black community. As a result of this dynamic, U.S.

black leaders faced more demands from their constituents to take stands on developments on the continent.

Several historians have argued that the black elite members' commitment to anticommunism served as their primary heuristic for this new era.[81] There is no doubt that anticommunism remained an important guiding principle for black leaders as they struggled to keep pace with changes on the continent. Moreover, it is clear that this commitment was strengthened by the fact that southern members of Congress and other proponents of Jim Crow laws renewed their efforts to paint the civil rights movement as Red in the 1950s and 1960s.

It is also clear that black leaders relied on other models to navigate these uncharted waters. In particular, black leaders also remained true to their traditional ideational commitment that blacks were Americans first and foremost. In other words, the black elite continued to push the line that the United States was the black Americans' permanent homeland. This commitment sometimes brought more established black leaders into conflict with younger activists and politicians who had come to see their roots in Africa as a more attractive basis for forging a positive self-identity than the traditional narratives about black contributions to the development of U.S. society.

Historians have seen the ascendency of this younger generation in the 1960s as the fount of a new black authenticity centered on Africa. As we have seen, the black community was well on its way to redefining itself through its connection to Africa even before the rise of the black power movement. And, even though they were constrained by their ideational commitments, mainstream black elites also worked to build this new black authenticity. Indeed, the old guard black leaders in the 1950s and 1960s consistently used their public pronouncements on foreign policy issues to reinforce the notion that black Americans shared a linked fate with their kith and kin in Africa. We can illustrate this by recovering the ways that black leaders responded to three of the events—the Defiance Campaign in South Africa, the Mau Mau uprising in Kenya, and the emergence of Ghana as an independent nation—we have already discussed.

Despite its weakened position as a result of U.S. government persecution, the CAA was the first black organization to respond to the Defiance Campaign. Indeed, Paul Robeson, now the primary CAA leader, issued the first statement by the organization of support for the ANC-led coalition on February 25, 1952.[82] When the Defiance Campaign started on April 6, 1952, the CAA organized solidarity protests in front of the South African mission to the United Nations in New York City.[83] Moreover, Robeson urged black Americans to follow the model of the Defiance Campaign in their own struggle. In the February edition of the CAA's *Spotlight on Africa*, for example, Robeson asked black Americans to "imagine" following the South African example by "joining together in a great and compelling action to put a STOP to Jim Crowism in all its forms everywhere in this land."[84]

Although there is no evidence that the CAA ever tried to build such a coalition to confront the forces of Jim Crow on the home front, it did attempt to forge alliances with other groups to support the protesters involved in the Defiance Campaign. On March 21, 1952, for example, William Alphaeus Hunton wrote to the leaders of the Americans for South African Resistance (AFSAR) about forming an alliance in support of the South African protesters.[85] The AFSAR was an integrated group of scholars, activists, and clergy members to which notable black leaders such as Charles S. Johnson, Mordecai Wyatt Johnson, A. Philip Randolph, and Bayard Rustin belonged. But because these men, and their white colleagues, intended the AFSAR to serve as an anticommunist counterpoint to the CAA, they flatly dismissed Hunton's calls for collaboration.[86]

Despite the fact that the AFSAR activists rejected the CAA's overtures, they shared the fundamental assumption of the organization that Americans—and particularly the black community—should support the Defiance Campaign by staging their own nonviolent social protests in the United States.[87] Indeed, on the day that the Defiance Campaign began in South Africa, AFSAR staged a giant rally at the Abyssinian Baptist Church, the pulpit of AFSAR board member Representative Adam Clayton Powell Jr. (D-N.Y.). During the rally, Powell spoke in terms that evoked a new authenticity when he urged his fellow black Americans to stand with black South Africans.[88]

In independent statements they made in the black press during the Defiance Campaign, other black leaders reinforced the notion that black Americans and South Africans were linked together in a common struggle against white supremacy. In her weekly column for the *Chicago Defender*, for example, Mary McLeod Bethune stated plainly that apartheid was the "counterpart" of the "insistence on segregation in the United States."[89] Although Bethune acknowledged that she was generally enthused by the rising "resistance of the colored peoples of the world to the pressures of racial discrimination," she was particularly heartened by ways that black Americans and South Africans were challenging their subordinate positions in their respective countries.[90]

As the response of the civil rights establishment to the Defiance Campaign demonstrates, the parallels between the experiences of blacks living under apartheid and those living under Jim Crow continued to support the notion that these two communities of color shared a special relationship. This does not mean, however, that black leaders had the luxury of focusing exclusively on South Africa. On the contrary, the rapid pace of change on the continent in the age of decolonization meant that the black activists and politicians faced a constant learning curve as they tried to merge their commitment to winning in the domestic arena with the dictates of third wave Pan-Africanism.

The first indications the black elite had that this learning curve could be incredibly steep came in the wake of Kenyan Mau Mau insurgency. As we have seen, the black press portrayed the Mau Mau in ambivalent tones. On the one hand, the press painted the uprising as a function of white oppression and sympathized with the desires of the indigenous peoples to own land and be rid of white domination. At the same time, black editorialists condemned the Mau Mau insurgents' use of violence to achieve these ends and their assaults on fellow blacks. The response of the mainstream black elite was similar. Some black leaders joined the press and the black masses in making public statements that placed the blame for the conflagration squarely on the shoulders of the settlers and demonstrated great empathy for black victims of the violent crackdowns by the colonial government as reprisals for the insurgency. For example, when news of the violent crackdowns by the British government on Kikuyu insurgents reached him in Washington, D.C., Adam Clayton Powell took to the House floor to sponsor a resolution calling on the U.S. government to cut foreign aid to Kenya to prevent the colonial government from using the money to continue its "massacres" of the indigenous Africans.[91] Similarly, A. Philip Randolph, who had spent so much of his early career fighting Marcus Garvey's variant of Pan-Africanism, used his position as head of the Brotherhood of Sleeping Car Porters (BSCP) to push the AFL to pass a resolution condemning the "arrogant and ruthless domination of the white colonial government officials and greedy white settlers" in Kenya.[92]

By drawing a clear link between the exploitative nature of colonialism and the "fires of nationalism that are raging and sweeping across the continent," the BSCP resolution minced no words.[93] This does not mean, however, that Randolph and his fellow union members condoned the violent tactics used by the insurgents. "The leaders of the African natives [in Kenya]," Randolph wrote in a letter to President Eisenhower that clarified the BSCP's position on the Mau Mau, "must be prevailed upon to see that violence and bloodshed cannot constitute a solution of their social, economic, and political problems."[94]

Not surprisingly, the NAACP, which had been committed to nonviolent civil disobedience since its inception in 1909, also walked this middle path. In 1953, the organization passed a resolution at its annual convention that simultaneously condemned the "terrorist methods" of both the British and the Mau Mau insurgents.[95]

Again, James Meriwether has argued that part of the black elite's response to the Mau Mau uprising was a "reluctance to be linked with 'savage' Africa."[96] Although there is no doubt that some black leaders saw the Mau Mau movement as evidence that Africans remained less civilized than their black American counterparts, this was by no means the dominant mode of thought among the black elite.

What, then, led the black elite to take such a cautious stand on the Mau Mau uprising when they faced a political context in which at least some constituents demanded that they embrace the revolution as a model for overthrowing white supremacy? According to the historical record, two factors were at work. First, the vast majority of black politicians and activists who advocated for black civil rights in the New Negro period and in the middle of the twentieth century simply did not believe that violent tactics would produce positive change for blacks in the United States. Indeed, although groups such as the SCLC, SNCC, and CORE gained wide recognition for their use of nonviolent social protests beginning in the 1950s, an ethos of nonviolence had already permeated the entire civil rights movement in the previous five decades. It was a commitment to this ethos that compounded the frustrations that members of the black elite felt over Garvey's wild pronouncements about confronting the European powers in Africa and reinforced their already deep skepticism of communism. Thus, the last thing that black leaders wanted to do with their pronouncements on the Mau Mau uprising was to suggest that the violent tactics of the insurgency might be an acceptable model for blacks in America.

Second, the tactics employed by their enemies in the United States also shaped the way that black leaders responded to the Mau Mau uprising. As discussed in chapter 3, southern politicians and their allies frequently attempted to smear the civil rights movement by claiming that communists were behind the protest actions that blacks initiated. This, however, was not the only rhetorical strategy that racists employed to try to discredit the movement or generate white resistance to civil rights gains. Indeed, as the historian Thomas Noer has demonstrated, the segregationists often evoked images of the "savage" African as a trope in their campaigns to convince the nation that blacks were not yet ready for full citizenship rights.[97] Thus, it was very important for black leaders to inoculate the domestic movement from associations that could play into the hands of those using this rhetorical strategy.

Whereas the Mau Mau uprising challenged the ability of mainstream black leaders to stay in synch with both the opinion makers who controlled the black press and a black public that was growing increasingly militant, the emergence of Ghana as an independent nation provided an opportunity for the black community to come together in celebration of a historic milestone. Indeed, while the black community was enthusiastically following the Ghanaian independence ceremonies in the pages of the *Chicago Defender*, *Pittsburgh Courier*, and other leading black newspapers, several prominent black leaders made the trip to Accra to witness the proceedings in person.[98] It is clear from the statements that these figures made to the press during and after the trip that they joined the broader community in seeing the transition of Ghana to independence as a crucial marker in the emergence of a new black authenticity that incorporated an identification with the independent states of modern Africa as a component of black identity in America.

Ralph Bunche, for example, who had so frustrated Du Bois when he refused to support his vision of a Fifth Pan-African Congress built around black racial identity, told the press that Ghanaian independence was an important marker of progress of both black Americans and Africans.[99] Similarly, A. Philip Randolph hailed Ghana as a "modern miracle in statecraft" that pushed his mind "back to the first Pan-African Conference called by Dr. W. E. B. Du Bois, great scholar and prophet of the new Africa."[100] Randolph's excitement about the transformation of Ghana even led him down the unlikely path of reconsidering his position on the nationalist dimensions of the Garvey movement. "I, also, in retrospect," Randolph told the readers of the *New York Amsterdam News*, "reconstructed the massive demonstrations for the cause of Africa for the Africans by the improbable crusader and organizer, Marcus Garvey."[101]

The black leaders who attended the festivities in Accra were also quick to use the transition experience of Ghana as a frame of reference for the black struggle in the United States. Randolph, for example, praised Ghana for showing the black world that it is possible to bring about political transformations without "recourse to violence and bloodshed."[102] "What has impressed me the most," John H. Johnson, the wealthy publishing magnate and civil rights activist, told the *Atlanta Daily World*, "is how Ghana achieved its freedom without bitterness." Johnson concluded his interview by stating that he saw "Martin Luther King's efforts in the South" as the "counterpart" to what Kwame Nkrumah had engineered in Ghana.[103]

King had just come from his major victory leading the Montgomery Bus Boycott using nonviolent direct action, so it is easy to see why Johnson made this connection. Moreover, King, whose success in Montgomery had vaulted him into the national spotlight with a cover story in *Time* magazine, was by all accounts in the black press the star among the U.S. delegation in Accra. Indeed, for many in the black press and back home in the United States, King's face-to-face meeting with Vice President Richard M. Nixon was the major story to come out of the first few days of the celebration.[104] In the wake of the Ghanaian independence ceremonies, King, who was then just thirty-six years old, emerged as one of the strongest voices for the new black authenticity and third-wave Pan-Africanism in his generation. This was because of King's ability to remain committed to the practice of nonviolence in United States while simultaneously accepting that the struggles against colonialism in Africa sometimes required alternative means of resistance. This, in turn, made him a perfect broker between the activists who came of age in the New Negro period and the black power generation.

Indeed, it was through the intervention of King that the old guard civil rights activists came to realize that the calls of the next generation for black power both on the home front and in Africa were really a call to move from protest to political empowerment through the electoral system and self-help projects. By the time of King's death in 1968, the phrase *black power* had become a slogan embraced by most black politicians.

Nothing reflects this unity more than the black political conventions of the late 1960s. The delegates to the conferences were in general agreement that the Voting Rights Act provided the black community with an unprecedented opportunity to impact the U.S. electoral system through voting-bloc behavior and the slating of candidates for office.[105] This course was pursued so vigorously in the closing years of the 1960s that, by the time black politicians and community activists gathered for another national conference in 1972, the famed Gary Convention, significant electoral gains had been made on both the local and national levels. As discussed in the next chapter, even though the black elite had reached the pinnacle of political power in the United States, U.S. foreign policy issues toward Africa continued to provide black politicians and activists with unique opportunities to serve their constituents.

・・・

The political context of black politics shifted in response to the decolonization movements that swept across Africa beginning in the 1950s. Indeed, both the black elite and the masses rewrote their prevailing notions of black authenticity in response to these decolonization movements. This new black authenticity was grounded in the notion that Africa was now the place to look for models for challenging white supremacy on the home front. As a result of this transformation, black Americans now saw their collective fate as linked with the new nations in Africa.

Although, the black elite and the rank-and-file generally agreed about the terms of this new authenticity, the paternalistic notion held by the black elites, that they were in control of the civil rights movement, did sometimes lead to conflict between these two segments of the community. These occasional breaks, however, were far less frequent that scholarship suggests is the case. Indeed, for the most part, there was widespread agreement within the black community about the importance of Africa for the domestic movement by the close of the UN Year of Africa.

5

"WE ARE A POWER BLOC"
The Congressional Black Caucus and Africa

> I listened to those who said this is going to hurt blacks [in South Africa]; it's going to hurt corporations. But human beings will struggle for their freedom, in peace if they can, in violence if they must.... That pales every single argument you have made. We must end the madness of apartheid.
>
> —Representative Ron Dellums (D-Calif.), House chamber, August 12, 1988

> For some reason, Mr. Archer [the chairman of the committee] will not allow the amendments that are necessary to protect the textile and apparel industry, when they know full well that's what the Senate is going to do. But I understand the game. They would like for it to be said that your black congressman couldn't protect your job, but your white senator did.
>
> —Representative James Clyburn (D-S.C.), remarks reported in *The Hill*, July 7, 1999

On July 16, 1999, Representative Sanford Bishop (D-Ga.; serving 1992–present) took to the floor of the House of Representatives to deliver a speech against the African Growth and Opportunity Act (AGOA). Because the bill advocated the creation of free trade linkages between the United States and African farmers, a speech by Bishop, a southern Democrat with strong ties to labor unions and agricultural interests, against the measure should have been anything but news worthy on Capitol Hill. On this day, however, reporters, lobbyists, and even other members of Congress crowded into the House chamber to hear Bishop's arguments against the bill.

This unusual attention was a function of the fact that Bishop was also a well-respected member of the Congressional Black Caucus (CBC), and his speech was the first (but not the last) to break ranks with the official CBC position in support of the bill. It is important to note that the interest in Bishop's speech did not come simply from the fact that he was breaking ranks with his comrades. On the contrary, individual CBC members have always demonstrated a considerable willingness to go their own way on important issues. Moreover, a number of recent studies have demonstrated that the unity that characterized the CBC of the 1970s and 1980s has been more difficult to maintain since the expansion of the CBC in the 1990s.[1] The interest in Bishop's speech stemmed from the fact that he was breaking ranks with the CBC on the AGOA—the one issue area on which Hill insiders and watchers expected the CBC to maintain the unity that had been their hallmark in previous decades is U.S. foreign policy toward Africa.

This expectation stemmed from the fact that the CBC's greatest legislative achievement was in the field of African affairs. In 1986, the CBC engineered the passage of the Comprehensive Anti-Apartheid Act (CAAA) over Ronald Reagan's veto. This was the first time in U.S. history that a racial or ethnic minority successfully challenged the authority of a sitting president on a foreign policy issue and won.[2] In the wake of this victory, members of Congress came to view U.S. policy toward Africa as the special domain of the CBC. Moreover, despite the fact that the group has not pushed any major legislation in this area since the CAAA, many black legislators continue to view this policy area as a rallying point for their caucus.[3]

Many scholars suggest that the rift within the CBC over the AGOA grew out of principled disagreements among its members about the best way to help Africa develop.[4] Without completely discounting the importance of these differences, I show in this chapter that CBC members who voted against the AGOA did so out of a desire to protect the interests of their constituents and gain reelection. In other words, the terms of the AGOA placed some CBC members under tremendous cross-pressures that made it impossible for them to both support the initiative and maintain their electoral coalitions.

In this chapter, I also demonstrate that such balancing acts have been an omnipresent feature of the experiences of black legislators since the first CBC engagements in African affairs in the late 1960s. Indeed, even the seventeen-year CBC campaign for a sanctions bill, which most previous studies cite as a prime example of foreign policy activism motivated by transnationalism, was shaped by this dynamic.[5] In other words, CBC members shifted their commitment to pushing sanctions legislation to balance their pursuit of transnationalist goals against their goals on the home front.

The analytic narrative presented here draws on evidence derived using both qualitative and quantitative research methods. An examination of published historical works forms the backdrop of this chapter. Most of the causal inferences I make in the chapter emerge from semistructured interviews with twenty-six members of the CBC.[6] Finally, I employ logistic regressions to bolster and refine the conclusions that emerge from the historical record and interview data.

Welcome to the House

Political scientists segment the history of black representation in the U.S. Congress into three distinct periods. The first period is the Reconstruction Era, running from 1870, when Joseph Rainey (R-S.C.; 1870–1879) became the first black person to serve in Congress, to 1900, when racial gerrymandering removed George White (R-N.C.; 1897–1900) from office. The second period is the Civil Rights Era, running from 1928, when the residents of the historic South Side neighborhood of Chicago made Oscar De Priest (R-Ill.; 1928–1934) the first African American to hold a seat in Congress in the twentieth century, to 1972, when opportunities stabilized for black Americans to send representatives of their choice to Congress. The final period, the Post–Civil Rights Era, runs from 1972 to the present. Scholars assume that legal struggles for inclusion are now over and that the most pressing questions about black political behavior in the Congress revolve around the content and quality of the representation elected officials offer their constituents.[7] The origins of the CBC sanctions campaign are rooted in the experiences of black legislators during the closing days of the Civil Rights Era.

The transition from the Civil Rights Era to the Post–Civil Rights Era began with the election of 1968. This poll, which was the first real test of the Voting Rights Act of 1965, increased the number of blacks in Congress from five to ten members. The hope that these gains would translate into the fulfillment of long overdue substantive demands was so palpable among black Americans that Representative Charles Diggs (D-Mich.) was compelled to call attention to these sentiments in the remarks he entered into the *Congressional Record* announcing the formation of the CBC. "Our concerns and obligations as members of Congress," stated Diggs, "do not stop at the boundaries of our districts; our concerns are national and international in scope."[8] He continued, "We are petitioned daily by citizens living hundreds of miles from our districts who look on us as Congressmen-at-large for black people and poor people in the United States."[9] Representative William L. Clay Sr. (D-Mo.; 1968–2000), one of the founders of the CBC, recalls a real sense of optimism permeating the group as their fledgling caucus set out to use the legislative process to address the very challenging problems that confronted black Americans in the late 1960s:

> We decided that the nine of us [Senator Edward M. Brooke, a Republican from Massachusetts, did not join the group], representing such a collage of talent and experience, and coming mostly from politically safe districts, now constituted a power-bloc deserving of respect in the institution. It was our opinion that the establishment of a caucus would lead to the solidarity of purpose and program necessary for us to realize this potential.[10]

Because scholars of Congress have long noted that the three-tiered committee system is the nerve system of the House of Representatives,[11] the CBC would have to master it to become a power bloc within the institution. Mastering the committee system requires the ability to guide bills from the lowest tier (subcommittees) to consideration at the two higher levels of the system (standing committees and the committee-of-the-whole). Because this process becomes easier when one has influence at these higher levels of decision making, fierce competition ensues among all representatives for membership on the most important standing and control committees.[12] Over time, the norm of seniority evolved to prevent the rationally egoistic behavior of members seeking committee assignments from paralyzing the House of Representatives.[13]

Despite the fact that the majority of CBC members lacked the seniority necessary to obtain plum committee assignments, the group had good reason to be optimistic about expanding its influence through coordinated action. The literature on the Congress also tells us that backbenchers, particularly those affiliated with the majority party, can expect to have their interests advanced by their partisans who occupy more potent institutional roles than they do. Indeed, because it is far better to be the chairperson of a standing committee than ranking-member, an honorific title reserved for the most senior member of the minority party serving on a committee, the leaders of the party-in-power have an incentive to make sure that they maintain a majority within the chamber.[14] The easiest way to do this is to help more vulnerable junior members shore up their chances at reelection. Logrolling (or vote-trading) is the most common tool employed by party organizations to give their partisans who are disadvantaged by the committee system chances to feed at the pork barrel.[15]

"When [American] political institutions handle racial issues," writes Dianne Pinderhughes, a leading scholar of minority politics, "conventional rules go awry."[16] Although penned in reference to machine politics in Chicago, Pinderhughes's aphorism translates well to the experiences of the black Americans who served in Congress during the Civil Rights Era. Not only did the black members who served during this period suffer the indignities of a segregated work environment,[17] but party leaders also excluded them from most of the opportunities for professional development that were normally extended to white members.[18]

Although passage of the Civil Rights Act of 1964 made it impossible to maintain Jim Crow rules within the institution, the House of Representatives in 1969 was still a racially charged environment that certainly was not changing quickly enough to accommodate a new power bloc of black legislators. "Democratic leaders not only expressed hostility to the idea of our forming the [Congressional Black] Caucus," stated Clay, "but it was clear by the way we were treated that most of our colleagues doubted our abilities and preferred the composition of the party before the election [of 1968]."[19] Clay continued, "It is certainly hard to consider yourself welcome in the [party] caucus when you call the leadership to talk about black issues and they simply hang up the phone on you."[20]

Virtually locked out of the party caucus in the 91st and 92nd Congresses, the CBC pursued a number of extra-institutional activities—such as convening conferences and producing reports on the state of black Americans—to compensate for their legislative impotence. Because all these activities essentially duplicated the efforts of groups such as the NAACP and the Urban League, many rank-and-file African Americans began to raise questions about the long-term potential of the CBC members as substantive representatives.[21] It was in the context of this crisis of performance legitimacy that black legislators decided to make passing a sanctions bill the highest priority of the CBC.

The Diggs Plan

Carol Swain, in her book on black political behavior in the U.S. Congress, depicts the CBC campaign for a sanctions bill as purely symbolic behavior.[22] Swain also argues that CBC members run the risk of alienating their constituents by "turning to foreign policy issues that appear easier for them to tackle than domestic issues";[23] in other words, she characterizes the foreign policy activism of black legislators as arising from a cynical politics aimed at distracting their constituents from their lack of efficacy on domestic issues. The historical record and testimony from three of the surviving founders of the CBC, however, challenge Swain's interpretation on both counts.

First, Representative Charles Diggs, the principal architect of the sanctions campaign, used his position as ranking member of the CBC to push his colleagues to take up the sanctions issue precisely because it was likely to be an uphill fight within the institution. There is also considerable evidence attesting that Diggs's colleagues bought into his plan mostly because they believed it would help them overcome the CBC's crisis of performance legitimacy and pave the way for them to generate particularistic benefits for their constituents. Thus, although it is true that none of the sanctions bills introduced in the 91st and 92nd Congresses contained provisions that delivered pork to their districts, the CBC members who sponsored these bills clearly believed that their actions in the foreign policymaking arena were ultimately about such substantive gains and not merely about symbols.

This claim gains greater coherence when placed in the context of the literature on legislative behavior. Political scientists have frequently noted the unique position that foreign policy questions occupy in the consciousness of most members of the House of Representatives. Robert Dahl, for example, describes foreign policy as one of the few issue areas in which members of Congress are free to act on their private preferences.[24] This is so, Dahl believes, because foreign policy questions remain so far removed from the issues that concern the proverbial man-on-the-street that members of Congress are rarely given much instruction from their constituents on them.²⁵ Dahl also suggests that, even though the executive branch circumscribes their ability to carve out leadership roles,²⁶ members of Congress cherish the opportunities for independent action that foreign policy questions afford them.²⁷

Writing some twenty years after Dahl, Richard Fenno found that few members of the House of Representatives relish opportunities to become involved in foreign policy debates. On the contrary, he reported that most members of Congress actively avoid service on the Foreign Affairs Committee because its work is devoid of opportunities to engage in the types of distributive behavior that individual members seek to strengthen their chances at reelection.²⁸ Fenno also finds, ironically, that members of the House of Representatives hold their colleagues who forgo the temptation to view their service in purely careerist terms by engaging the "important" and "exciting" issues that come before the Foreign Affairs Committee in high esteem.²⁹

It was this cluster of attitudes that Representative Diggs hoped to exploit by encouraging his colleagues in the CBC to become engaged in foreign affairs. Indeed, by the time his colleagues anointed him the first chair of the CBC in 1969, Diggs had accumulated fifteen years of personal experiences within the chamber that suggested this was possible.

Diggs won election to the House of Representatives from the Thirteenth Congressional District in Michigan in 1954. This is extremely significant because it means that he served his apprenticeship in the institution in the middle of the Civil Rights Era, a time when the racial climate of the Capitol was even more hostile to black members than in the period when the CBC emerged. Indeed, it was common practice at this time for white members of Congress (mostly southern segregationists in the Democratic Party) to use the epithet *nigger* in the course of legislative business.³⁰ As if exposure to this language during the course of legislative business were not enough, black members and their staffers frequently found themselves victimized by racist verbal assaults.³¹ Moreover, because segregation of the races was official policy within the halls of Congress, every day at work reminded black legislators in a number of more subtle ways that their white counterparts (mostly their partisans) viewed them as second-class citizens.³²

When Diggs arrived on Capitol Hill, he found that his two black colleagues coped with the limitations imposed on them by the racist environment of the House chamber in very different ways. Representative William Dawson (D-Ill.; 1942–1970) was the consummate party loyalist.³³ "I play with my team [the Democratic party]," Dawson was once overheard remarking to a group of his constituents who pressed him about why he did not use his position in the House to speak out more aggressively against segregation.[34] Political scientists attribute Dawson's behavior to his being deeply ensconced in the powerful Chicago Democratic machine.[35] The leaders of the machine used their influence with the national party to protect his status in the House of Representatives. In return for this patronage, Dawson did not make any waves about race matters.[36]

Without a political machine to advocate on his behalf, Adam Clayton Powell Jr. (D-N.Y.; 1944–1970) had to take a circuitous path around the racist southern Democrats (or Dixiecrats) who controlled the committee structure.[37] First, he made himself a national figure by speaking out aggressively on race issues in the press.[38] He then used the fealty that he earned from the black community for lifting this heavy mantle to bolster his reputation with liberal Democrats and Republicans in the chamber.[39] Finally, Powell also demonstrated a willingness to buck the party system in very public ways to achieve his legislative and political objectives.[40]

Diggs's service record, both as a student leader at Fisk University and as a member of the Michigan legislature, demonstrated that his personality was far better suited to protest than accommodation.[41] Given his temperament, it is not at all surprising that Diggs gravitated toward the maverick Powell when he arrived on Capitol Hill in 1955. Happy to have another race man[42] in the Congress, Powell gladly took on the responsibility of mentoring his young colleague.[43] It was through this relationship that Diggs first came to believe that foreign policy activism was an important resource for black members seeking influence within the racist environs of the House of Representatives.

Powell's masterful performance at the Bandung Conference was the critical juncture through which he made an internationalist out of Diggs. In January 1955, the emerging nations of Asia and Africa announced that they would gather at the resort town of Bandung, Indonesia, to discuss their place in the world order.[44] Believing that it was in the best interests of the United States to recognize the conference,[45] Powell lobbied the Eisenhower administration to send him to Bandung as its official observer.[46] Fearing that the resolutions coming out of this gathering would contain unfavorable appraisals of the foreign and domestic (race) policies of his administration, Eisenhower balked at Powell's request.[47] Undaunted by the objections of his political ally in the White House,[48] Powell headed to the conference on his own accord.[49]

As predicted, the Eisenhower administration's shabby record of countenancing racial discrimination at home and abroad quickly emerged as a major theme in the plenary sessions at Bandung.[50] When Powell arrived on the scene on the second day of the meetings, he promptly called a press conference to address the charges against the United States.[51] Virtually everyone attending the conference expected Powell to deliver a speech that would further inflame the anti-U.S.

sentiments of the gathering by detailing the hardships of black Americans.[52] Powell surprised them all by offering a stirring defense of the record of the Eisenhower regime on civil rights and presenting the United States as a land where "[being] a Negro is no longer a stigma."[53]

Reactions to Powell's speech at home were swift and varied. Although a few Republican-leaning black newspapers showered praise on Powell,[54] most press outlets in the black community ran articles and editorials that registered a deep annoyance with the Harlemite for having "sold the colored people down the river."[55] By contrast, the mainstream (white) press in both the North and the South unequivocally lauded Powell for doing, as Ralph McGill, an influential southern journalist, called it, "a great service for the country."[56] When Powell returned to work on Capitol Hill, he found that his popularity with the mainstream press had expanded his influence within the House chamber.[57]

Powell's behavior at Bandung was not a calculated move designed to build political capital in the House of Representatives.[58] On the contrary, a sincere desire to protect the Eisenhower administration from losing ground in the Cold War motivated Powell's actions at the conference.[59] Nevertheless, he certainly did relish the positive externalities that his performance generated for him in the chamber. Indeed, in the aftermath of this episode, Powell began to look for ways to use the foreign policymaking arena to continue to bolster his growing influence in the House.[60] Diggs's former colleagues and staff members suggest that Powell also encouraged Diggs to look to the international context for opportunities to build his own reputation in House.[61] According to the documentary record, two years later Powell literally pushed his young protégé into the foreign policymaking arena.

In 1957, Britain's Gold Coast colony was set to become the first nation in sub-Saharan Africa to join the community of independent nations. Finally recognizing that Powell's interpretation of the importance of the new states in the Cold War struggle was correct, the Eisenhower administration decided to send a full delegation, headed by Vice President Richard M. Nixon, to the independence ceremonies.[62] When Powell requested that he be a member of this delegation, the White House moved with great alacrity to fulfill his request.[63] It soon became clear, however, that partisan politics was going to prevent Powell from making the trip.[64] Because Powell had already suggested to the administration that Representative Diggs would also make a fine delegate, the Michigander went to Ghana in Powell's place.[65]

The fact that nothing extraordinary happened for Diggs on this trip to Ghana did not stop him and Powell from parlaying his experience in Africa into a seat on the House Foreign Affairs Committee.[66] Diggs was an outstanding member of this committee in the period between 1957 and the formation of the CBC. Although he was still too junior to leave much of mark in terms of legislative output, Diggs quickly earned the respect of his colleagues for both his mastery of substantive issues and his political skills.[67] And these skills helped Diggs achieve one of the most significant victories of his legislative career.

During the height of the search by the Lyndon Johnson administration for a clear policy on South Africa, the *New York Times* reported that the *USS Roosevelt* intended to dock in Cape Town for refueling. Coming just one day before the third ANLCA conference, this report greatly antagonized the organization, which immediately wrote to President Johnson in protest. The Johnson administration argued that the *Roosevelt*'s refueling mission was a legitimate action under the embargo and decided not to budge on this issue. With the ANLCA and the administration at loggerheads, Representative Diggs decided to get involved. Diggs generated a letter opposing the stopover; had it co-signed by thirty-five House Democrats, three House Republicans, and three powerful senators; and forwarded it to President Johnson.

With Jacob Javits, Walter Mondale, and other powerful figures signing the Diggs letter, the administration had to take notice. Indeed, one day after the president received the letter, two members of his foreign policy team—Deputy Defense Secretary Cyrus R. Vance and Navy Secretary Paul H. Nitze—were sent to meet with the signatories. After this meeting, the administration announced that, although it would go ahead with the *Roosevelt*'s docking in Cape Town, it had reformulated its policy. Not only would all future refueling be done at sea, but also the captain of the *Roosevelt* was instructed to cancel shore leave unless he was given a guarantee by the Pretoria government that black sailors would be treated as equals by the people of South Africa. Because there was no way this was going to happen, the Navy was in effect canceling the *Roosevelt*'s leave.[68]

In light of Diggs's personal history, it is not surprising that he pushed the five new black members who won election to the House in 1968 to cut their legislative teeth in foreign affairs. Indeed, oral tradition among the founding members of the CBC clearly paints Diggs, who was the first CBC chairperson, in the role of mentor and leader.[69] It also makes explicit that the robust sanctions campaign that emerged in the 91st and 92nd Congresses was a direct result of Diggs's ability to convince them that such activism would accelerate their rise to power in the House. "Diggs, being the great leader that he was," Representative William Clay remembered, "reckoned that getting us involved in foreign policy would make a big splash on the Hill." Clay continued, "[Diggs] knew that there would be no way that the [party] leadership could continue to doubt our abilities or ignore [the CBC] because of our race if we demonstrated real competence in that arena."[70]

This is not to say that the black legislators lacked a genuine interest in obtaining justice for blacks in South Africa. On the contrary, most CBC members issued statements to the popular press and entered remarks into the *Congressional*

Record throughout this phase of the sanctions campaign that revealed that they felt deep empathy for blacks suffering under apartheid. Moreover, these same statements also show that sentiments derived from transnationalism intensified these feelings for many CBC members.[71]

These sentiments were simply not enough of a push factor on their own, however, to generate the incredibly robust movement for a sanctions bill that emerged within the CBC during the 92nd Congress. Representative Louis Stokes (D-Ohio; 1968–1998), another pivotal figure in the formation of the CBC, clearly recalled that, in the absence of Charles Diggs, any political impulses that he and his colleagues derived from transnationalism would have taken a backseat to servicing the needs of their home districts. According to Stokes,

> We all came to the Congress with some diffuse interest in the South Africa problem. In other words, we knew that it was important, but it certainly did not register with most of us the way that say health care, full employment and education for our constituents did. It really was not until our ranking member, Congressman Charles Diggs, chairman of the Subcommittee on Africa at the time, showed us the importance of the connection between [the South Africa] issue and the achievement of our domestic goals that [passing] sanctions legislation [became] part of our legislative agenda.[72]

But, as soon as the connection between passing a sanctions bill and achieving their domestic goals became somewhat muddled, the vast majority of CBC members significantly scaled back their activism on the issue.

New Directions

As we have seen, the early efforts of CBC members to pass a sanctions bill were not merely a ploy designed to distract their constituents from their inability to deliver on the domestic front. In addition, the sharp decline in bill sponsorship in the 93rd and 94th Congresses (see fig. 5.1) was primarily a response to signals that the black legislators received from their white colleagues that led them to question the utility of the Diggs plan as a means for raising the CBC profile in the House chamber. The changes in sponsorship shown in figure 5.1 can also be considered, in a wider context, to be a function of CBC members' efforts to balance their ideological commitment to the sanctions issue against the kinds of electoral, policy-oriented, and institutional goals that scholars of the legislative process, such as Fenno, David Mayhew, and Keith Krehbiel, see as the driving force behind the behavior of most members of Congress.[73]

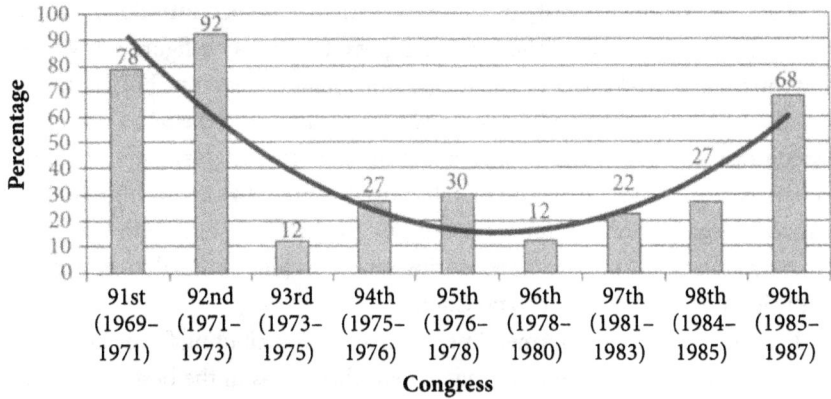

FIGURE 5.1 Percentage of CBC members sponsoring sanctions bills, 1969–1987. CBC, Congressional Black Caucus.
Source: *Congressional Record*

Even with Diggs firmly in control of the Subcommittee on Africa, the CBC's push for a sanctions bill floundered because, despite the respect that Diggs commanded within the beltway on issues of U.S. foreign policy toward Africa,[74] few white members of the 92nd Congress were ready to buy into the sanctions framework. On the contrary, the vast majority of white members (on both sides of the aisle) were far more comfortable standing with the Nixon administration as he moved to return relations between the United States and the white-minority regimes in southern Africa to the status quo ante that existed before the Kennedy administration. Diggs and his protégés in the CBC received this message quite strongly when a large bipartisan majority in both houses of Congress passed the Byrd Amendment on April 20, 1972. The bill, named for Senator Harry Byrd (D-Va.; 1965–1982), its chief sponsor, cleared the Nixon Defense Department to import strategic materials from Rhodesia (now Zimbabwe) in direct contravention of an embargo resolution that had recently passed the UN General Assembly.[75]

In the wake of the Byrd Amendment, it became painfully obvious to CBC members that their campaign for a sanctions bill was far out of line with the prevailing mood of the House of Representatives. If the sanctions campaign were purely (or even primarily) a function of transnationalism, such a signal would have had no affect on the behavior of the CBC members who had demonstrated a commitment to the issue before the Byrd Amendment became law. But the passing of the Byrd Amendment did alter the behavior of the majority of CBC members in two significant ways, showing that the early sanctions movement was primarily a response to institutional imperatives.

First, the vast majority of CBC members simply stopped introducing sanctions bills after the close of the 92nd Congress. Returning to figure 5.1, we see that thirteen members of the CBC (92 percent) made at least one bill calling for sanctions a part of their individual legislative portfolios in the 92nd Congress. By contrast, only one other CBC member in the 93rd Congress, Representative Robert Nix Sr. (D-Pa.; 1957–1978), felt moved enough by the issue to join the stalwart Diggs in sponsoring a sanctions bill. By the close of the 94th Congress, the number of CBC members sponsoring sanctions bills declined to 20 percent of the level established in the 92nd Congress.

The passage of the Byrd Amendment was also a contributing factor in Diggs's and his colleagues' coming to the agreement that it was in the best interests of the CBC for him to relinquish the role of chairperson to Representative Stokes.[76] Representative Clay described the role that the Byrd Amendment played in leading to this shift in the following terms:

> The exciting thing about being in Congress is that when something grabs your conscience, like southern Africa did with all of us [CBC members] in the early 1970s, is that you are sometimes in a position to help. You always have to remember, though, that it can cause real [political] problems when pressing these issues takes you too far afield from responding to the immediate demands of your constituents; so striking a balance is definitely the key to being successful in those cases. The problem with our first big push for sanctions was that we were so far ahead of everybody [on the issue] that it really made it hard for us sometimes. In other words, it is certainly no fun to go home and face a lot of questions about what you are doing [in Washington, D.C.]. These pressures pushed all of us in new directions after the [Byrd] Amendment.[77]

For most CBC members, moving in "new directions" primarily meant moving away from issues that did not resonate directly with their constituents.[78]

It is important to note that it became easier for CBC members to pursue their own legislative priorities based on constituent demands in the 93rd Congress. This was so because the Democratic Caucus had passed a set of institutional reforms at the close of the 92nd Congress that diminished the Dixiecrats' stranglehold on both the committee assignments of their junior colleagues and the legislative process.[79] These reforms were essential to normalizing the experiences that black legislators had in the House.[80] This is one of the chief reasons that scholars tend to see them as completing the transition from the Civil Rights Era to the Post–Civil Rights Era in the historiography of black representation.[81]

There were two crucial differences between Diggs and most of his colleagues in the CBC in the 93rd Congress. First, his interest in South Africa was anything but diffuse. On the contrary, Diggs possessed a firm ideological commitment to getting a sanctions bill through Congress. Second, Diggs, who was incredibly safe in his district,[82] had wide latitude by virtue of his seniority on the Foreign Relations Committee to continue to pursue this goal. Not surprisingly, then, Diggs pushed even harder to make sanctions the law of the land once his colleagues moved away from the issue after the Byrd Amendment.

Diggs personally sponsored more sanctions bills in the 93rd Congress than during any other time in his career. He also continued to use his institutional position as a senior member of the House Foreign Relations Committee as a platform for keeping the issue before his colleagues on the Hill.[83] When these measures failed to generate a new enthusiasm for sanctions under the Capitol dome, Diggs realized that only a "massive groundswell of support" at the grassroots level would convince his colleagues in the Democratic Caucus to come around to his viewpoint.[84]

At the start of the 94th Congress, Diggs took his first step toward generating this groundswell when he formed the Black Forum on Foreign Policy along with several prominent black activists and intellectuals.[85] He also embarked on a barnstorming tour of Democratic-leaning districts with substantial black populations.[86] Although he billed this tour as an effort to raise black Americans' consciousness about their "stake in Africa," Diggs never failed to find the time to urge his listeners to contact their representatives about sanctions legislation.[87] And because reapportionments were already shifting the black population into majority-minority districts in the mid-1970s,[88] these new demands fell disproportionately on the ears of Diggs's fellow CBC members.

Evidence that the consciousness-raising efforts that Diggs (and the Black Forum on Foreign Policy) initiated were beginning to work came in 1976. In that year, grassroots mobilization in the black community surged in response to media coverage of the Soweto uprisings.[89] As the small spike in figure 5.1 at the 95th Congress illustrates, many CBC members reincorporated sanctions bills into their legislative portfolios once their constituents began to demand action.[90] Representative Clay described the link between constituent demands and this sudden flurry of activity on the House floor:

> Although we knew that we faced an uphill battle to get a bill [through Congress]—given the deference that our [white] colleagues had toward the President—we were just happy that our constituents had caught up [with us] on the issue in such a short time. Most of us were safe

> politically... so it was really about doing the right thing. At the same time, I did [not] know of anyone in the Caucus who wanted to go home and face the opposite of the question that we talked about earlier: what are you doing for South Africa?[91]

Thus, the surge in bill sponsorship in the 95th Congress was primarily an attempt on the part of CBC members to engage in what David Mayhew calls "position-taking" through legislative action.[92]

Historians have corroborated Clay's remark about the CBC push for a sanctions bill being an uphill fight because of the deference that his white colleagues afforded the executive branch on foreign policy issues in the mid-1970s. According to most secondary sources, few outside the CBC believed that the Congress should drive U.S. foreign policy toward South Africa in the late 1970s.[93] As a result, all the sanctions bills that CBC members placed in the hopper in the 95th Congress died well short of passage.

The percentage of CBC members introducing legislation calling for sanctions declined markedly after the 95th Congress (see fig. 5.1). Representative Stokes recalled that a desire not to appear to be pursuing symbolic issues to the detriment of substantive commitments contributed to this shift.

> Every member of the [Congressional Black] Caucus has their own set of legislative priorities, interests and pet projects in their districts—mine have often been in the field of public health. No matter what we are doing as a group, members are always going to pursue these priorities. Thus, if there was a shift in behavior [after the 95th Congress], I suspect part of it was that members were falling back on these core interests. This is not to say that we lost interest in sanctions. Sometimes, with these big [national] issues, it is necessary to take time to regroup and develop new strategies.[94]

Had CBC members initiated the campaign for sanctions to send purely symbolic signals to their constituents, there would have been no incentive for them to be so sensitive to public opinion in their districts. There also would have been little incentive for them to invest much time in the development of "new strategies" to push a sanctions bill through Congress.

According to the historical record, this period of reflection led most CBC members to share Diggs's view that they must bolster their legislative efforts with extra-institutional behavior. Indeed, the majority of CBC members attended the Black Foreign Policy Forum Leadership Conference on Southern Africa in the fall of 1976, illustrating the sea change that had taken place in the group since it had deposed Diggs in the 92nd Congress.[95]

TransAfrica was by far the most significant development to come out of the Leadership Conference on Southern Africa.[96] Under the leadership of Randall Robinson, who had previously served as a staff aide for Clay and Diggs, TransAfrica emerged as the most effective lobby for Africa in U.S. history[97] for two reasons. First, the organization was able to draw on a deep reservoir of financial, logistical, and moral support from the CBC (and other black politicians) while it was still in its infancy.[98] Second, Robinson, who had cut his political teeth as a leader of the student protests against apartheid that sprang up at Harvard University in the early 1970s,[99] quickly proved to be a master at unifying the ethnically and ideologically diverse groups that became the core of the Free South Africa Movement (FSAM).[100]

In November 1984, TransAfrica initiated a campaign of nonviolent protests against apartheid.[101] Mostly staged at the South African embassy in Washington, D.C., and frequently drawing on the popular appeal of celebrities, these marches and sit-ins were made-for-media events.[102] When not staging public protests, TransAfrica encouraged its supporters to keep the pressure on both the Congress and the White House through mass letter-writing campaigns.[103] By the close of the year, the FSAM had become such a potent force in U.S. politics that it forced virtually every Democrat on the Hill to try to establish anti-apartheid credentials.[104] Representative Ronald V. Dellums (D-Calif.; 1971–1998), who emerged as the most active CBC member on the sanctions issue after a federal investigation forced Representative Diggs to resign from the House in 1980,[105] described the impact of the FSAM:

> It was very interesting to see colleagues from both sides of the aisle and of *all races*, who had previously paid little attention to our efforts, scramble to get arrested in front of the South African embassy and introduce sanctions bills when the [effects of the] movement hit home in their districts. It really was amazing how quickly the environment [in Washington, D.C.] changed.[106]

Dellums's reference to "*all races*" indicates that the spike in CBC members' sponsoring sanctions bills in the 99th Congress (see fig. 5.1) was also partly a function of the political dynamics created by the FSAM.

Dellums also makes it clear that members of Congress who demonstrated a greater commitment to the sanctions issue in the wake of the pressures generated by the FSAM faired very well in subsequent elections. "Members of the House [who supported the push for sanctions]," Dellums writes in his memoir, "no longer had to worry about disinvestment as a barrier to their reelection (and fear of defeat provides the greatest motivation for members in evaluating their vote on an issue)."[107] Only one member of the CBC who sponsored a sanctions bill lost his bid for reelection, corroborating Dellums's recollection of the period.[108] This also challenges Swain's thesis that anti-apartheid activism carried some political risks for black members of Congress.

Representative Clay, however, cautioned against seeing the increase in bill sponsorship rates among CBC members in the 99th Congress as a product of individual black legislators' desires to claim credit for the CAAA. "Most of us [in the CBC]," Representative Clay stated, "had been in the Congress for many years and were in very safe districts."[109] He continued,

> Although there certainly was this sense of urgency among our constituents, I really don't think that anyone would have lost an election just because they did not have their own version of the bill in the [Congressional] Record. Besides, the CBC had played a big role in the Free South Africa Movement—getting arrested at the [South African] embassy, leading community rallies, etc.—so most of us were incredibly visible on this issue before we even got to a point where we could get a vote on the [House] floor.[110]

Katherine Tate's analysis of reelection rates for the period confirms Clay's impressions about the safety of most CBC members. Indeed, she finds that black incumbents who served between the 94th and 99th Congresses had a reelection rate of 96.84 percent; moreover, this rate surpassed even the 93.52 percent that all House incumbents enjoyed during the same period.[111]

So, if reelection was not the prime motivation, why did most CBC members go to the floor with sanctions bills in the 99th Congress? Representative Dellums believes that, like the legislators portrayed in both Mayhew's and Fenno's writings that pursue committee assignments that will yield no particularistic benefits for their districts, a desire to make good public policy motivated most members of the CBC in the 99th Congress. Indeed, Dellums recalled that his colleagues went to the House floor primarily to push Democratic leaders to pass a tough sanctions law.

> By the middle of the [legislative] session, it was clear to just about everyone in Washington that America wanted some action [on apartheid]. Suddenly, you had people in every branch of government—from our Democratic colleagues in the House to [President Ronald] Reagan—talking about reform measures. Most of these proposals fell far short of what we [in the CBC] wanted—a total economic withdrawal from South Africa—so we had to stay vigilant to make sure that we got a real sanctions law.[112]

Representative Clay largely concurred with this analysis. "We did not work so hard on this issue for a decade," he stated, "to allow Reagan to get off the hook with some weak executive order or to allow the [Democratic] leadership to cut a deal with the Senate."[113] Although the CBC ultimately had to accept some compromises with Senate, most scholars agree that its efforts ensured that the CAAA was not a toothless measure.[114] Were the CBC campaign for a sanction bill about generating a symbolic outcome, it is hard to imagine a scenario in which they would not have accepted one of these earlier compromises. After all, even these measures went far beyond what anyone in the CBC had thought was possible before the rise of the FSAM.[115]

Representative Clay suggested that a second institutional imperative also motivated CBC members to return to the floor with sanctions bills in the 99th Congress:

> Above all else, we [the CBC] wanted to pass the CAAA to help free blacks in South Africa from a racist dictatorship; and it was such a great joy to all of us [in the CBC] to be able to finally deliver this victory. At the same time, we were also aware of the fact that getting this law on the books was going to be historic and make a real impact on party politics in [Washington,] D.C. So part of what you see with members drafting legislation and staying so active on this issue was a desire to preserve our control over this important issue. This was going to be one of our biggest legislative victories as a group... and we were not going to allow it to slip away. We also refused to allow others in our party push us to the side on this issue.[116]

Essentially, Clay's argument is that a desire to claim credit as a group played some role in motivating CBC members to reintegrate sanctions bills into their legislative portfolios in the 99th Congress.

Mainstream media coverage of the politics behind implementing the CAAA between 1986 and 1988 suggests that the CBC succeeded in this task. Figure 5.2 summarizes the results of a content analysis of thirty-six *New York Times* and *Washington Post* articles on the CAAA. As we can see, the CBC, with eleven mentions, was second among the political actor most frequently attributed credit for the CAAA. Indeed, only Representative Dellums, who introduced the version of the bill that passed the House of Representatives on June 19, 1986, received more mentions in the press.[117] Moreover, both the Democratic Party in Congress and House Speaker Thomas P. (Tip) O' Neill (D-Mass.; 1953–1986) received infrequent mentions. Surprisingly, the analysis also reveals that in the wake of the CAAA no one in the media remembered the important role that Representative Diggs had long played as the congressional conscience on the sanctions issue between the 93rd and the 97th Congresses.

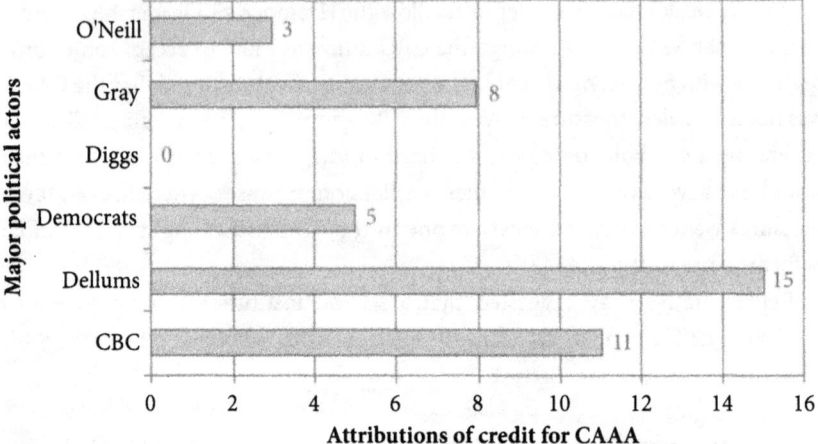

FIGURE 5.2 *NY Times* and *Washington Post* coverage of the CAAA, 1986–1988; numbers of articles attributing credit for the bill to six political actors. CAAA, Comprehensive Anti-Apartheid Act; CBC, Congressional Black Caucus.
Sources: *New York Times; Washington Post*

Growth and Decline

The CBC experienced considerable growth after 1986. Indeed, the continued enforcement of the Voting Rights Act of 1965 (and its extensions) and the creation of majority-minority districts through gerrymandering more than doubled the size of the CBC during the next twenty years. A number of studies have explored the effects of this growth on the CBC. The conventional wisdom within this burgeoning literature is that, despite the fact that all CBC members are Democrats, the increasing variation in both their personal backgrounds and the nature of their constituencies made it increasingly difficult for the group to maintain the unity that was its hallmark in the 1970s and 1980s. At the same time, the literature on black representation also suggests that the CBC has been able to hang together more effectively on issues that have traditionally defined the identity of the group.[118]

As we have seen, the role of the CBC in formulating U.S. foreign policy toward Africa is obviously one of these issue areas. Despite this fact, the behavior of the CBC in this arena has not come under as much scrutiny from scholars as we might expect. On the contrary, most scholars of black politics have returned their gaze to the behavior of the CBC in African affairs only in the wake of the controversy over the AGOA.

Figure 5.3 charts the growth of the CBC along with the number of CBC members sponsoring bills related to U.S. foreign policy toward Africa between 1969 and 2003. As we can see, despite the growth of the organization, black legislators have not pushed very many initiatives in U.S. foreign policy toward Africa.

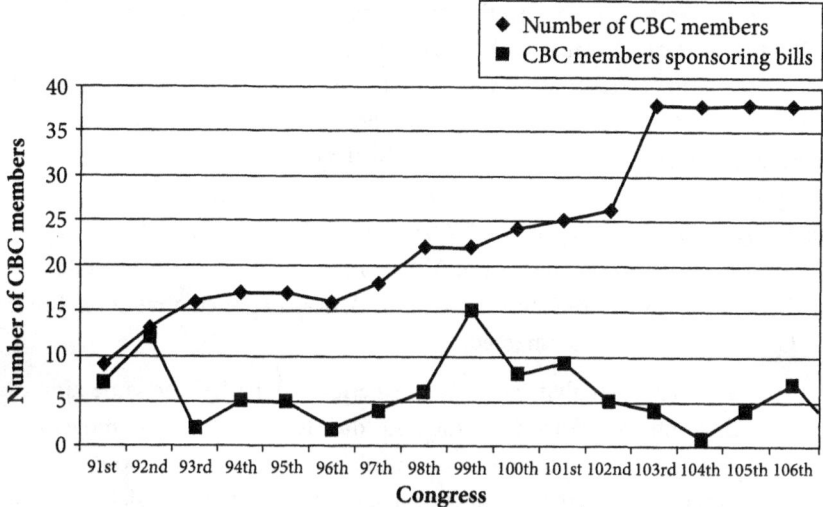

FIGURE 5.3 CBC growth and number of CBC members sponsoring Africa-related bills, 1969–2003. CBC, Congressional Black Caucus.
Source: *Congressional Record*

Indeed, CBC activism in African affairs after the close of the 99th Congress quickly returned to roughly the levels that were present in the 93rd through 98th Congresses. The average number of CBC members sponsoring Africa-related bills was 4.0 per session in the 93rd–98th Congresses and 4.75 per session in the 100th–107th Congresses. Nevertheless, there is a critical difference between the two periods. In the 93rd–99th Congresses, the CBC roster averaged seventeen members per session. By contrast, in the 100th–107th Congresses, the ranks of the CBC had grown to an average of thirty-three members per session. In light of this expansion, the overall CBC activism in the field of African affairs actually declined by 11 percent in the 100th–107th Congresses.

This finding presents yet another challenge to the view that CBC activism in U.S. foreign policy toward Africa is primarily a function of transnationalism. After all, the 1980s and 1990s were decades when Africa's humanitarian, political, and economic crises led the U.S. government into increasing contact with the continent. Although some black members of Congress worked on behalf of the continent with nonprofit organizations and the executive branch, the lack of floor activity from the CBC remains an empirical puzzle that challenges the covering law of black elite behavior in the U.S. foreign policymaking arena.

My alternative theory that Africa-related foreign policy activity reflected U.S. domestic concerns holds the potential to explain this shift. The twenty-six elite interviews that I conducted with CBC members between 1996 and 2003 also support this claim. Indeed, twenty-three of the twenty-six (88 percent) CBC members I interviewed reported that they pursued few initiatives in U.S. foreign policy toward Africa because they were concerned about how these issues would affect their primary responsibilities to their constituents. Moreover, twenty of the twenty-six (77 percent) respondents reported that their ability to sponsor legislation related to Africa was hampered by the fact that few issues in U.S. foreign policy toward Africa resonate with their constituents in the same way that the struggle for democracy in South Africa did in the 1970s and 1980s.

Describing the shifting interest in Africa of his constituency since the demise of the white-minority regimes in southern Africa, Representative John Lewis (D-Ga.; 1986–present) commented,

> It is fair to say that most black Americans don't feel the same kind of link with Africa today as they did during our civil rights movement and throughout their de-colonization movement....In other words, because of the progress that was made both here and abroad, in terms of ending colonialism and segregation, we are witnessing something of a breakdown in that sense of solidarity that blacks in Africa and America shared when they were fighting against white domination.[119]

In this era of diminished constituency interest in Africa, the role of those CBC members who serve as the opinion leaders in African affairs has again become very pronounced. "The reality of the situation," said Mel Foote, an experienced lobbyist on behalf of Africa, "is that the unified front that the CBC often projects to other members of Congress or to the public on African foreign policy issues typically stems from the group following the lead of one or two highly informed members."[120] For some of these opinion leaders, the tendency of their colleagues to take a backseat on issues related to U.S. foreign policy toward Africa is just as frustrating as that which Representative Diggs experienced in the 1970s. Describing his time as Vice Chairman of the CBC in 105th Congress, Representative Earl Hilliard (D-Ala.; 1992–2002) stated:

> In 1993, I wrote to every member of the [Congressional Black] Caucus asking them to participate in a program to facilitate communication between the CBC and the African diplomatic corps by pairing-up every black member of Congress with the head of an African diplomatic delegation. Although there are thirty-eight Caucus members and more than fifty African nations, we only got eighteen CBC members to participate. Do I think that we should have had more participation? We certainly should, and it is something that I am committed to working on. The fact of the matter, though, is that most members are so oriented inwards, toward their own districts, that they just don't feel enough of a connection with Africa to join such a program.[121]

This district-level focus described by Representative Hilliard is clearly observable in the legislative history of the AGOA.

Balancing Acts

The AGOA did not emerge from the CBC. On the contrary, Representative Jim McDermott (D-Wash.; 1992–present) first introduced the bill in 1996. Borrowing from the NAFTA framework, Representative McDermott hoped that the bill would shift U.S. foreign policy toward Africa from a donor framework to a development focus driven by trade and private-sector investment.[122] The bill immediately drew the support of the African diplomatic corps, the opinion leaders of the CBC on U.S. policy in Africa, and many other prominent House Democrats and Republicans. Because McDermott had introduced the bill late in the second session of the 104th Congress, however, the leadership of the House tabled the measure for consideration in the next Congress. With so many powerful forces in the beltway already working for passage of the AGOA, the measure seemed destined to sail through the 105th Congress.

This did not happen, however, because deep opposition to the AGOA suddenly emerged from U.S. trade unionists. The opposition centered on one of the central provisions of the AGOA that called for lowering tariffs on textiles from Africa. Fearing that the reduction of protective barriers would further weaken the already soft domestic sector, the union movement initiated a vigorous campaign to sink the bill.[123] Not surprisingly, many southern Democrats with ties to labor unions and agricultural interests responded to this campaign by voting to kill the AGOA.[124]

Despite the context provided by the opposition of labor to the AGOA, scholars of black politics have persisted in seeing the actions of the CBC members who opposed the bill through the lens of transnationalism. According to these studies, black opposition to the AGOA grew out of concerns that the bill did not do enough to help Africa.[125] The problem with this view is that the CBC members who opposed the AGOA were largely forthcoming about the fact that they did so because they viewed the measure as a threat to their constituencies. Consider, for example, the following excerpt from Representative Bishop's famous speech:

> I want an Africa trade bill, but I want a good Africa trade bill.... This [procedural] rule will prevent that. I am disappointed that many Members of the House are not allowed to address the very real concerns that we have about the loss of over 400,000 jobs in the U.S. textile and apparel

industry that has taken place across this country since 1995 and would be exacerbated by this bill. Despite my attempts last year and this year in the Committee on Rules and on the [House] floor to make sure that the African Growth and Opportunity Act does not do more harm than good, the bill as reported is not beneficial to all parties concerned.[126]

Moreover, even the CBC members who supported the AGOA saw a desire to protect the home front as the primary motivation of the dissidents. "Sanford, Jesse [Jackson], Jr. [(D-Ill.)], and Jim [Clyburn (D-S.C.)] have been very outspoken about their inability to support the African Growth and Opportunity Act because of their fear that the bill will take jobs out of their districts," stated Representative Carolyn C. Kilpatrick (D-Mich.; 1997–present) in an interview shortly before the measure came to the floor of the House for a vote. "I can't agree with their claims," she continued; "however, I do understand that members face constituency pressures, and that losing one job within a district could be politically problematic. In the end, who can argue with a member's desire to protect their district? It is pretty clear, then, that these district-level priorities are going to split the vote of the Caucus on this issue."[127]

Quantitative analyses of the voting behavior of CBC members confirm the prescience of Kilpatrick's remark. A direct comparison of CBC members who voted for the AGOA and those who voted against it based on the mean number of jobs in their districts linked to textile industries, shows that the twenty-one CBC members who voted in favor of the bill had an average of 17,000 jobs in their districts linked to textiles. By contrast, the fifteen black members of Congress who voted against the bill had an average of 51,000 jobs in the textile industry or a closely linked sector in their districts.[128]

Table 5.1 reports the results of logistic regressions on CBC members' individual roll call votes on the AGOA. These results further demonstrate that district-level factors drove the decision making of black legislators on this measure.[129] Indeed, CBC members whose districts had higher unemployment rates, lower median incomes, and were located in the southern United States—the seat of the U.S. textile industry—were far more likely to vote against the AGOA.[130] Neither the percentage of black voters residing within a member's district nor their individual ratings on the American Federation of Labor and Congress of Industrial Organization's (AFLCIO) scorecard on key labor votes for the 109th Congress were statistically significant predictors.

Using the logistic regression technique, we can also estimate the impact of individual predictor variables on the likelihood that the dependent variable—in this case that a CBC member voted yes (or no) on the roll call vote for the AGOA—

Table 5.1 Results of Logistic Regression Analyses of CBC Members' Roll Call Votes on AGOA

VARIABLE	COEFFICIENT	STANDARD ERROR
AFLCIO	−0.0859	0.0649
%BLACK	0.0169	0.0342
MEDINCOME	0.0003**	0.0001
MOV1998	0.0395	0.0241
SOUTHREG	−3.698*	1.682
UNEMPLOYMENT	−0.8198*	0.3633

$N = 36$
$R^2 = .37$

Notes: * indicates statistically significant at the 0.05 level; ** indicates statistically significant at the 0.01 level. %BLACK, size of the black population in the districts of CBC members (continuous variable ranging from 0 to 100); AFLCIO, ranking of the CBC members' voting records on issues that the AFL-CIO deems critical for U.S. labor (continuous variable ranging from 0 to 100); AGOA, African Growth and Opportunity Act; CBC, Congressional Black Caucus; MEDINCOME, median income in the districts of CBC members (continuous variable); MOV1998, CBC members' margins of victory in the 1998 midterm election (continuous variable); SOUTHREG, dummy variable for the southern region (coded 1 for districts in the South and 0 for all others); UNEMPLOYMENT, size of the jobless population in the districts of CBC members (continuous variable ranging from 0 to 100).

occurs.[131] The logistic regression model calculates the odds ratios associated with the value of each predictor variable, and the best way to interpret these odds ratios is as the relative amount (or probability) by which the odds of the outcome increase or decrease in the presence of the predictor variable. The odds ratios for the three statistically significant variables (MEDINCOME, SOUTHREG, and UNEMPLOYMENT) in the logistic regression model of the CBC members' votes on the AGOA shows that the probability that a CBC member voted for the AGOA is 0.62 if the constituents living his or her district had annual household incomes that exceeded the median income for the thirty-six districts in the sample. By contrast, CBC members whose districts were located in the southern United States had only a 0.14 probability of voting in favor of the AGOA. Finally, black legislators whose constituents had higher than average unemployment rates had a 0.32 probability of voting to pass the AGOA. Thus, the statistical analyses provide further evidence that the CBC members who took stands against the AGOA did so primarily out of a desire to defend the interests of their constituents on the home front. These voting records are completely consistent with the strategic behavior model of black engagement with issues in U.S. foreign policy toward Africa that I develop throughout this book.

. . .

Most studies of ethnic and racial groups' seeking to influence U.S. foreign policy toward their ancestral homelands see the motivations of these groups through the lens of transnationalism. This chapter has demonstrated that sentiments derived from transnationalism are not always a sufficient condition for group mobilization. More specifically, the analytic narrative presented here shows that the initial push by the CBC for sanctions legislation grew more out of rationalist concerns derived from institutional imperatives than from affective ties to Africa. In light of this evidence, it is best to understand the early sanctions campaign as a two-level game in which winning in the domestic environment (the House chamber) took precedence over achieving the desired outcome in the international context. Moreover, my findings suggest that black members of Congress pushed the sanctions issue through two distinct streams of activism and not, as scholars have tended to assume, one long movement.

The analytic narrative also refines our understanding of black political behavior in the Congress. Most studies of the CBC suggest that inexperience led the group to develop collective goals that centered primarily on symbolic issues before the group became institutionalized at the end of the 93rd Congress.[132] The narrative presented here undermines this conventional wisdom and shows that the early activism by the CBC on the sanctions issue was part of a complex strategy for achieving institutional clout that was devised by its most experienced member, Charles Diggs. Moreover, because the Diggs plan was predicated on the notion that CBC members' work on such a difficult issue would earn the respect of their white colleagues, the narrative dispels the myth that black legislators invariably press African issues because they are, as Carol Swain argues, "easier to tackle" than the tough issues in their home districts.[133] Finally, the fact that most of the black legislators withdrew from the sanctions campaign when it proved to be a losing internal strategy but returned to the issue when calls for activism emanated from their own districts proves that black members of Congress are indeed responsive to the demands of their constituents.

The analysis of the disagreements that emerged within the CBC over the AGOA also demonstrates that transnationalism is often an insufficient basis for mobilizing the black elite in the U.S. foreign policymaking arena. Indeed, following the pattern established by CBC members in the 93rd–99th Congresses, those CBC members who deemed the AGOA a threat to their constituencies refused to support the measure. This finding also contradicts Swain's thesis that black members of Congress place symbolic action in the realm of African affairs above their duty to serve as effective representatives of their constituents in the domestic arena.

CONCLUSION

> [T]he concept of race has changes so much and presented so much of a contradiction that as I face Africa I ask myself: what is it between us that constitutes a tie that I can feel better than I can explain.
>
> —W. E. B. Du Bois, *Dusk of Dawn: An Essay toward an Autobiography of a Race Concept* (1940).

> But can a people (its faith in an idealized American creed notwithstanding) live and develop for over three hundred years simply by reacting? Are American Negroes simply the creation of white men, or have they at least helped to create themselves out of what they found around them?
>
> —Ralph Ellison, "Review of Gunnar Myrdal's *An American Dilemma*," *Antioch Review* (1944).

The elite members of ethnic and racial minority groups have sought to influence U.S. foreign policy toward their ancestral homelands since at least the nineteenth century.[1] For more than two generations, political scientists and diplomatic historians have argued that transnationalism is the best theoretical vantage point for understanding the actions of these elites in the U.S. foreign policymaking arena.[2] According to this perspective, when the elite members of ethnic and racial minorities seek to carve out a distinctive voice on issues in U.S. foreign policy toward their ancestral homelands they are engaging in expressive behavior aimed at reifying their affective ties to these nations.[3] In this book, I demonstrate the limitations of this model and develop an alternative theory.

This is not to say that commitments derived from transnationalism are unimportant in spurring the elite members of minority groups to engage with issues in U.S. foreign policy toward their ancestral homelands. On the contrary, there is a wealth of empirical evidence suggesting that these sentiments often play an important, and sometimes even *necessary*, role in the equation. At the same time, as the analytic narratives from the historical record demonstrate, sentiments derived from affective ties are rarely *sufficient* on their own to motivate these leaders to take up the work of advocating for their ancestral homelands in the U.S.

foreign policymaking arena. Thus, we gain greater theoretical purchase on this dimension of minority politics through the alternative theoretical perspective developed in this book.

The central axiom in the alternative theory holds that the decisions that minority elites make about mobilizing in the foreign policymaking arena on behalf of their ancestral homelands emerge from strategic calculations that seek to balance the value of the engagement against the costs accrued in the domestic arena. In short, the behavior of minority elites in the U.S. foreign policymaking arena conforms to the "logic of two-level games."[4] Thus, the most robust expressions of transnationalism in the U.S. foreign policymaking arena occur when such activism dovetails with the goals that elite members of ethnic and minority groups are pursuing in the domestic arena. By contrast, when expressions of transnationalism hold the potential to generate cross-pressures or threaten to undermine the goals that these leaders are pursuing on the home front, they typically disengage from serious efforts on behalf of their ancestral homelands.

In this book, I have provided both demonstrations of the shortcomings of the expressive behavior model and empirical tests of my alternative theory through analytic narratives based on the black experience in the U.S. foreign policymaking arena between 1816 and 2000. I used multiple data sources to develop the analytic narratives featured in the book; moreover, I used both qualitative and quantitative methods to test the core propositions of my strategic behavior model, and the model held up very well through these tests.

Beyond providing evidence in support of the strategic behavior model of minority group activism in the U.S. foreign policymaking arena, the analytic narratives presented in this book also make at least three other contributions to the field of political science. First, they demonstrate the considerable gains that are possible by studying ethnic and racial politics through a perspective that merges insights from the APD and REP subfields. Indeed, scholars can gain a fuller sense of stability and change in identity politics by deploying the APD concepts of critical junctures and increasing returns with Walton's notion of the political context variable. It is only through such a synthesis that we can finally begin model the interplay between the prevailing structures of race relations and racial hierarchies in societies—what Desmond King and Rogers Smith, both APD scholars, call "racial orders"[5]—and the behavior of political actors seeking to maintain and challenge these orders. In addition, the analytic narratives point to a way to extend the scope of the core theories that animate scholarship in the REP subfield. The leading scholars in this area have always turned to developments in political and social history to improve their theory-building enterprises.[6] Further gains are possible by following the lead of APD scholars in using path-dependence more frequently in the study of social movements, political behavior, and representation in minority communities.[7]

The second broad contribution of this study is its potential to reorient the very robust literature on the behavior of the elite members of ethnic and racial minority groups within the U.S. foreign policymaking arena. Within this literature, developed by political scientists and historians in the 1980s and 1990s,[8] there is broad consensus on two issues: (1) that the leaders of ethnic and racial minority groups remain mobilized around issues in U.S. foreign policy that affect their ancestral homelands (or regions) and (2) that this mobilization is a function of their affective ties to these homelands. In other words, an affect-rich attachment is both a necessary and sufficient condition to spur elites to pursue transnationalist goals in the U.S. foreign policymaking arena. The findings presented throughout this book show that framing the motivations of the leaders of ethnic and racial groups in this way obscures a great deal of the complexity of their behavior in the U.S. foreign policymaking arena. Indeed, strategic considerations derived from the domestic environment play a prominent role in determining whether a group will mobilize on behalf of its kith and kin abroad. In the absence of a direct connection to the domestic goals of the group, affective ties are often insufficient to motivate black Americans to represent the interests of Africa in the U.S. foreign policymaking arena. In short, it is best to think of the behavior of ethnic and racial elites in the U.S. foreign policymaking arena as conforming to the logic of two-level games.[9]

Third, bringing strategic considerations into the analysis also sheds new light on the long-standing debate between irredentists and democratic-pluralists about the implications of transnationalism for domestic unity. Because the scholars and practitioners of politics who make up the irredentist community believe that loyalty is a zero-sum game, they see expressions of transnationalism as emblematic of an assimilation crisis that threatens to Balkanize the United States.[10] Moreover, because they see domestic tranquility as the key to success on the world stage, irredentists tend to recommend either the establishment of new norms to minimize the voices of ethnic and racial groups in the foreign policymaking arena and or the scaling back of engagements abroad.[11] Democratic-pluralists, on the other hand, completely reject the contention that the expansion of ethnic and racial group influence in the foreign policymaking arena has had a deleterious effect on U.S. unity. Instead, they argue that expressions of transnationalism in the foreign policymaking arena are often the first signs that newly incorporated groups understand the rules of the democratic political game in the United States.[12] In making their case for this interpretation of transnationalism, democratic-pluralists tend to stress that the objectives ethnic and racial groups pursue in the foreign policymaking arena are typically consistent with preexisting U.S. goals in their ancestral homelands.[13]

This study bolsters the claims of the democratic-pluralists. Were the irredentists right, and expressions of transnationalism pointed to a broader assimilation crisis in the United States, the subjects of my study would have demonstrated no sensitivity whatsoever to the demands of the domestic context. On the contrary, nothing could be farther from the truth. In both the nineteenth and twentieth centuries, black Americans not only remained cognizant of how their expressions of transnationalism were perceived by their fellow citizens, but they also tended to set real limits on their activism in the foreign policymaking arena to avoid jeopardizing valuable political capital in the domestic arena. Indeed, my research reveals that in a number of cases black Americans refused to mobilize on behalf of Africa in the foreign policymaking arena because such actions threatened to undermine their interests in the domestic environment. The tendency of black Americans to engage in this type of balancing behavior to protect the interests of the race at home is undeniable evidence of assimilation.

As we have seen, public opinion scholars reached a consensus in the late 1980s that middle- and upper-income blacks think very differently about racial-group membership than do their white counterparts.[14] In short, middle- and upper-income blacks demonstrate a strong sense of linked fate with other members of their racial group. Michael Dawson claims that this is a function of the fact that "until at least the late 1960s, individual African Americans' life chances were over determined by the ascriptive feature of race." As a result, Dawson argues, black Americans developed a "black utility heuristic" to "economize" the decision-making process about policies and political candidates. "This heuristic suggests that as long as race remains dominant in determining the lives of individual blacks, it is rational for American Americans to follow group cues in interpreting and acting in the political world."[15] In addition, Dawson asserts that the "tendency of African Americans to follow racial cues has been reinforced historically by institutions developed during the forced separation of blacks from whites during the post-Reconstruction period."[16]

Several scholars have argued recently that black members of Congress rely on this heuristic to guide their behavior in the institution.[17] "The Congressional Black Caucus," Tate writes, "would declare its mission as national with a primary focus on the needs and interests of Black Americans."[18] Similarly, Richard Fenno writes that black legislators see themselves as "representing a national constituency of black citizens who live beyond the border of any one member's district, but with whom all black members share a set of race-related concerns."[19]

The tendency for the black elite to exhibit a strong sense of linked fate with their constituents did not start with black members of Congress who served in the Post–Civil Rights Era. As the historian Kevin Gaines demonstrated in his seminal work on black leadership, *Uplifting the Race*, this norm has been deeply rooted among black activists and politicians since at least the late nineteenth century.[20] Gaines's work is also important because it shows that the good intentions of the black elite are sometimes merged with paternalism and other biases against the rank-and-file.

Carol Swain goes even farther in her study of black members of Congress. Indeed, she asserts that the disproportionate attention that black members of Congress give to racial issues often diminishes their performance as representatives. Moreover, Swain claims that black members of Congress often pursue goals in the U.S. foreign policymaking arena to distract their constituents from focusing on the fact that they lack efficacy within the institution.[21]

As I show in this book, linked fate does indeed play a very important role in the motivations of black politicians and activists as they navigate the U.S. foreign policymaking arena. And there is also evidence that the paternalism of members of the black elite did sometimes put them at odds with their constituents. For the most part, however, it is clear that black politicians and activists always tried very hard to deliver the best representation possible to their constituents. Thus, there is no evidence to substantiate claims that the black elite were or are aloof to the concerns of the rank-and-file.

That black leaders tried very hard to stay in line with the preferences of their constituents in the latter half of the twentieth century gives us some basis for speculating about the future of Pan-Africanism. The stark decline in the black elite's engagement with issues in U.S. foreign policy toward Africa since the late 1980s has prompted several scholars to argue that Pan-Africanism is a moribund ideology.[22] Indeed, I myself have argued in one such piece that deracialization is the future of Pan-Africanism.[23]

The baseline assumption driving this prediction is that the relatively low level of engagement with issues in U.S. foreign policy toward Africa by the black masses since the Free South Africa Movement means that there is little pressure on black leaders to act in this field.[24] Moreover, because the black elite are now fully incorporated in U.S. political institutions, they no longer have to pursue their agendas through strategies designed to generate second-image effects. Indeed, the CBC is now an institutionalized power bloc within the House of Representatives, and its members have considerable individual and collective resources at their disposal.

Despite all this, a few black members of Congress continue to emerge as regular champions of African interests in the U.S. foreign policymaking arena. Like Diggs, Dellums, and the other members of the CBC who kept the sanctions issue alive in the House of Representatives after the Byrd Amendment, these men and women conform to Fenno's classic conception of the policy wonk, found in his famous work on the motivations of members of Congress.[25] It is clear, however, that these CBC opinion leaders on Africa are in the minority. Indeed, since the passage of the AGOA in the 106th Congress, the average proportion of CBC members sponsoring at least one substantive bill about U.S. relations with Africa has hovered around 6 percent per two-year session.

What may ultimately reverse this trend is the steady influx of immigrants from Africa into majority-minority congressional districts.[26] As these groups grow and mobilize within these districts, we can expect them to demand that their homeland issues become a greater part of the legislative portfolios of their black representatives to Congress. Of course, there is also the possibility that African immigrants will follow the path of their Afro-Caribbean counterparts in the New York 11th Congressional District and use their burgeoning numbers to compete with native-born blacks for control of these districts.[27] Regardless of the outcomes of these potential competitions, we can expect them to increase the volume of legislative activity around issues in U.S. relations with Africa.

One question looms large here, as at the end of every social science study: How generalizable or portable are these theoretical claims? The case of black Americans is exceptional in many ways. Instead of arising from the free choices of people seeking to better their life chances, the black diaspora was created through the forced migration of African peoples from the continent of their ancestry. Moreover, blacks were the only diaspora group whose ancestral heritage was used as a tool to press them into a system of chattel slavery in the United States. For many scholars working across disciplinary boundaries, these facts are enough to justify the development of distinct theoretical paradigms to explain trajectories in the experience of black Americans.

Although I am sympathetic to this approach in some instances, I do not believe that it is appropriate when theorizing about transnationalism. On the contrary, I believe that much of my theoretical perspective can be extended beyond the black case to apply to other ethnic and racial groups that have attempted to influence U.S. foreign policies toward their ancestral homelands. This is so because such groups share with blacks two fundamental realities of life in America: that survival in the United States, at least politically, is predicated on the successful completion of a period of assimilation and that, because of the nature of U.S. political institutions, all minority groups remain powerless to unilaterally generate outcomes in the foreign policymaking arena.

The black experience is exceptional because the period of assimilation has been longer and filled with more obstacles than those of just about every other ethnic and racial group that has entered the United States from foreign shores. Despite this, as we have seen, blacks quickly formed bonds of attachment to the

United States and adopted the democratic ideology of the founders as their political creed. Building on the work of scholars such as Sheldon Stryker and Michael Dawson, I suggest that these bonds of attachment (or identity salience) grew primarily out of the social relationships that blacks maintained with others living in close proximity to them and the experiences that they shared as a community.[28]

Although blacks never forgot their African heritage, the affective ties that they formed to the United States clearly superseded their primordial ties to Africa. If black Americans could form such strong ties to the United States during their systematic exclusion from the polity, then why should it to be any different for groups created largely through the free choices of immigrants seeking to better their life chances? In my view, we should expect similar dynamics to be at work with other groups.

Notes

INTRODUCTION

1. Guy Gugliotta, "Squaring Off over African Trade; Jackson's Bill Challenges Rangel's Measure," *Washington Post*, February 24, 1999, A4; Alvin B. Tillery, Jr., field notes, February 23, 1999.
2. See, for example, Samuel P. Huntington, "The Erosion of American National Interests," *Foreign Affairs* 76, no. 5 (1997): 28–50; Yossi Shain, *Marketing the American Creed Abroad: Diasporas in the U.S. and Their Homelands* (New York: Cambridge University Press, 1999); Tony Smith, *Foreign Attachments: The Power of Ethnic Groups in the Making of American Foreign Policy* (Cambridge, Mass.: Harvard University Press).
3. Stephen Vertovec, "Conceiving and Researching Transnationalism," *Ethnic and Racial Studies* 21, no. 1 (1999): 447–62; Alejandro Portes, Luis Gaurnizo, and Patricia Landolt, "The Study of Transnationalism: Pitfalls and Promise of an Emergent Research Field," *Ethnic and Racial Studies* 22, no. 2 (1999): 217–35; Rainer Baubock, "Towards a Political Theory of Migrant Transnationalism," *International Migration Review* 37, no. 3 (2003): 700–723.
4. Steven Vertovec, "Transnationalism and Identity," *Journal of Ethnic and Migration Studies* 27, no. 4 (2001), 573.
5. Aihwa Ong, *Flexible Citizenship: The Cultural Logic of Transnationality* (Durham: Duke University Press, 1999), 1–25; Shain, *Marketing the American Creed Abroad*, 1–17; Vertovec, "Transnationalism and Identity," 573–82.
6. See, for example, Ronald Walters, "African-American Influence on U.S. Foreign Policy toward South Africa," in *Ethnic Groups and U.S. Foreign Policy*, ed. Mohammed Ahrari (Westport, Conn.: Greenwood Press, 1987), 65–83; Hanes Walton, *African American Power and Politics* (New York: Columbia University Press, 1997), 352–69; Elliott P. Skinner, *African Americans and U.S. Policy toward Africa 1850–1925: In Defense of Black Nationality* (Washington, D.C.: Howard University Press, 1992); Penny Von Eschen, *Race against Empire: Black Americans and Anti-Colonialism* (Ithaca: Cornell University Press, 1997), 69–122; Smith, *Foreign Attachments*, 60–64.
7. The term *covering law* is widely used in physics and the positive social sciences to denote a universal explanation. For a brief intellectual history of the concept and the debate within the social sciences about the possibility of establishing such laws, see Harold Kinkaid, "Defending Laws in the Social Sciences," in *Readings in the Philosophy of Science*, ed. Michael Martin and Lee C. McIntyre (Cambridge, Mass.: MIT Press, 1994), 111–31.
8. See, for example, Jesse Jackson Jr., "Hope for Africa," *Nation*, February 25, 1999.
9. Dave Boyer, "African Trade Bill Opens Rift in Congressional Black Caucus," *Washington Times*, July 16, 1999, A3; Thomas L. Friedman, "Foreign Affairs, Africa: Aid or Harm?" *New York Times*, March 28, 2000, 23.
10. Juliet Eilperin, "House Passes Measure on Trade with Africa," *Washington Post*, July 17, 1999, E1.
11. Robert D. Putnam, "Diplomacy and Domestic Politics: The Logic of Two-Level Games," *International Organization* 42 (1988): 427–61.

12. Scholars have used the term *transnationalism* for only approximately three decades. The phenomenon, however, long predates the rise of this academic nomenclature. Indeed, the African, Jewish, and Irish diasporas all had well-developed transnationalist perspectives or ideologies—Pan-Africanism, Zionism, and Fenianism, respectively—by the late nineteenth century. In this book, I occasionally use the terms *Pan-African* or *Pan-Africanism* to refer to the transnationalist behavior. I limit my use of these terms to the behavior of black elites that they themselves would be most likely to describe in such terms. For an interesting discussion of the epistemological issues related to the study of historical movements with transnationalist aims, see Nancy Foner, "What's New about Transnationalism? New York Immigrants Today and at the Turn of the Century" *Diaspora* 6, no. 3 (1997): 354–75.

13. Hanes Walton, *Invisible Politics: Black Political Behavior* (Albany: SUNY Press, 1985), 1–19; Charles Henry, *Culture and African American Politics* (Bloomington: University of Indiana Press, 1990), 12–37; Michael Dawson, *Behind the Mule: Race and Class in African American Politics* (Princeton: Princeton University Press, 1994), 1–45; Melissa Harris-Lacewell, *Barbershops, Bibles, and BET: Everyday Talk and Black Political Thought* (Princeton: Princeton University Press, 2004), 86–109.

14. Scholars working in the fields of international relations and diplomatic history describe a foreign policy issue as *domesticated* when it gains the attention of the mass public on the domestic level. For an excellent treatment of this concept, see Von Eschen, *Race against Empire*, 158–60.

15. See, among the many works that make this point about African Americans' identification with Africa during this period, Robert Weisbord, *Ebony Kinship: Africa, Africans and Afro-Americans* (Westport, Conn.: Greenwood Press: 1973); Manning Marable, *Race, Reform, Rebellion: The Second Reconstruction in Black America, 1945–1990* (Jackson: University of Mississippi Press, 1991); William L. Van Deburg, *New Day in Babylon: The Black Power Movement and American Culture, 1965–1975* (Chicago: University of Chicago Press, 1992).

16. For examples of studies that base their theoretical claims on interview data gleaned from black politicians, see Walters, "African-American Influence," 65–83; Walton, *African American Power and Politics*, 352–69.

17. For examples of studies that make explicit comparisons between the black experience and those of European-descent ethnic groups, see Walters, "African-American Influence," 65–83 Skinner, *African Americans*, 1–21.

18. For a treatments of the differences between covering laws in the physical sciences and in the social sciences, see Carl G. Hempel, "The Function of Laws in General History," *Journal of Philosophy* 39, no. 2 (1942): 35–48; Harold Kincaid, "Defending Laws in the Social Sciences," *Philosophy of the Social Sciences* 20, no. 1 (1990): 56–83.

19. Walters, "African-American Influence," 65–83; Walton, *African American Power and Politics*, 352–69.

20. Barbara Geddes, "How the Cases You Choose Affect the Answers You Get: Selection Bias in Comparative Politics," *Political Analysis* 2, no. 1 (1990): 131–50.

21. Ibid., 132–35.

22. Ibid., 90.

23. Scholars that argue that exogenous shocks were sometimes an important force shaping black elite behavior between 1935 and 1960 include Brenda Gayle Plummer, *Rising Wind: Black Americans and U.S. Foreign Affairs, 1935–1960* (Chapel Hill: University of North Carolina Press, 1996), 180–214; Von Eschen, *Race against Empire*, 122–67; James Meriwether, *Proudly We Can Be Africans: Black Americans and Africa, 1935–1961* (Chapel Hill: University of North Carolina Press, 2002); Skinner, *African Americans*, 1–48.

24. For example, James Rosenau, *Public Opinion and Foreign Policy* (New York: Random House, 1961).

25. See, for example, Lester Milbrath, "Interest Groups and Foreign Policy," in *Domestic Sources of Foreign Policy*, ed. James Rosenau (New York: The Free Press, 1967).

26. Robert D. Putnam, "Diplomacy and Domestic Politics: The Logic of Two-Level Games," *International Organization* 42 (1988): 427–61.

27. Patricia Gurin, Shirley Hatchett, and James S. Jackson, *Hope and Independence: Blacks' Response to Electoral and Party Politics* (New York: Russell Sage Foundation, 1989); Dawson, *Behind the Mule*, 56–72; Katherine Tate, *From Protest to Politics: The New Black Voters in American Elections* (Cambridge, Mass.: Harvard University Press, 1994), 23–29.

28. Dawson, *Behind the Mule*, 57.

29. Ibid.

30. Ibid.

31. Ibid., 58.

32. Carol Swain, *Black Faces, Black Interests: The Representation of African Americans in Congress* (Cambridge, Mass.: Harvard University Press, 1993); Richard Fenno, *Going Home: Black Representatives and Their Constituents* (Chicago: University of Chicago Press, 2003); Katherine Tate, *Black Faces in the Mirror: African Americans and Their Representatives in the U.S. Congress* (Princeton: Princeton University Press, 2003).

33. Tate, *Black Faces in the Mirror*, 127.

34. Fenno, *Going Home*, 7.

35. Kevin Gaines, *Uplifting the Race: Black Leadership, Politics, and Culture in the Twentieth Century* (Chapel Hill: University of North Carolina Press, 1996), 1–19.

36. For an introduction to the concept second image, see Kenneth Waltz, *Man, the State, and War: A Theoretical Analysis* (New York: Columbia University Press, 2001), 80–124.

37. William R. Scott, *Sons of Sheba's Race: Afro-Americans and the Italo-Ethiopian War, 1935–1941* (Bloomington: University of Indiana Press, 1993); Plummer, *Rising Wind*, 37–80; Von Eschen, *Race against Empire*, 96–122.

38. Von Eschen, *Race against Empire*, 96–122, uses the term *domesticating* to describe the hypermobilization that took place in U.S. black communities in the 1940s around U.S. foreign policy issues related to colonialism.

39. Samuel P. Huntington, "The Erosion of American National Interests," *Foreign Affairs* (October 1997): 28–50; Bruce D. Porter, "Can American Democracy Survive?" *Commentary* (November 1993): 37–40; James Schlesinger, "Fragmentation and Hubris: A Shaky Basis for American Leadership," *National Interest* 49 (fall 1997): 3–10. For a much more systematic and less bleak account—but one that is still deeply skeptical—of the rise of racial and ethnic group power in U.S. foreign policy formulation, see Smith, *Foreign Attachments*.

40. Nell Painter, *Exodusters: Black Migration to Kansas after Reconstruction* (New York: Norton, 1977), 133–50.

41. Swain, *Black Faces, Black Interests*, 216.

42. Gaines, *Uplifting the Race*; Fenno, *Going Home*; Tate, *Black Faces in the Mirror*.

43. For excellent accounts of the rise of the quantitative movement in U.S. political science, see Robert A. Dahl, "The Behavioral Approach in Political Science: Epitaph for a Monument to a Successful Protest," *American Political Science Review* 55, no. 4 (1961): 763–72; Heinz Eulau, *Behaviorism in Political Science* (New York: Atherton, 1969).

44. D. W. Miller, "Storming the Palace in Political Science: Scholars Join Revolt against the Domination of Mathematical Approaches to the Discipline," *Chronicle of Higher Education*, September 21, 2001; Kristen Renwick Monroe, "Introduction," in *Perestroika! The Raucous Rebellion in Political Science*, ed. Kristen Renwick Monroe (New Haven: Yale University Press, 2005), 1–12.

45. Michael Dawson and Cathy Cohen, "Problems in the Study of the Politics of Race," in *Political Science: The State of the Discipline*, Vol. 3, ed. Ira Katznelson and Helen Milner (New York: W. W. Norton, 2002), 490–97; Karen Orren and Stephen Skowronek, *The Search for American Political Development* (New York: Cambridge University Press, 2004); Paul Pierson, *Politics in Time: History, Institutions, and Social Analysis* (Princeton: Princeton University Press, 2004).

46. Desmond King and Rogers Smith, "Racial Orders in American Political Development," *American Political Science Review* 99, no. 1 (February 2005): 75–92. For a recent work that succeeds in achieving such a synthesis, see Paul Frymer, *Black and Blue: African Americans, the Labor Movement, and the Decline of the Democratic Party* (Princeton: Princeton University Press, 2008).

47. Walton, *African American Power and Politics*, 1–9, 41–77.

48. My focus on elite attitudes is rooted in a long tradition in American political science that makes a connection between shifts in elite discourse and trends in mass opinion. For an excellent summary of this tradition and a well-developed theory of this connection, see John Zaller, *The Nature and Origins of Mass Opinion* (New York: Cambridge University Press, 1992), 6–39. The generalizations that I make in this book about *elite behavior* and *elite attitudes* are references to majority perspectives.

49. Orren and Skowronek, *Search for American Political Development*.

50. For a discussion of how this approach differs from other case-driven and narrative designs, see Robert H. Bates, Avner Greif, Margaret Levi, Jean-Laurent Rosenthal, and Barry R. Weingast, *Analytic Narratives* (Princeton: Princeton University Press, 1998), 10–22.

51. Stephen Van Evera, *A Guide to Methods for Students of Political Science* (New York: Cornell University Press, 1997), 58–63; Alexander George and Andrew Bennett, *Case Studies and Theory Development in the Social Sciences* (Cambridge, Mass.: MIT Press, 2005), 181–204.

52. George and Bennett, *Case Studies*, 205–32.

53. Van Evera, *Guide to Methods*, 64. For an extensive treatment of the method, see George and Bennett, *Case Studies*, 205–33.

54. For an extensive treatment of the role of secondary sources in historically oriented social science, see Theda Skocpol and Margaret Somers, "The Uses of Comparative History in Macrosocial Inquiry," *Comparative Studies in Society and History* 22, no. 2 (1980): 174–97.

55. The consensus view among historically oriented social scientists regarding the appropriateness of conducting archival research has shifted considerably over the last two decades. For excellent statements on this evolution, see Edwin Amenta, "What We Know about the Development of Social Policy: Comparative and Historical Research in Comparative and Historical Perspective," in *Comparative Historical Analysis in the Social Sciences*, ed. James Mahoney and Dietrich Rueschemeyer (New York: Cambridge University Press, 2003), 91–131; Theda Skocpol, "Doubly Engaged Social Science: The Promise of Comparative Historical Analysis," in *Comparative Historical Analysis in the Social Sciences*, ed. James Mahoney and Dietrich Rueschemeyer (New York: Cambridge University Press, 2003), 407–29. For an excellent work on race relations in the APD literature that uses archival research, see Daniel Kryder, *Divided Arsenal: Race and the American State during World War II* (New York: Cambridge University Press, 2000).

56. In chapter 5, I use logistic regressions to analyze the roll-call votes of CBC members. For an introduction to this method, see Alfred Demaris, *Logit Modeling: Practical Applications* (New York: Russell Sage, 1992).

57. Klaus Krippendorf, *Content Analysis: An Introduction to Its Methodology* (Thousand Oaks: Sage, 2004); Robert Franzoni, *From Words to Numbers: Narrative, Data, and Social Science* (New York: Cambridge University Press, 2004).

58. Cathy Cohen, *The Boundaries of Blackness: Aids and the Breakdown of Black Politics* (Chicago: University of Chicago Press, 1999); Martin Gilens, *Why Americans Hate Welfare: Race, Media, and the Politics of Antipoverty Policy* (Chicago: University of Chicago Press, 1999).

59. Floyd J. Miller, *The Search for Black Nationality: Black Emigration and Colonization 1787–1863* (Chicago: University of Illinois Press, 1975); P. Olisanwuche Esedebe, *Pan-Africanism: The Idea and Movement, 1776–1963* (Washington, D.C.: Howard University Press, 1982); Skinner, *African Americans*.

60. Skinner, *African Americans*, 42–68.

61. See, for example, Tony Martin, *Marcus Garvey: Hero* (Dover, Mass.: The Majority Press, 1983), 96–114; Rod Bush, *We Are Not What We Seem: Black Nationalism and Class Struggle in the American Century* (New York: New York University Press, 1999), 93–99.

62. Ben F. Rogers, "W.E.B. Du Bois, Marcus Garvey, and Pan-Africa," *Journal of Negro History* 40 (April 1955): 154–65154–165; Skinner, *African Americans*, 423–68; Nikhil Pal Singh, *Black Is a Country: Race and the Unfinished Struggle for Democracy* (Cambridge, Mass.: Harvard University Press, 2004), 58–61.

63. The NAACP, Brotherhood of Sleeping Car Porters, Congress of Racial Equality (CORE), National Council of Negro Women, Southern Christian Leadership Conference (SCLC), and the Student Nonviolent Coordinating Committee (SNCC) are the Big-Six organizations in the literature on the civil rights movement.

64. Plummer, *Rising Wind*; Von Eschen, *Race against Empire*; Mary Dudziak, *Cold War Civil Rights: Race and the Image of American Democracy* (Princeton: Princeton University Press, 2000); Thomas Borstelmann, *The Cold War and the Color Line: American Race Relations in the Global Arena* (Cambridge, Mass.: Harvard University Press, 2001).

65. Plummer, *Rising Wind*, 94–125; Von Eschen, *Race against Empire*, 122–45.

66. See, for example, Borstelmann, *Cold War and the Color Line*, 135–72.

67. Walters, "African-American Influence," 65–83; Lako Tongun, "Pan-Africanism and Apartheid: African American Influences on U.S. Foreign Policy," in *Imagining Home: Class, Culture and Nationalism in the African Diaspora*, ed. Robin D. Kelley and Sidney J. Lemelle (New York: Verso, 1994), 243–83; Walton, *African American Power*, 352–69.

CHAPTER 1. "NOT ONE WAS WILLING TO GO!"

1. Elliot Skinner, *African Americans and U.S. Policy toward Africa, 1850–1924: In Defense of Black Nationality* (Washington, D.C.: Howard University Press, 1992), 64–65.

2. Alexander Crummell to Charles A. Dunbar (1864), in *Apropos of Africa: Sentiments of Negro American Leaders on Africa from the 1800s to the 1950s*, ed. Adelaide Cromwell Hill and Martin Kilson (London: Frank Cass, 1969), 87–93.

3. Ibid., 90.

4. Ibid., 93.

5. Alexander Crummell to W. A. Crowther, March 6, 1878, reprinted in *African Repository* 54, no. 1 (1878), 1–2.

6. For the origins of this view, see Nell Irvin Painter, *Exodusters: Black Migration to Kansas after Reconstruction* (New York: W. W. Norton and Company, 1976).

7. Skinner, *African Americans*, 70–85.

8. Michael C. Dawson, *Behind the Mule: Race and Class in African-American Politics* (Princeton: Princeton University Press, 1994), 3–45.

9. Cathy Cohen, *The Boundaries of Blackness: AIDS and the Breakdown of Black Politics* (Chicago: University of Chicago Press, 1999).

10. Skinner, *African Americans*, 12.

11. Sidney Kaplan and Emma Nogrady Kaplan, *The Black Presence in the Era of the American Revolution* (Amherst: University of Massachusetts Press, 1989), 206–9;

P. Olisanwuche Esedebe, *Pan-Africanism: From Idea to Movement, 1776–1963* (Washington, D.C.: Howard University Press, 1982), 8–10.

12. Esedebe, *Pan-Africanism*, 8. See also Sheldon H. Harris, *Paul Cuffe and the African Return* (New York: Simon and Schuster, 1972).

13. Harris, *Paul Cuffe and the African Return*, 50–52; Floyd J. Miller, *The Search for Black Nationality: Black Emigration and Colonization, 1787–1863* (Urbana: University of Illinois Press, 1975), 27–28; Lamont D. Thomas, *Paul Cuffe: Black Entrepreneur and Pan-Africanist* (Urbana: University of Illinois Press, 1986), 49–51; Skinner, *African Americans*, 27.

14. Henry N. Sherwood, "Paul Cuffe," *Journal of Negro History* 8 (1923): 169–82; Miller, *Search for Black Nationality*, 31–33.

15. Miller, *Search for Black Nationality*, 34–35.

16. Ibid.; Thomas, *Paul Cuffe*, 82–85.

17. Cuffe neither believed nor hoped that all free blacks would leave the United States for Africa. On the contrary, his plan was to take just enough black Americans to Africa to stimulate the economic development of Sierra Leone so that it could challenge the southern United States in the production of cotton. In his view, this competition would undercut the basis of slavery in the United States by driving down the demand for cotton in Great Britain. For a detailed analysis of Cuffe's views, see Miller, *Search for Black Nationality*, 25–29.

18. Ibid., 35–37; *The Annals of the Congress of the United States*, 13th Congress, 1st and 2nd Sess., 569–70, 572.

19. *Annals of the Congress*, 13th Congress, 1st and 2nd Sess., 569–70, 572.

20. Ibid., 601.

21. Ibid., 861–63.

22. Miller, *Search for Black Nationality*, 40–41; Thomas, *Paul Cuffe*, 100–103.

23. Thomas, *Paul Cuffe*, 113–18.

24. Miller, *Search for Black Nationality*, 47–50.

25. Philip J. Staudenraus, *The African Colonization Movement, 1816–1865* (New York: Columbia University Press, 1961), 34; Harris, *Paul Cuffe and the African Return*, 59.

26. See, for example, Edwin S. Redkey, *Black Exodus: Black Nationalist and Back-to-Africa Movements, 1890–1910* (New Haven: Yale University Press, 1969); Painter, *Exodusters*.

27. Staudenraus, *African Colonization Movement*, 22–27; Harris, *Paul Cuffe and the African Return*, 60–64; Skinner, *African Americans*, 26–32.

28. Staudenraus, *African Colonization Movement*, 23–35.

29. Ibid., 24.

30. Ibid., 31.

31. Ibid., 34; *Annals of the Congress*, 14th Congress, 2nd Sess., 481–83, 639, 939–41.

32. Paul Pierson, "Big, Slow-Moving, and... Invisible: Macrosocial Processes in the Study of Comparative Politics," in *Comparative Historical Analysis in the Social Sciences*, ed. James Mahoney and Dietrich Rueschemeyer (New York: Cambridge University Press, 2003), 188. The critical junctures concept in political analysis was developed by David Collier and Ruth Berins Collier, *Shaping the Political Arena: Critical Junctures, the Labor Movement, and Regime Dynamics in Latin America* (Princeton: Princeton University Press, 1991).

33. Staudenraus, *African Colonization Movement*, 32–34; Leon Litwack, *North of Slavery* (Chicago: University of Chicago Press, 1961), 24.

34. The point here is that the economic concept path-dependence is also a key component of critical junctures arguments in political science. For excellent examinations of the relationship between the two concepts, see James Mahoney, "Path Dependent Explanations of Regime Change," *Studies in Comparative and International Development* 36,

no. 1 (2001), 111–41; Paul Pierson, *Politics in Time: History, Institutions, and Social Analysis* (Princeton: Princeton University Press, 2004), 17–54.

35. Henry Noble Sherwood, "The Formation of the American Colonization Society," *Journal of Negro History* 2 (1917): 221–25; Miller, *Search for Black Nationality*, 48–50; Skinner, *African Americans*, 31.

36. James Forten to Paul Cuffe, January 25, 1817, Paul Cuffe Papers, Box 4, Free Library, New Bedford, Mass.

37. Louis Mehlinger, "The Attitude of the Free Negro toward African Colonization," *Journal of Negro History* 1 (1916): 277.

38. Ibid., 272.

39. Russell Parrot, quoted in Mehlinger, "Attitude of the Free Negro," 272–73.

40. Ibid., 272.

41. The House Foreign Relations Committee scrapped the initial ACS position because of opposition that the proposal encountered from a few southern members of Congress. Two years later, however, the Congress authorized President James Monroe to "spend $100,000 for resettling captured slaves in Africa." For a full account of the path to congressional authorization, see Staudenraus, *African Colonization Movement*, 48–58.

42. Mehlinger, "Attitude of the Free Negro," 272–74; Benjamin Quarles, *Black Abolitionists* (New York: Da Capo, 1997 [1969]), 16–18.

43. *Freedom's Journal* 1, no. 3 (1827): 12. For excellent scholarly treatments of the rise of black periodicals and the role they played in the abolitionist movement, see Charles S. Johnson, "The Rise of the Negro Magazine," *Journal of Negro History* 13, no. 1 (1928): 7–21; Bella Gross, "Freedom's Journal and the Rights of All," *Journal of Negro History* 17, no. 3 (1932): 241–86; Quarles, *Black Abolitionists*, 18–20; Mia Bay, *The White Image in the Black Mind: African American Ideas about White People, 1830–1925* (New York: Oxford University Press, 2001), 32–38.

44. Charlotte G. O'Kelly, "Black Newspapers and the Black Protest Movement: Their Historical Relationship, 1827–1945," *Phylon* 43, no. 3 (1982): 1–14; Ella Forbes, "African-American Resistance to Colonization," *Journal of Black Studies* 21, no. 2 (1990): 210–23; Gayle T. Tate, "Free Black Resistance in the Antebellum Era, 1830 to 1860," *Journal of Black Studies* 28, no. 6 (1998): 764–82; Bay, *White Image in the Black Mind*, 32–38.

45. The five periodicals analyzed are *Freedom's Journal* (1827–1829), *Colored American* (1837–1842), *Frederick Douglass' Paper* (1851–1860), *Anglo-African Magazine* (1859–1865), and *Christian Recorder* (1852–present). For an excellent treatment of these newspapers and their meaning to the black community in the antebellum period, see O'Kelly, "Black Newspapers," 1–14.

46. *Congressional Globe*, 37th Congress, 2nd Sess., Washington, D.C., February 4, 1862.

47. See, for example, Skinner, *African Americans*, 63–65.

48. *Frederick Douglass' Paper*, January 11, 1862.

49. Hanes Walton, *Black Republicans: The Politics of the Black and Tans* (Metuchen, N.J.: The Scarecrow Press, 1975); William Gillette, *The Right to Vote* (Baltimore: Johns Hopkins University Press, 1969); Brooks D. Simpson, *The Reconstruction Presidents* (Lawrence: University of Kansas Press, 1998), 140–45.

50. Walton, *Black Republicans*, 21; Simpson, *Reconstruction Presidents*, 142–43.

51. For a thorough examination of why the congressional Republicans abandoned radicalism, see William Gillette, *Retreat from Reconstruction, 1869–1879* (Baton Rouge: Louisiana State University Press, 1979); Patrick Riddleberger, "The Abandonment of the Negro during Reconstruction," *Journal of Negro History* 45, no. 2 (April 1960): 88–102. For an excellent place to start a survey of the major historical literature on the subject, see Richard Allen Gerber, "The Liberal Republicans in 1872 in Historiographical Perspective," *Journal of American History* 62, no. 1 (June 1975): 40–73.

52. Herbert Shapiro, "Afro-American Responses to Race Violence during Reconstruction," *Science and Society*, no. 36 (summer 1972): 158–70; Herbert Shapiro, *White Violence and Black Response: From Reconstruction to Montgomery* (Amherst: University of Massachusetts Press, 1988), 5–29; Joel Williamson, *After Slavery* (Chapel Hill: University of North Carolina Press, 1965), 266–73.

53. See the *Shreveport Daily Times* and the *New Orleans Daily Picayune* of September 3, 1874. See also Oscar H. Lestage Jr., "The White League of Louisiana and Its Participation in Reconstruction Riots," *Louisiana Historical Quarterly* 28 (July 1935).

54. The events of the Eufaula Riot are meticulously described by numerous witnesses in *Affairs in Alabama*, 43rd Congress, 2nd Sess., House Report no. 262, U.S. Government Printing Office, Washington, D.C., 1875. See also Harry P. Owens, "The Eufaula Riot of 1874," *Alabama Review* (July 1963): 224–37.

55. Vernon Wharton, *The Negro in Mississippi, 1865–1890* (Chapel Hill: University of North Carolina Press, 1947), 188–98.

56. Testimony of Elias Hill in *Affairs in South Carolina*, 43rd Congress, 2nd Sess., Report of the Joint Select Committee to Investigate Affairs in the Late Insurrectionary States, U.S. Government Printing Office, Washington, D.C., 1875, 47.

57. Ibid., 46.

58. Shapiro, *White Violence and Black Response*, 13.

59. Testimony of Henry Frazier in *Affairs in Alabama*, 43rd Congress, 2nd Sess., House Report, U.S. Government Printing Office, Washington, D.C., 1875, 213.

60. I base this conclusion on the fact that many of the letters that southern blacks wrote to the ACS seeking assistance with repatriation stressed their ability and preference for agricultural work once they got to Liberia. See, for example, Isidore Turner (Eufaula, Alabama) to ACS, August 2, 1878, American Colonization Society Papers, Library of Congress, Washington, D.C.

61. Testimony of Henry Adams, 46th Congress, 2nd Sess., Senate Report no. 693, U.S. Government Printing Office, Washington, D.C., 1880, 177.

62. Ibid., 114.

63. Painter, *Exodusters*, 138.

64. Staudenraus, *African Colonization Movement*, 251; Kenneth C. Barnes, *Journey of Hope: The Back-to-Africa Movement in Arkansas in the Late 1800s* (Chapel Hill: University of North Carolina Press, 2004), 8, 20–22.

65. Redkey, *Black Exodus*, 40–46; Painter, *Exodusters*, 138–44; Skinner, *African Americans*, 68–80.

66. Skinner, *African Americans*, 68–80.

67. Painter, *Exodusters*, 135–50.

68. *Charleston News and Courier*, April 16, 1878. I first learned of this article from reading George Brown Tindall's excellent article, "The Liberian Exodus of 1878," *South Carolina Historical Magazine* 53, no. 3 (July 1952): 133–45.

69. Testimony of Henry Adams, 105.

70. Victor Ullman, *Martin Delany: The Beginnings of Black Nationalism* (Boston: Beacon Press, 1971), 411.

71. Ibid.

72. Ibid., 412–14.

73. James A. Padgett, "Ministers to Liberia and Their Diplomacy," *Journal of Negro History* 22, no. 1 (1937): 50–92.

74. Ullman, *Martin Delany*, 414.

75. Ibid.

76. Frederick Douglass to Martin R. Delany, August 31, 1871, in *The Life and Writings of Frederick Douglass*, ed. Philip Sheldon Foner (New York International Publishers, 1975), 1:276–81.

77. Skinner, *African Americans*, 68–69.
78. Douglass to Delany, August 31, 1871, 277.
79. Thomas Holt, *Black over White: Negro Political Leadership in South Carolina during Reconstruction* (Urbana: University of Illinois Press, 1979), 175–80.
80. See Walton, *Black Republicans;* Edmund L. Drago, *Black Politicians and Reconstruction Georgia: A Splendid Failure* (Baton Rouge: Louisiana State University Press, 1982), 30–50.
81. Blanche K. Bruce to editor of the *Commercial,* reprinted in the *Christian Recorder,* March 7, 1878.
82. Ibid.
83. Bishop Benjamin T. Tanner et al., "A Emigration," *Christian Recorder,* May 16, 1878.
84. Ibid.
85. "The Emigration Movement," *Christian Recorder,* April 18, 1878.
86. Barnes, *Journey of Hope,* 25–29.
87. *New York Times,* March 27, 1880; ibid., 26.
88. Barnes, *Journey of Hope,* 26.
89. *New York Times* editorial, quoted in ibid.
90. *New York Times,* April 20, 1880; Barnes, *Journey of Hope,* 27.
91. Barnes, *Journey of Hope,* 27.
92. Ibid.
93. *New York Times,* April 25, 1880; ibid., 28.
94. Barnes, *Journey of Hope,* 33.
95. Grant endorsed James Milton Turner for the ministerial post in Liberia on February 17, 1871. The endorsement note is in *Letters of Application and Recommendations of the Grant Administration,* Record Group 59, National Archives and Records Administration [hereafter NARA], Washington, D.C. See also Padgett, "Ministers to Liberia and Their Diplomacy," 58.
96. See, for example, Padgett, "Ministers to Liberia and Their Diplomacy," 58–72; Gary B. Kremer, *James Milton Turner and the Promise of America* (Columbia: University of Missouri Press, 1991); Skinner, *African Americans,* 68–80.
97. Kremer, *James Milton Turner,* chap. 3; Skinner, *African Americans,* 68–91.
98. Painter, *Exodusters,* 140.
99. James Milton Turner to Department of State, March 30, 1872, no. 40, *Dispatches from U.S. Ministers to Liberia, 1863–1906,* Record Group 59, Roll 3, NARA, Washington, D.C.
100. Turner's efforts to convince the United States to aid the Americo-Liberians in their 1875 conflict with the Grebo people appear in the dispatches that he mailed in September and October 1875. See, particularly, communications nos. 180 and 184 in *Dispatches from U.S. Ministers to Liberia, 1863–1906,* Record Group 59, Roll 5, NARA, Washington, D.C.
101. Kremer, *James Milton Turner,* 40–57.
102. Turner to Department of State, March 30, 1872.
103. Skinner, *African Americas,* 73–75.
104. James Milton Turner to Hamilton Fish, May 25, 1872, no. 45, *Dispatches from U.S. Ministers to Liberia, 1863–1906,* Record Group 59, Roll 3, NARA, Washington, D.C.
105. C. A. Newcombe to Ulysses S. Grant, January 28, 1871, in *Letters of Application and Recommendations of the Grant Administration,* Record Group 59, Roll 3, NARA, Washington, D.C.
106. James Milton Turner to Secretary of State William Evarts, September 3, 1877, Dispatch no. 273, *Foreign Relations of the United States,* 1877, 370–75.

107. *African Repository* 54 (January 1878); *African Repository* 55 (January 1879); see also Kremer, *James Milton Turner*, 94–95.

108. Turner to Evarts, September 3, 1877.

109. "Of an emigration that arrived in December 1871, numbering 243 persons," Turner reported to the secretary of state, "45 or 50 persons have died of fever, many are acclimating, thirty-five or forty are intending to return, the remainder are quite despondent, and those who remain here will be little else than a burden on the country." Turner to Fish, May 25, 1872.

110. Barnes, *Journey of Hope*, 149.

111. Where possible, for this sample I randomly selected letters from each month in the years covered, 1870–1900. Of course, Liberia Fever did not strike black communities evenly in all years. On the contrary, the correspondence from freed blacks was torrential during some periods—such as the height of the Counter-Reconstruction—and virtually nonexistent at other times. When sampling by month was impossible, I used an every-five-microform-frame rule within the period. The final sample contained 360 items, which is the equivalent of one letter per month for 1870–1900.

112. James Milton Turner to Department of State, April 15, 1878, no. 266, *Dispatches from U.S. Ministers to Liberia, 1863–1906*, Record Group 59, Roll 7, NARA, Washington, D.C.

113. Kremer, *James Milton Turner*, 98–100.

114. Frederick Douglass, "Light from Liberia," *Frederick Douglass' Paper*, March 25, 1855, 1.

115. Skinner, *African Americans*, 90.

116. For an account of Delany's admission to and experiences at Harvard Medical School, see Ullman, *Martin Delany*, 115–21. For treatments of Delany's early advocacy of emigrationism, see Skinner, *African Americans*, 48–52; Robert S. Levine, *Martin Delany, Frederick Douglass, and the Politics of Representative Identity* (Chapel Hill: University of North Carolina Press, 1997), 184–88.

117. Martin Robinson Delany, *The Condition, Elevation, Emigration, and Destiny of the Colored People of the United States* (Philadelphia: King and Baird, 1852), 173–88.

118. Ullman, *Martin Delany*, 11–13, 174–76; Forbes, "African-American Resistance to Colonization," 222; Levine, *Martin Delany*, 80–83.

119. Delany, *Condition, Elevation, Emigration, and Destiny*, 169.

120. Cyril E. Griffith, *The African Dream: Martin R. Delany and the Emergence of the Pan-African Thought* (College Park: Pennsylvania State University Press, 1975), 33–35; Ullman, *Martin Delany*, 194–210.

121. Robert M. Kahn, "The Political Ideology of Martin Delany," *Journal of Black Studies* 14, no. 4 (1984): 415–40; Skinner, *African Americans*, 49–51; Levine, *Martin Delany*, 182–83.

122. Ullman, *Martin Delany*, 216–20; Skinner, *African Americans*, 49–51; Levine, *Martin Delany*, 183–84.

123. Griffith, *African Dream*, 35–39; Ullman, *Martin Delany*, 219–20; Skinner, *African Americans*, 49–51.

124. Martin R. Delany and Robert Campbell, *The Search for a Place: Black Separation and Africa* (Ann Arbor: University of Michigan Press, 1969 [1860]), 120–22; Griffith, *African Dream*, 46–47; Ullman, *Martin Delany*, 224–27; Skinner, *African Americans*, 51.

125. A. H. M. Kirk-Greene, "America in the Niger Valley: A Colonization Centenary," *Phylon* 23 (fall 1962): 225–39; Skinner, *African Americans*, 53.

126. Skinner, *African Americans*, 411.

127. Ibid., 510–12.

128. Griffith, *African Dream*, 107–8; Ullman, *Martin Delany*, 502–4; Skinner, *African Americans*, 85.

129. George Brown Tindall, *South Carolina Negroes, 1877–1900* (Columbia: University of South Carolina Press, 1952), 153–55; Ullman, *Martin Delany,* 503; Skinner, *African Americans,* 85.

130. Tindall, *South Carolina Negroes,* 153–55; Griffith, *African Dream,* 108.

131. Tindall, *South Carolina Negroes,* 155–63; Griffith, *African Dream,* 108–10.

132. Tindall, *South Carolina Negroes,* 163–68; Skinner, *African Americans,* 85–87.

133. Mungo M. Ponton, *The Life and Times of Henry M. Turner* (Atlanta: A. B. Caldwell Publishing, 1917), 33–36; Edwin S. Redkey, "Bishop Turner's African Dream," *Journal of American History* 54, no. 2 (September 1967), 273.

134. Ponton, *Life and Times,* 36–39.

135. Ibid., 49–51; John Dittmer, "The Education of Henry McNeal Turner," in *Black Leaders of the Nineteenth Century,* ed. Leon Litwack and August Meier (Urbana: University of Illinois Press, 1988), 255.

136. Drago, *Black Politicians and Reconstruction Georgia,* 35–50; Dittmer, "Education of Henry McNeal Turner," 257.

137. E. Merton Coulter, "Henry McNeal Turner: Georgia Negro Preacher-Politician during the Reconstruction Era," *Georgia Historical Quarterly* 48 (December 1964): 383–85.

138. Dittmer, "Education of Henry McNeal Turner," 259; Redkey, *Black Exodus,* 27.

139. Skinner, *African Americans,* 84.

140. Henry McNeal Turner, quoted in the *African Repository* 51 (April 1875). Emphasis added.

141. Griffith, *African Dream,* 108, 114–16.

142. Redkey, *Black Exodus,* 45–46.

143. Ibid.

144. Professor John H. Sampson to *Christian Recorder,* January 18, 1883.

145. Reverend Benjamin T. Tanner to *Christian Recorder,* February 22, 1883. See also Redkey, "Bishop Turner's African Dream," 276.

146. Rayford Logan, *The Betrayal of the Negro: From Rutherford B. Hayes to Woodrow Wilson* (New York: Collier Books, 1965), 48–50.

147. Benjamin Harrison, "Inaugural Address," in *A Compilation of the Messages and Papers of the Presidents, 1789–1902,* ed. James D. Richardson (Washington, D.C.: National Bureau of Art and Literature, 1907), 9:8.

148. *Congressional Record,* 51st Congress, 1st Sess., Washington, D.C., 3760. For an excellent secondary account, see Richard E. Welch Jr., "The Federal Elections Bill of 1890: Postscripts and Prelude," *Journal of American History* 52, no. 3 (1965): 511–26.

149. *Congressional Record,* 51st Congress, 1st Sess., 125, 155–57, 338, 802.

150. Redkey, *Black Exodus,* 63–64. See also *African Repository* 66 (April 1890): 53–55.

151. Redkey, *Black Exodus,* 64–66.

152. As the leading black weekly and the forum where Bishop Turner most frequently expressed his views, the *Christian Recorder* received numerous articles from black politicians opposed to the Butler bill. See, for example, the issues for January 23, February 6, and April 24, 1890.

153. *Congressional Record,* 51st Congress, 1st Sess., 857, 966–71. See also Redkey, *Black Exodus,* 64–65.

154. Recognizing that the Republicans valued the passage of the McKinley tariff act more than anything else, Senate Democrats threatened to filibuster the measure unless the force bills were taken off the table. For an excellent treatment of this episode, see Welch, "Federal Elections Bill of 1890," 511–26.

155. Bishop Turner actually increased his propagandizing in the black community after the defeat of the Butler bill in 1890. In 1891, the Council of AME Bishops sent Turner

on a mission to Africa to bring congregations there under greater centralization. When Turner returned to the United States in early 1892, he again immersed himself in the private-sector efforts of the ACS and other groups. Turner's letters to the *Christian Recorder* during his stay in West Africa are a fascinating read; see the *AME Church Review* 8 (April 1892).

156. Redkey, *Black Exodus*, 99–194. For treatments of how the Republicans' decision to withdraw the Lodge Federal Elections bill led to a second Counter-Reconstruction in the South, see William Alexander Mabry, "Disfranchisement of the Negro in Mississippi," *Journal of Southern History* 4, no. 3 (August 1938): 318–33; Willie D. Halsell, "The Bourbon Period in Mississippi Politics, 1875–1890," *Journal of Southern History* 11, no. 4 (November 1945): 519–37.

157. Stewart E. Tolnay, *A Festival of Violence: An Analysis of Southern Lynchings, 1882–1930* (Urbana: University of Illinois Press, 1995).

158. Roy Garvin, "Benjamin, or 'Pap,' Singleton and His Followers," *Journal of Negro History* 33, no. 1 (1948): 7–23; Painter, *Exodusters*, 184–202; Randall B. Woods, "Integration, Exclusion, or Segregation?: The 'Colorline' in Kansas, 1878–1900," *Western Historical Quarterly* 14, no. 2 (1983): 181–98.

159. Booker T. Washington, "Atlanta Exposition Address," in *Selected Speeches of Booker T. Washington*, ed. E. Davidson (New York: Doubleday, 1932), 31–37.

160. August Meier, *Negro Thought in America, 1880–1915: Racial Ideologies in the Age of Booker T. Washington* (Ann Arbor: University of Michigan Press, 1969), 19–58, argues that Washington's message was a natural fit for the black masses in the last decade of the nineteenth century because they had already turned away from politics to focus on moral and economic development.

CHAPTER 2. "HIS FAILURE WILL BE THEIRS"

1. Marcus Garvey to W. E. B. Du Bois, July 16, 1920, in *The Marcus Garvey and Universal Negro Improvement Association Papers*, ed. Robert A. Hill (Los Angeles: University of California Press, 1983) [hereafter *Garvey and UNIA Papers*], 2:426.

2. W. E. B. Du Bois to Marcus Garvey, July 22, 1920, in *Garvey and UNIA Papers*, 2:431–32.

3. Garvey approached, among others, Robert R. Moton, the second principal of Tuskegee and the leading conservative foil to Du Bois and the NAACP, about accepting the post of leader of American blacks. See Elliot Skinner, *African Americans and U.S. Policy toward Africa, 1850–1924* (Washington, D.C.: Howard University Press, 1992), 435–36.

4. For an excellent overview of black transnationalism during the period 1850–1930, see Wilson Jeremiah Moses, *The Golden Age of Black Nationalism, 1850–1925* (Hamden, Conn.: Archon Books, 1978).

5. Ben F. Rogers, "William E.B. Du Bois, Marcus Garvey, and Pan-Africa," *Journal of Negro History* 20, no. 2 (1955): 154–65; P. Olisanwuche Esedebe, *Pan-Africanism: From Idea to Movement, 1776–1963* (Washington, D.C.: Howard University Press, 1982), 78–85; Skinner, *African Americans*, 456–61; Rod Bush, *We Are Not What We Seem: Black Nationalism and Class Struggle in the American Century* (New York: New York University Press, 1999), 93–99.

6. For an excellent summary of the literature that reduces the conflicts between black social movement leaders to clashing personalities, see Ramon G. Vela, "The Washington-Du Bois Controversy and African American Protest: Ideological Conflict and Its Consequences," *Studies in American Political Development* 16, no. 1 (2002): 88–109.

7. Rogers, "William E.B. Du Bois," 154–65; Skinner, *African Americans*, 423–68; Nikhil Pal Singh, *Black Is a Country: Race and the Unfinished Struggle for Democracy* (Cambridge, Mass.: Harvard University Press, 2004), 58–61.

8. See, for example, Tony Martin, *Race First: The Ideological and Organizational Struggles of Marcus Garvey and the Universal Negro Improvement Association* (Westport, Conn.: Greenwood Press, 1976); Esedebe, *Pan-Africanism*, 67–80; Bush, *We Are Not What We Seem*, 93–97.

9. Edwin S. Redkey, *Black Exodus: Black Nationalist and Back-to-Africa Movements, 1890–1910* (New Haven: Yale University Press, 1969), 63–64; Robert Weisbord, *Ebony Kinship: Africa, Africans, and the Afro-American* (Westport, Conn.: Greenwood Press, 1973), 29–31; Skinner, *African Americans*, 77, 142–43.

10. For reactions to the demise of the Butler emigration bill among the black elite, see *Christian Recorder*, January 23, February 6, and April 24, 1890. Nadir is the term used by Rayford Logan, the pioneering black historian, for the period between the Counter-Reconstruction and the rise of the modern civil rights movement. The term is now used for this period in much of the literature on the U.S. black experience. Rayford W. Logan, *The Negro in American Life and Thought: The Nadir, 1877–1901* (New York: Dial Press, 1954).

11. *Congressional Record*, 51st Congress, 1st Sess., Washington, D.C., 857, 966–71. See also Redkey, *Black Exodus*, 64–65.

12. For accounts of Washington's rise to prominence, see Samuel R. Spencer Jr., *Booker T. Washington and the Negro's Place in American Life* (Boston: Little, Brown and Company, 1955), 13–28; Louis H. Harlan, *Booker T. Washington: The Making of a Black Leader, 1856–1901* (New York: Oxford University Press, 1972), 1–51; Michael Rudolph West, *The Education of Booker T. Washington: American Democracy and the Idea of Race Relations* (New York: Columbia University Press, 2006), 185–227.

13. Booker T. Washington, "Atlanta Exposition Address," in *Selected Speeches of Booker T. Washington*, ed. E. Davidson (New York: Doubleday, 1932), 31–32.

14. Booker T. Washington to President Theodore Roosevelt, March 21, 1908, in *The Booker T. Washington Papers*, ed. Louis R. Harlan and Raymond W. Smock (Urbana: University of Illinois Press, 1980) [hereafter *Washington Papers*], 9:476; President Theodore Roosevelt to Booker T. Washington, April 14, 1908, in *Washington Papers*, 9:499. See also Edward O. Erhagbe, "African Americans and the Defense of African States against European Imperial Conquest: Booker T. Washington's Diplomatic Efforts to Guarantee Liberia's Independence 1907–1911," *African Studies Review* 39, no. 1 (1996): 56–57; Louis Harlan, "Booker T. Washington and the White Man's Burden," *American Historical Review* 71, no. 2 (1966): 454; Skinner, *African Americans*, 313–14.

15. Skinner, *African Americans*, 335–40.

16. In 1899, a group of white philanthropists from Boston paid for Washington and his wife to go to Europe. Although the trip was intended to be a vacation, the irrepressible principal of Tuskegee could not pass up the opportunity to spread his message in Europe by accepting a few prestigious speaking engagements. The content of these addresses was widely circulated in the European press and added greatly to Washington's acclaim in Europe. See Booker T. Washington, *Up from Slavery: An Autobiography* (New York: W. W. Norton, [1901] 1995), 121–33.

17. Booker T. Washington to Grace Luling, January 28, 1905, in *Washington Papers*, 8:184–85. For analyses of Washington's views of indigenous Africans and their suitability for "industrial education," see Harlan, "Booker T. Washington," 441–67; W. Manning Marable, "Booker T. Washington and African Nationalism," *Phylon* 35, no. 4 (1974): 398–406; Ibrahim Sundiata, *Brothers and Others: Black Zion, Black Slavery, 1914–1940* (Durham: Duke University Press, 2003), 7.

18. Esedebe, *Pan-Africanism*, 47–53; Skinner, *African Americans*, 164–71.

19. Henry Sylvester Williams to Booker T. Washington, June 1, 1900, in *Washington Papers*, 8:184–85. See also Owen Charles Mathurin, *Henry Sylvester Williams and the Origins of the Pan-African Movement, 1869–1911* (Westport, Conn.: Greenwood Press, 1976), 50–52; Skinner, *African Americans*, 169–71, 336.

20. W. E. B. Du Bois, "An Address to the Nations of the World," in *W.E.B. Du Bois: A Reader*, ed. David Levering Lewis (New York: Henry Holt, 1995), 639. For an excellent analysis of the ideological and intellectual crosscurrents in the document, see Adolph Reed Jr., *W.E.B. Du Bois and American Political Thought: Fabianism and the Color Line* (New York: Oxford University Press, 1997), 79–83.

21. Du Bois, "Address to the Nations," 640.

22. Ibid. For excellent treatments of the conference and the political context that shaped "An Address to the Nations of the World," see Clarence Contee, "The Emergence of Du Bois as an African Nationalist," *Journal of Negro History* 54, no. 1 (1969): 48–63; Skinner, *African Americans*, 172–76.

23. Wilson Jeremiah Moses, *The Golden Age of Black Nationalism, 1850–1925* (Hamden, Conn.: Archon Books, 1978), 59–81; Ibrahim K. Sundiata, *Black Scandal: America and the Liberian Labor Crisis, 1929–1936* (Philadelphia: ISHI Press, 1980); Tunde Adeleke, *UnAfrican Americans: Nineteenth-Century Black Nationalists and the Civilizing Mission* (Lexington: University of Kentucky Press, 1998), 13–31.

24. See *Report of the Pan-African Conference* (London, 1900), W. E. B. Du Bois Papers, Box 10, Fisk University Collection, Nashville, Tenn. See also Contee, "Emergence of Du Bois," 58; Esedebe, *Pan-Africanism*, 47–56.

25. *Report of the Pan-African Conference*. See also Immanuel Geiss, *The Pan-African Movement* (New York: Methuen, 1974), 192–98.

26. Contee, "Emergence of Du Bois," 58.

27. Skinner, *African Americans*, 167–73.

28. August Meier, *Negro Thought in America, 1880–1915: Racial Ideologies in the Age of Booker T. Washington* (Ann Arbor: University of Michigan Press, 1965), 113, 164–65; David Levering Lewis, *W.E.B. Du Bois: Biography of a Race, 1868–1919* (New York: Henry Holt, 1995), 297–343.

29. Geiss, *Pan-African Movement*, 233–62; Esedebe, *Pan-Africanism*, 81–92; Skinner, *African Americans*, 381–422; Lewis, *W.E.B. Du Bois: Biography*, 561–63.

30. Minutes of the Board of Directors of the NAACP, November 11, 1918, Records of the NAACP, Box A12, Library of Congress, Washington, D.C.

31. W. E. B. Du Bois, "Memorandum on the Future of Africa," Records of the NAACP, Box A12, Library of Congress, Washington, D.C. See also Clarence Contee, "Du Bois, the NAACP, and the Pan-African Congress of 1919," *Journal of Negro History* 57, no. 1 (January 1972): 13–28; Moses, *Golden Age of Black Nationalism*, 1978, 140–45; Reed, *W.E.B. Du Bois*, 82–89.

32. The fact that Du Bois had press credentials from his position with the *Crisis* was the only reason that he was able to make the trip. See Skinner, *African Americans*, 399.

33. Richard B. Moore, "Du Bois and Pan-Africa," in *Black Titan: W.E.B. Du Bois*, ed. John Henrik Clarke (Boston: Beacon Press, 1970), 202–3; Lewis, *W.E.B. Du Bois: Biography*, 567–70.

34. W. E. B. Du Bois, *Crisis* 18 (May 1919): 8; *New York Times*, February 2 and 16, 1919; Contee, "Du Bois, the NAACP," 13–28; Rogers, "William E.B. Du Bois," 154–65; Manning Marable, *W.E.B. Du Bois: Black Radical Democrat* (Boston: Twanye, 1986), 100–102; Skinner, *African Americans*, 399–401.

35. Contee, "Du Bois, the NAACP," 13–28; Geiss, *Pan-African Movement*, 235–40; Marable, *W.E.B. Du Bois*, 101–3; Lewis, *W.E.B. Du Bois: Biography*, 574–76.

36. Du Bois provides extremely rich commentary on the proceedings of the Congress in the *Crisis* 17 (April 1919). See also Geiss, *Pan-African Movement*, 238–41; John D. Hargreaves, "Maurice Delafosse on the Pan-African Congress of 1919," *African Historical Studies* 1, no. 2 (1968): 233–41; Skinner, *African Americans*, 404–8.

37. Esedebe, *Pan-Africanism*, 81–82; Geiss, *Pan-African Movement*, 240.

38. Sylvia M. Jacobs, *Black American Perspectives on the European Partitioning of Africa, 1880–1920* (Westport, Conn.: Greenwood Press, 1981).

39. Ibid., 250–60; Geiss, *Pan-African Movement*, 240–62; Skinner, *African Americans*, 406–11.

40. Amy Jacques Garvey, *Garvey and Garveyism* (New York: Octagon Books, 1963), 3; E. David Cronon, *Black Moses: The Story of Marcus Garvey and the Universal Negro Improvement Association* (Madison: University of Wisconsin Press, 1955), 6–15; Martin, *Race First*, 3–4.

41. A. Garvey, *Garvey and Garveyism*, 9–11; Cronon, *Black Moses*, 12–14; Colin Grant, *Negro with a Hat: The Rise and Fall of Marcus Garvey* (New York: Oxford University Press, 2008), 13.

42. Cronon, *Black Moses*, 14–16; Martin, *Race First*, 3–4; Grant, *Negro with a Hat*, 14–18.

43. Martin, *Race First*, 4; Cronon, *Black Moses*, 15; Grant, *Negro with a Hat*, 18–19.

44. Grant, *Negro with a Hat*, 19.

45. Robert H. Brisbane, "Some New Light on the Garvey Movement," *Journal of Negro History* 36, no. 1 (1951): 53–62; Cronon, *Black Moses*, 14–16; Rupert Lewis, *Marcus Garvey: Anti-Colonial Champion* (Trenton: African World Press, 1988), 41–42.

46. Martin, *Race First*, 4; Grant, *Negro with a Hat*, 22–24.

47. Brisbane, "Some New Light," 56–58; Cronon, *Black Moses*, 15–16; Martin, *Race First*, 4–6; Grant, *Negro with a Hat*, 34–51.

48. Brisbane, "Some New Light," 57.

49. Martin, *Race First*, 5–7; Grant, *Negro with a Hat*, 44–47.

50. Marcus Garvey, *The Philosophy and Opinions of Marcus Garvey*, ed. Amy Jacques Garvey (New York: Antheneum Publishing, 1992 [1923]), 2:126. See also Cronon, *Black Moses*, 16.

51. Marcus Garvey, "The Negro's Greatest Enemy," *Current History* 18, no. 6 (1923), 952; Cronon, *Black Moses*, 16–18; Martin, *Race First*, 6; Grant, *Negro with a Hat*, 52–54.

52. Martin, *Race First*, 6; Cronon, *Black Moses*, 17–18; Skinner, *African Americans*, 382–83; Grant, *Negro with a Hat*, 52–56.

53. Cronon, *Black Moses*, 17–20; Skinner, *African Americans*, 383–84; Grant, *Negro with a Hat*, 65–71.

54. Grant, *Negro with a Hat*, 63–69.

55. M. Garvey, *Philosophy and Opinions*, 2:127.

56. A. Garvey, *Garvey and Garveyism*, 8–10; Cronon, *Black Moses*, 39–41; Grant, *Negro with a Hat*, 73–76.

57. Cronon, *Black Moses*, 44–47; Grant, *Negro with a Hat*, 88–105.

58. Grant, *Negro with a Hat*, 109.

59. Although Garvey had a substantial following, the consensus among most historians is that his claims to have 2 million members were dubious. For works in this vein, see Cronon, *Black Moses*, 45–49; Grant, *Negro with a Hat*, 164. Martin, *Race First*, 12–13, is an example of a work that accepts Garvey's count.

60. Cronon, *Black Moses*, 43–44; Martin, *Race First*, 22–41, 151–74.

61. Cronon, *Black Moses*, 21.

62. See, for example, Rogers, "William E.B. Du Bois," 154–65; Elliot M. Rudwick, "Du Bois vs. Garvey: Race Propagandists at War," *Journal of Negro Education* 28, no. 4 (1959): 421–29; John Henrik Clarke, "Marcus Garvey: The Harlem Years," *Transition* 46 (1974): 14–19; Manning Marable, *W.E.B. Du Bois: Black Radical Democrat* (Boulder: Paradigm Publishers, 2005), 36–42.

63. Rogers, "William E.B. Du Bois," 154–65; Skinner, *African Americans*, 335–40.

64. Marcus Garvey, "Editorial Letter to the *Negro World*," New York, March 27, 1919, and "Synopsis of UNIA Meeting," *Negro World*, March 29, 1919, *Garvey and UNIA Papers*, 1:391–93.

65. W. E. B. Du Bois, "Back to Africa," in *W.E.B. Du Bois: A Reader*, ed. David Levering Lewis (New York: Henry Holt, 1995), 333–39.

66. Grant, *Negro with a Hat*, 89.

67. Marcus Garvey to W. E. B. Du Bois, April 30, 1915, in *Garvey and UNIA Papers*, 1:157.

68. Marcus Garvey to W. E. B. Du Bois, April 25, 1916, in *Garvey and UNIA Papers*, 1:187–90.

69. W. E. B. Du Bois to Marcus Garvey, May 1, 1916, in *Garvey and UNIA Papers*, 1:190.

70. M. Garvey, "Editorial Letter to the *Negro World*," March 27, 1919.

71. W. E. B. Du Bois, "Marcus Garvey," *Crisis* 20 (December 1920): 58–60. For an extensive treatment of this controversy, see Skinner, *African Americans*, 413–14. Skinner concludes that the weight of the historical evidence rests with Du Bois.

72. "Interview with W.E.B. Du Bois by Charles Mowbray White," August 22, 1920, in *Garvey and UNIA Papers*, 2:620–21.

73. E. G. Woodward to James Weldon Johnson, September 25, 1920, NAACP Papers, Series I, Box C304, Library of Congress, Washington, D.C.

74. F. Randolph to E. G. Woodward, October 2, 1920, NAACP Papers, Series I, Box C304, Library of Congress, Washington, D.C.

75. Charles Beasley to Assistant Field Secretary of NAACP, January 11, 1921, NAACP Papers, Series I, Box C304, Library of Congress, Washington, D.C.

76. Walter White, Assistant Field Secretary, NAACP, January 11, 1921, NAACP Papers, Series I, Box C304, Library of Congress, Washington, D.C.

77. The count data presented in figure 2.1 exclude all editorials and letters written by notable black leaders and official representatives of organizations such as the NAACP and Urban League.

78. W. E. B. Du Bois, *Dusk of Dawn: An Essay toward an Autobiography of a Race Concept* (New York: Schocken Books, 1968), 277–78.

79. W. E. B. Du Bois, "The Rise of the West Indian," *Crisis* 20 (September 1920): 214–15.

80. William Pickens to Marcus Garvey, July 24, 1922, quoted in the *Chicago Defender*, July 29, 1922, 8.

81. Quoted in Philip S. Foner, *American Socialism and Black Americans: From the Age of Jackson to World War II* (Westport, Conn.: Greenwood Press, 1977), 329.

82. Du Bois, "Marcus Garvey" (December 1920), 58.

83. Ibid., 59.

84. Ibid., 60

85. Cronon, *Black Moses*, 50; Martin, *Race First*, 152.

86. Martin, *Race First*, 152.

87. Cronon, *Black Moses*, 52–54; Grant, *Negro with a Hat*, 204.

88. Cronon, *Black Moses*, 54–55; Martin, *Race First*, 152–54; Judith Stein, *The World of Marcus Garvey: Race and Class in Modern Society* (Baton Rouge: Louisiana State University Press, 1986), 90–91; Grant, *Negro with a Hat*, 204–5.

89. Martin, *Race First*, 153; Grant, *Negro with a Hat*, 204.

90. Hugh Mulzac, *A Star to Steer By* (New York: International Publishers, 1963), 82; Martin, *Race First*, 153; Grant, *Negro with a Hat*, 205.

91. Cronon, *Black Moses*, 53–54; Grant, *Negro with a Hat*, 205.

92. Grant, *Negro with a Hat*, 205.

93. Cronon, *Black Moses*, 54; Grant, *Negro with a Hat*, 205.
94. Cronon, *Black Moses*, 78–80; Stein, *World of Marcus Garvey*, 92–95; Grant, *Negro with a Hat*, 208–10.
95. Grant, *Negro with a Hat*, 210.
96. Claude McKay, *Harlem: Negro Metropolis* (New York: Harcourt Brace, 1940), 99. See also Cronon, *Black Moses*, 55; Martin, *Race First*, 153; Grant, *Negro with a Hat*, 211.
97. Cronon, *Black Moses*, 55–56; Grant, *Negro with a Hat*, 217.
98. Stein, *World of Marcus Garvey*, 91–92; Grant, *Negro with a Hat*, 221.
99. Quoted in Mulzac, *Star to Steer By*, 82.
100. Grant, *Negro with a Hat*, 222.
101. Stein, *World of Marcus Garvey*, 90–91; ibid., 227.
102. Cronon, *Black Moses*, 81–82; Martin, *Race First*, 154; Grant, *Negro with a Hat*, 227.
103. Cronon, *Black Moses*, 82; Stein, *World of Marcus Garvey*, 91; Grant, *Negro with a Hat*, 228.
104. Martin, *Race First*, 154; Grant, *Negro with a Hat*, 228.
105. Grant, *Negro with a Hat*, 228.
106. Cronon, *Black Moses*, 83–84; ibid., 228.
107. Cronon, *Black Moses*, 82–83; Martin, *Race First*, 154; Stein, *World of Marcus Garvey*, 91; Grant, *Negro with a Hat*, 233.
108. Cronon, *Black Moses*, 81, 84; Grant, *Negro with a Hat*, 240–41.
109. Cronon, *Black Moses*, 56–58, 88–90; Stein, *World of Marcus Garvey*, 94–95; Grant, *Negro with a Hat*, 233–40.
110. Cronon, *Black Moses*, 96–97; Stein, *World of Marcus Garvey*, 95–96.
111. Cronon, *Black Moses*, 100–101.
112. J. Edgar Hoover to Special Agent Ridgeley, Washington, D.C., October 11, 1919, in *Garvey and UNIA Papers*, 2:72.
113. Cronon, *Black Moses*, 94.
114. Ibid., 99–101; Grant, *Negro with a Hat*, 324–25.
115. See Martin, *Race First*, 162–66 for an account that suggests that the mail fraud case was largely without merit.
116. Cronon, *Black Moses*, 100; Grant, *Negro with a Hat*, 324.
117. Grant, *Negro with a Hat*, 325.
118. *Negro World*, January 21, 1922.
119. Grant, *Negro with a Hat*, 326.
120. See, for example, Martin, *Race First*, 27–28, 231–33.
121. Cronon, *Black Moses*, 52–54.
122. W. E. B. Du Bois, "The Demagog," *Crisis* 23 (April 1922). See also Grant, *Negro with a Hat*, 326.
123. Garvey's meetings with Clarke and other southern racists were widely reported in both the mainstream and black presses. See, for example, *New York Times*, July 10, 1922; *Chicago Defender*, July 8 and 22, 1922.
124. Cronon, *Black Moses*, 106–8.
125. Rogers, "William E.B. Du Bois," 158, 165.
126. "Garveyism in Africa," The Marcus Garvey and Universal Negro Improvement Association Papers, ed. Robert A. Hill (Los Angeles: University of California Press, 2006), 10:3.
127. Stein, *World of Marcus Garvey*, 48; Grant, *Negro with a Hat*, 172.
128. Stein, *World of Marcus Garvey*, 49; Grant, *Negro with a Hat*, 172.
129. Grant, *Negro with a Hat*, 172.
130. Ibid., 177–78.

131. "British Military Report," *Garvey and UNIA Papers*, 1:405–8.
132. Grant, *Negro with a Hat*, 178.
133. Ibid., 181.
134. Ibid.
135. M. Garvey, "Editorial Letter to the *Negro World*," *Garvey and UNIA Papers* (March 27, 1919), 1:391; "Synopsis of UNIA Meeting," March 29, 1919.
136. Du Bois, "Marcus Garvey," (December 1920):60.
137. Skinner, *African Americans*, 414.
138. Rupert Lewis, *Marcus Garvey: Anti-Colonial Champion* (Trenton: Africa World Press, 1988), 96–97; Martin, *Race First*, 124.
139. Martin, *Race First*, 124.
140. A. Garvey, *Garvey and Garveyism*, 106–7; George Huggins, "Marcus Garvey and the League of Nations," in *Garvey: Africa, Europe, the Americas*, ed. Rupert Lewis and Maureen Warner-Lewis (Kingston, Jamaica: University of the West Indies, 1986), 152–65.
141. Marcus Garvey, quoted in "Report by Bureau Agent H.J. Lenon," January 18, 1921, in *Garvey and UNIA Papers*, 3:133–34.
142. Marcus Garvey to Gabriel Moore Johnson, January 18, 1921, in *Garvey and UNIA Papers*, 3:135.
143. Marcus Garvey, quoted in "Report by Bureau Agent H.J. Lenon," 3:133–34.
144. W. E. B. Du Bois, "Marcus Garvey," *Crisis* 21 (January 1921), 114.
145. Quoted in Kevin Gaines, *Uplifting the Race: Black Leadership, Politics and Culture in the Twentieth Century* (Chapel Hill: University of North Carolina Press, 1996), 240.
146. These passages are based on the account in Skinner, *African Americans*, 444–46.
147. Nathaniel R. Richardson, *Liberia's Past and Present* (London: Diplomatic Press, 1959), 135; ibid., 444–45. On Harding's return to the practice of appointing black politicians to positions of importance in the black community, see W. E. B. Du Bois, "The Political Rebirth of the Office Seeker," *Crisis* 21 (January 1921): 104. Harding's appointment of Solomon Porter Hood, a black man, to the post of minister resident to Liberia is chronicled in James A. Padgett, "Ministers to Liberia and Their Diplomacy," *Journal of Negro History* 22, no. 1 (1937): 87–88.
148. Charles King, "An Open Letter from the President of Liberia," *Crisis* 22 (June 1921), 53.
149. Skinner, *African Americans*, 444–46, 447–49; Sundiata, *Brothers and Others*, 72–78.
150. Skinner, *African Americans*, 444–46.
151. Sundiata, *Brothers and Others*, 78–79, 101–4.
152. Joseph E. Harris, *African American Reactions to War in Ethiopia, 1936–1941* (Baton Rouge: Louisiana State University Press, 1994), 2–3. See also Bishop Alexander Walters, *My Life and Work* (New York: Revell, 1917), 253; Contee, "Emergence of Du Bois," 48–63; Robert Pankhurst, "Menelik and the Utilisation of Foreign Skills in Ethiopia," *Journal of Ethiopian Studies* 5 (1967): 65–67.
153. Harris, *African American Reactions*, 6.
154. Weisbord, *Ebony Kinship*, 87–89.
155. Ibid., 89.
156. William R. Scott, *The Sons of Sheba's Race: African Americans and the Italo-Ethiopian War, 1935–1941* (Bloomington: Indiana University Press, 1993), 12–23.
157. The Philadelphia Pacific Movement to Emperor Haile Selassie, quoted in Harris, *African American Reactions*, 38.
158. See *New York Times*, September 10, 1935; *Amsterdam News*, October 12, 1935 and January 11, 1936; *Pittsburgh Courier*, October 30, 1935; Scott, *Sons of Sheba's Race*, 112; Weisbord, *Ebony Kinship*, 97.

159. See, for example, Scott, *Sons of Sheba's Race*, 211–14.
160. The evolution of the U.S. neutrality policy during the second Italian-Ethiopian War is thoroughly explored in Brice Harris Jr., *The United States and the Italo-Ethiopian Crisis* (Stanford: Stanford University Press, 1964), 53–62.
161. Scott, *Sons of Sheba's Race*, 64–70.
162. James H. Meriwether, *Proudly We Can Be Africans: Black Americans and Africa, 1935–1961* (Chapel Hill: University of North Carolina Press, 2002), 34–39.
163. Harris, *African American Reactions*, 42–44.
164. Ibid., 48.
165. Ibid.
166. Scott, *Sons of Sheba's Race*, 138.
167. See *New York Times*, July 15, 1935; *Pittsburgh Courier*, July 20, 1935; *New York Age*, July 20, 1935. See also Scott, *Sons of Sheba's Race*, 136–37.
168. Scott, *Sons of Sheba's Race*, 136–37.
169. Ibid.
170. Indeed, if we are to accept the accounts of Roosevelt's aides, it is clear that the thirty-second president even rooted for Ethiopia to score an unlikely victory over the fascist Mussolini. See Harris, *United States*, 53–62.
171. Scott, *Sons of Sheba's Race*, 138.
172. Ibid., 141.
173. See Brenda Gayle Plummer, *Rising Wind: Black Americans and U.S. Foreign Affairs, 1935–1960* (Chapel Hill: University of North Carolina Press, 1996), 53; Scott, *Sons of Sheba's Race*, 145–46.

CHAPTER 3. PROTECTING "FERTILE FIELDS"

1. *New York Times*, June 7, 1946; *New Africa* (June 1946); Hollis Lynch, *Black American Radicals and the Liberation of Africa: The Council on African Affairs, 1937–1955* (Ithaca: Cornell University Press, 1978), 32–33.
2. Lynch, *Black American Radicals*, 32.
3. John Foster Dulles to Paul Robeson, chairman, Council on African Affairs, December 7, 1946, William Alphaeus Hunton Papers [hereafter Hunton Papers], Box 1, Folder 16 (CAA 1945–55), New York Public Library, New York [hereafter NYPL]; Council on African Affairs (CAA) Press Release, April 9, 1947, Hunton Papers, Reel 2, NYPL. *New Africa* 5, no. 6 (1946); *New York Times*, June 7, 1946; *Pittsburgh Courier*, October 26, 1946; *Chicago Defender*, November 2, 1946; Lynch, *Black American Radicals*, 34–35; Penny Von Eschen, *Race against Empire: Black Americans and Anti-Colonialism* (Ithaca: Cornell University Press, 1997), 87–95.
4. Lynch, *Black American Radicals*, 32.
5. For treatments of the rise of Truman's national security regime, see Robert Messer, *The End of an Alliance: James F. Byrnes, Roosevelt, Truman, and the Origins of the Cold War* (Chapel Hill: University of North Carolina Press, 1982); Michael J. Hogan, *A Cross of Iron: Harry Truman and the Origins of the National Security State, 1945–1954* (New York: Cambridge University Press, 1998).
6. *Pittsburgh Courier*, May 3, 1947; Lynch, *Black American Radicals*, 35.
7. Attorney General Tom Clark, quoted in Lynch, *Black American Radicals*, 36. See also David Caute, *The Great Fear: The Anti-Communist Purge under Truman and Eisenhower* (New York: Simon and Schuster, 1978), 32.
8. For Robeson's remarks on the nature of "Soviet Democracy," see *New Africa* (December 1945). For an excellent treatment of Robeson's views during this period, see Martin Duberman, *Paul Robeson: A Biography* (New York: The New Press, 1989), 303–6.

9. Hunton Papers, Box 1, Folder 16 (CAA Correspondence), NYPL; *New York Times*, February 3, February 4, and April 6, 1948; *Pittsburgh Courier*, February 14, 1948. See also Lynch, *Black American Radicals*, 36–37; Von Eschen, *Race against Empire*, 114–18; Duberman, *Paul Robeson*, 330–33; Gerald Horne, *Black and Red: W.E.B. Du Bois and the Afro-American Response to the Cold War, 1944–1963* (Albany: State University of New York Press, 1985), 115–19.

10. *New York Times*, May 29, June 20, and September 29, 1948. See also Lynch, *Black American Radicals*, 37.

11. Lynch, *Black American Radicals*, 39.

12. Duberman, *Paul Robeson*, 333; James H. Meriwether, *Proudly We Can Be Africans: Black Americans and Africa, 1935–1961* (Chapel Hill: University of North Carolina Press, 2002), 81–88.

13. Lynch, *Black American Radicals*, 39; Von Eschen, *Race against Empire*, 134–42.

14. Brenda Gayle Plummer, *Rising Wind: Black Americans and U.S. Foreign Affairs, 1935–1960* (Chapel Hill: University of North Carolina Press, 1996), 171–89; Von Eschen, *Race against Empire*, 109–18; Meriwether, *Proudly We Can Be Africans*, 82–89.

15. Plummer, *Rising Wind*, 210–214; Mary Dudziak, *Cold War Civil Rights: Race and the Image of American Democracy* (Princeton: Princeton University Press, 2000), 3–18, 18–47; Thomas Borstelmann, *The Cold War and the Color Line: American Race Relations in the Global Arena* (Cambridge, Mass.: Harvard University Press, 2001); Meriwether, *Proudly We Can Be Africans*, 84–89.

16. Horne, *Black and Red*, 91–92; Von Eschen, *Race against Empire*, 120; Nikhil Pal Singh, *Black Is a Country: Race and the Unfinished Struggle for Democracy* (Cambridge, Mass.: Harvard University Press, 2004), 174–211.

17. Von Eschen, *Race against Empire*, 109–21.

18. Meriwether, *Proudly We Can Be Africans*, 83.

19. Horne, *Black and Red*, 75–82.

20. "Du Bois Quits as Crisis Editor," *Atlanta Daily World*, June 12, 1934, 1; Elliot M. Rudwick, "Du Bois' Last Year as Crisis Editor," *Journal of Negro History* 57, no. 4 (1958): 526–33.

21. W. E. B. Du Bois, "The History of Race Provincialism," *Pittsburgh Courier*, April 25, 1936, A1.

22. W. E. B. Du Bois, "Memorandum on the Future of Africa," November 27, 1918, Records of the NAACP, Box A12, Library of Congress, Washington, D.C. See also Clarence G. Contee, "Du Bois, the NAACP, and the Pan-African Congress of 1919," *Journal of Negro History* 57, no. 1 (1972): 13–28.

23. Du Bois, "Memorandum on the Future of Africa."

24. *Report of the Pan-African Conference* (London, 1900), W. E. B. Du Bois Papers, Box 10, Fisk University Collection, Nashville, Tenn.

25. Minutes of the Board of Directors of the NAACP, November 11, 1918, Records of the NAACP, Box A12, Library of Congress, Washington, D.C.

26. Du Bois provides extremely rich commentary on the proceedings of the congress in the *Crisis* 17 (April 1919). See also P. Olisanwuche Esedebe, *Pan-Africanism: From Idea to Movement, 1776–1963* (Washington, D.C.: Howard University Press, 1982), 81–82; Immanuel Geiss, *The Pan-African Movement* (New York: Methuen, 1974), 238–40.

27. For an analysis of the achievements and press coverage of congress, see Contee, "Du Bois, the NAACP," 13–28; John D. Hargreaves, "Maurice Delafosse on the Pan-African Congress of 1919," *African Historical Studies* 1, no. 2 (1968): 233–41.

28. George Padmore, *History of the Pan-African Congress: Colonial and Colored Unity* (London: Hammersmith, 1963), 6; Bernard Magubane, *The Ties That Bind: African American Consciousness of Africa* (Trenton: African World Press, 1987), 154; Geiss, *Pan-African Movement*, 251–56.

29. W. E. B. Du Bois, *The World and Africa* (New York: International Publishers, 1946), 242–43; Geiss, *Pan-African Movement*, 248–62.

30. Elliot Rudwick, *W.E.B. Du Bois: Voice of the Black Protest Movement* (Urbana: University of Illinois Press, 1982), 254–71; David Levering Lewis, *W.E.B. Du Bois: The Fight for Equality and the American Century, 1919–1963* (New York: Henry Holt, 2000), 279–91.

31. W. E. B. Du Bois, *The Autobiography of W.E.B. Du Bois: A Soliloquy on Viewing My Life from the Last Decade of Its First Century* (New York: International Publishers, 1968), 291.

32. William R. Scott, *The Sons of Sheba's Race: African Americans and the Italo-Ethiopian War, 1935–1941* (Bloomington: Indiana University Press, 1993), 106–24; Plummer, *Rising Wind*, 40–48.

33. Scott, *Sons of Sheba's Race*, 124–27; Meriwether, *Proudly We Can Be Africans*, 34–37.

34. Alexander DeConde, *Ethnicity, Race, and American Foreign Policy: A History* (Boston: Northeastern University Press, 1992), 69–99; Tony Smith, *Foreign Attachments: The Power of Ethnic Groups in the Making of American Foreign Policy* (Cambridge, Mass.: Harvard University Press, 2000), 30–35, 50–54.

35. Walter White to Secretary of State Cordell Hull, March 20, 1935, Records of the NAACP, Series II, Box C192, Library of Congress, Manuscript Division, Washington, D.C.

36. NAACP telegram to Ambassador Maxim Litivinov, League of Nations, Geneva, Switzerland, May 22, 1935, and Walter White to Charles Hamilton Houston, Washington, D.C., May 22, 1935, Records of the NAACP, Series II, Box C192, Library of Congress, Manuscript Division, Washington, D.C. See also Scott, *Sons of Sheba's Race*, 125–26.

37. Walter White to Rayford Logan, July 8, 1935, Records of the NAACP, Series II, Box C192, Library of Congress, Manuscript Division, Washington, D.C. See also Meriwether, *Proudly We Can Be Africans*, 28.

38. Walter White, "Secretary's Report," July 1935, Records of the NAACP, Library of Congress, Manuscript Division, Washington, D.C., Series II, Box C192.

39. Lewis, *W.E.B. Du Bois*, 346–49; Meriwether, *Proudly We Can Be Africans*, 37.

40. Meriwether, *Proudly We Can Be Africans*, 37.

41. Ibid.

42. Ibid., 40.

43. NAACP, "Statement on the Italian-Ethiopian War," October 19, 1935, Records of the NAACP, Series II, Box C192, Library of Congress, Manuscript Division, Washington, D.C.

44. Horne, *Black and Red*, 22–24; Von Eschen, *Race against Empire*, 118–20; Singh, *Black Is a Country*, 178–79.

45. Charles Flint Kellog, *NAACP: A History of the National Association for the Advancement of Colored People, 1909–1920* (Baltimore: Johns Hopkins University Press, 1967); August Meier and John H. Bracey, "The NAACP as Reform Movement, 1909–1965: To Reach the Conscience of America," *Journal of Southern History* 59 (1993): 3–30.

46. Manfred Berg, "Black Civil Rights and Liberal Anticommunism: The NAACP and the Early Cold War," *Journal of American History* 94, no. 1 (June 2007), 78.

47. Irving Howe and Louis Coser, *The American Communist Party: A Critical History* (Boston: Beacon Press, 1957), 12–19.

48. Earl Ofari Hutchinson, *Blacks and Reds: Race and Conflict, 1919–1990* (East Lansing: Michigan State University Press, 1995), 9.

49. *Worker's Council* 1 (December 15, 1921); Hutchinson, *Blacks and Reds*, 9.

50. Hutchinson, *Blacks and Reds*, 10.

51. Ibid., 9–10.

52. For an excellent recent account of this history of exclusion, see Paul Frymer, *Black and Blue: African Americans, the Labor Movement, and the Decline of the Democratic Party* (Princeton: Princeton University Press, 2007), 1–44.

53. Hutchinson, *Blacks and Reds*, 10–11; Phillip S. Foner, *Organized Labor and the Black Worker, 1619–1973* (New York: Praeger, 1974), 154–56.

54. Foner, *Organized Labor and the Black Worker*, 154–56.

55. Abram L. Harris, "Negro Labor's Quarrel with White Workingmen," *Current History* 21 (September 1926): 903.

56. Foner, *Organized Labor and the Black Worker*, 155–57.

57. Hutchinson, *Blacks and Reds*, 11–12.

58. Note that the disappointment that many black workers felt with their treatment at the hands of mainstream labor did not translate into large gains for the CP-USA.

59. Theodore Draper, *American Communism and Soviet Russia* (New York: Viking Press, 1969), 18–22.

60. Ibid.

61. Berg, "Black Civil Rights and Liberal Anticommunism," 79.

62. Ibid.

63. Hutchinson, *Blacks and Reds*, 13.

64. *New York Amsterdam News*, January 3, 1923.

65. Hutchinson, *Blacks and Reds*, 15.

66. *Baltimore Afro-American*, August 11, 1922.

67. Claude McKay, *Crisis* 23 (December 1922): 65.

68. Claude McKay, *A Long Way from Home* (New York: Lee Furman, 1937), 160–65.

69. W. E. B. Du Bois, "The Class Struggle," *Crisis* 22 (August 1921): 151.

70. Berg, "Black Civil Rights and Liberal Anticommunism," 79.

71. Ibid.

72. Hutchinson, *Blacks and Reds*, 16–17.

73. Ibid.

74. Ibid., 17.

75. Ibid.

76. Ibid., 18.

77. "President General's Reply," Garvey and UNIA Papers, 3: 681, quoted in *Negro World*, August 27, 1921.

78. Colin Grant, *Negro with a Hat: The Rise and Fall of Marcus Garvey* (New York: Oxford University Press, 2008), 310–11.

79. Hutchinson, *Blacks and Reds*, 18.

80. Ibid., 19.

81. Ibid.

82. Ibid.

83. Ibid., 20.

84. Ibid., 19.

85. Robert Minor, quoted in ibid.

86. *New York Times*, January 17, 1926.

87. Hutchinson, *Blacks and Reds*, 23.

88. Ibid.

89. Ibid., 118.

90. Ibid.

91. Ibid.

92. Berg, "Black Civil Rights and Liberal Anticommunism," 79.

93. Ibid.

94. Quoted in ibid.

95. Quoted in ibid.
96. Hutchinson, *Blacks and Reds*, 118.
97. Ibid.
98. Berg, "Black Civil Rights and Liberal Anticommunism," 80.
99. M. J. Heale, *American Anti-Communism: Combating the Enemy Within, 1830–1970* (Baltimore: Johns Hopkins University Press, 1990), 124–25.
100. Ibid., 124.
101. Ibid.
102. "'Treason' in Strike Is Laid to Murphy," *New York Times*, October 22, 1938; Sidney Olson, "Judge Is Dies; Witness Raises Politics Issue; Reds Rush Denials," *Washington Post*, October 22, 1938.
103. Sidney Olson, "Roosevelt Calls Dies Quiz Unfair," *Washington Post*, October 26, 1938; "The Dies Committee," *Washington Post*, October 27, 1938; "Good Logic—Apply It," *Wall Street Journal*, October 27, 1938.
104. See, for example, "Roosevelt Condemns Dies Group," *Atlanta Daily World*, October 26, 1938.
105. "Weekly Topic," *Chicago Defender*, December 10, 1938.
106. Ibid.
107. Hutchinson, *Blacks and Reds*, 129–31.
108. R. J. Burgess, "Letter to the Editor," *Chicago Defender*, July 1, 1933, 15.
109. "Treat Negro as Equal or Make Him a Radical," *Pittsburgh Courier*, March 21, 1931, 15.
110. "Mr. White on Communism," *Chicago Defender*, January 16, 1932, 14.
111. "Making a Fertile Field," *Chicago Defender*, August 2, 1930, 14.
112. Dudziak, *Cold War Civil Rights*, 9–13; Borstelmann, *Cold War*, 45–48.
113. Harry S. Truman, "Lincoln Memorial Speech," *Public Papers of the United States: Harry S. Truman, Containing the Public Messages, Speeches, and Statements of the President, January 1 to December 31, 1947* (Washington, D.C.: U.S. Government Printing Office, 1947), 311–13; *New York Times*, June 30, 1947.
114. Harry S. Truman, "Special Message to the Congress on Civil Rights," February 2, 1948, *Public Papers of the United States: Harry S. Truman, Containing the Public Messages, Speeches, and Statements of the President, 1948* (Washington, D.C.: U.S. Government Printing Office, 1964), 121–26.
115. Harry S. Truman, "Establishing the President's Committee on Equality of Treatment and Opportunity in the Armed Services, Executive Order 9981," *Federal Register* 13, July 26, 1948, 4313.
116. Robert Zangrando, *The NAACP Crusade against Lynching, 1909–1950* (Philadelphia: Temple University Press, 1980), 201–2; Dudziak, *Cold War Civil Rights*, 87–89; Borstelmann, *Cold War*, 65–69.
117. Dudziak, *Cold War Civil Rights*, 89–90.
118. Richard T. Rutten, *Quest and Response: Minority Rights and the Truman Administration* (Lawrence: University of Kansas Press, 1973), 261–64; Dudziak, *Cold War Civil Rights*, 67.
119. For excellent treatments of the political context and the internal dynamics of the Warren Court leading up to the *Brown v. Board of Education* ruling, see Richard Kluger, *Simple Justice: The History of Brown v. Board of Education and the Black Struggle for Equality* (New York: Vintage Books, 2004); Michael Klarman, *Brown v. Board of Education and the Civil Rights Movement* (New York: Oxford University Press, 2007).
120. Mary Dudziak, "Desegregation as a Cold War Imperative," *Stanford Law Review* 41 (November 1988): 61–120; Philip A. Klinkner and Rogers Smith, *The Unsteady March: The Rise and Decline of Racial Equality in America* (Chicago: University of Chicago Press, 1999), 202–42.

121. Dudziak, *Cold War Civil Rights*, 102–7.

122. Harold R. Isaacs, "World Affairs and U.S. Race Relations: A Note on Little Rock," *Public Opinion Quarterly* 22 (1958): 364–70; Mary Dudziak, "The Little Rock Crisis and Foreign Affairs: Race, Resistance, and the Image of American Democracy," *Southern California Law Review* 70 (1997): 1641–716; Cary Fraser, "Crossing the Color Line in Little Rock: The Eisenhower Administration and the Dilemma of Race for U.S. Foreign Policy," *Diplomatic History* (2000): 233–64; Dudziak, *Cold War Civil Rights*, 115–52.

123. Horne, *Black and Red*, 201–22; Von Eschen, *Race against Empire*, 107–9; Dudziak, *Cold War Civil Rights*, 43–46, 67; Borstelmann, *Cold War*, 85–134; Meriwether, *Proudly We Can Be Africans*, 82–87.

124. Horne, *Black and Red*, 41–73; Von Eschen, *Race against Empire*, 114–18, 146–50.

125. Thomas J. Noer, *Cold War and Black Liberation: The United States and White Rule in Africa, 1948–1968* (Columbia: University of Missouri Press, 1985), 144–54; Thomas Borstelmann, *Apartheid's Reluctant Uncle: The United States and Southern Africa in the Early Cold War* (New York: Oxford University Press, 1993).

126. Von Eschen, *Race against Empire*, 118.

127. Ibid.

128. See, for example, Aaron Wildavsky, "The Two Presidencies," *Transaction* 4, no. 2 (1996): 7–14; John Spanier and Eric M. Uslaner, *How Foreign Policy Is Made* (New York: Praeger, 1974), 28–54.

129. Anthony Downs, *Inside Bureaucracy* (Boston: Little, Brown, 1967); William A. Niskanen Jr., *Bureaucracy and Representative Government* (Chicago: Aldine-Atherton, 1971); Kenneth Meier, *Politics and Bureaucracy: Policymaking in the Fourth Branch of Government* (North Scituate, Mass., 1979); James Q. Wilson, *Bureaucracy* (New York: Basic Books, 1989).

130. Daniel P. Carpenter, *The Forging of Bureaucratic Autonomy: Reputations, Networks, and Policy Innovation in Executive Agencies, 1862–1928* (Princeton: Princeton University Press, 2001).

131. Theodore Sorenson, *Kennedy* (London: Hodder and Stoughton, 1965), 96.

132. Noer, *Cold War and Black Liberation*, 63, 67; David Halberstam, *The Best and the Brightest* (New York: Random House, 1972), 99–101.

133. Sorenson, *Kennedy*, 96.

134. Noer, *Cold War and Black Liberation*, 63–65; Whitney W. Schneidman, *Engaging Africa: Washington and the Fall of Portugal's Colonial Empire* (Lanham: University Press of America, 2004), 19–21.

135. Report of the Task Force on the Portuguese Territories in Africa, July 12, 1961, NSF: Angola, Box 5, John Fitzgerald Kennedy Library, Boston, Mass. [hereafter JFKL]; Noer, *Cold War and Black Liberation*, 79–81; Rusk to American Embassy Lisbon, July 28, 1961, NSF: Angola, Box 5, JFKL.

136. Quoted in *New York Times*, October 26, 1961, 16.

137. Abram Chayes, Legal Advisor, Department of State, Oral History Interview, transcript, JFKL; Jean Edward Smith, *The Defense of Berlin* (Baltimore: Johns Hopkins University Press, 1963), 240–47; Arthur Schlesinger, *A Thousand Days: John F. Kennedy in the White House* (Boston: Houghton Mifflin, 1965), 383–84.

138. Noer, *Cold War and Black Liberation*, 65.

139. Bundy to Johnson, July 28, 1961, NSF: Africa, Box 2, JFKL.

140. See, for example, G. Mennen Williams to Kenneth Holland, January 24, 1960, Williams Papers, Box 1, National Archives and Records Administration [hereafter NARA], College Park, Md. See also Vernon McKay, "A Tribute to Governor Williams," *Report of the Fifth Annual Meeting of the African Studies Association*, special issue of *African Studies Bulletin* 5, no. 4 (1962): 2–5.

141. John Abernathy, Special Assistant to G. Mennen Williams, to Williams, May 29, 1962, Williams Papers, Box 1, NARA, College Park, Md.
142. "Advisory Council Meeting," June 13 and 14, 1962, Williams Papers, Box 15, NARA, College Park, Md.
143. Ibid., 5–57; Paula P. Pfeffer, *A. Philip Randolph: Pioneer of the Civil Rights Movement* (Baton Rouge: Louisiana State University Press, 1990), 142, 150, 152.
144. George Houser, "Summary of Meeting Held on May 16 on Afro-American Leadership Conference on American Policy toward Africa," May 22, 1962, Records of the NAACP, Box A198, Library of Congress, Washington, D.C. For evidence of Houser's use of the PACA proceedings to mobilize black leaders, see Minutes of the Steering Committee of the American Committee on Africa, June 20, 1962, A. Philip Randolph Papers, Box 1, Library of Congress, Washington, D.C.
145. John Morsell, NAACP staff member, to Roy Wilkins, July 23, 1962, Records of the NAACP, Box A198, Library of Congress, Washington, D.C.; Call Committee of the ANLCA to Black Leaders, August 21, 1962, Records of the NAACP, Box A198, Library of Congress, Washington, D.C. See also George Houser, *No One Can Stop the Rain: Glimpses of Africa's Liberation Struggle* (New York: Pilgrim Press, 1989), 266.
146. Dorothy Height, *Open Wide the Freedom Gates* (New York: Public Affairs Books, 2003), 230–31.
147. *New York Times*, November 24, November 25, November 26, and December 2, 1962; ANLCA "Resolutions," NAACP-ANLCA, Box A198, Library of Congress, Washington, D.C., November 23, 1962. See also Roy Wilkins, "Keynote Address before the ANLCA Conference," November 23, 1962, 1–3, NAACP-ANLCA, Box A198, Library of Congress, Washington, D.C.
148. *New York Times*, November 26, 1962.
149. ANLCA, "Resolutions," NAACP-ANLCA, Box A194, Library of Congress, Washington, D.C., November 23, 1962; Roy Wilkins to Kennedy, November 26, 1962, Records of the NAACP, Box A194, Library of Congress, Washington, D.C.
150. G. Mennen Williams to Roy Wilkins, December 1, 1962, Williams Papers, Box 16, NARA, College Park, Md.
151. Williams to Dean Rusk, December 3, 1962, Williams Papers, Box 16, NARA, College Park, Md.
152. Theodore Brown, Executive Director of the ANLCA, to Call Committee Members, March 29, 1963, NAACP-ANLCA, Box A194, Library of Congress, Washington, D.C.
153. Williams to Robert Manning, April 22, 1963, Williams Papers, Box 16, NARA, College Park, Md.
154. J. Wayne Fredericks to Dean Rusk, June 6, 1963, and Williams to Rusk, June 7, 1963, Williams Papers, Box 16, NARA, College Park, Md.

CHAPTER 4. "THE TIME FOR FREEDOM HAS COME"

1. Brian Urquhardt, *Ralph Bunche: An American Life* (New York: W. W. Norton, 1993), 339.
2. "Riot in Gallery Halts UN Debate," *New York Times*, February 16, 1961; James H. Meriwether, *Proudly We Can Be Africans: Black Americans and Africa, 1935–1961* (Chapel Hill: University of North Carolina Press, 2002), 233.
3. "Angry African Students Storm Embassies," *Chicago Defender*, February 15, 1961; "Belgium and United States Key Targets in Protests of Lumumba's Slaying in Congo," *Atlanta Daily World*, February 15, 1961.
4. "Riot in Gallery Halts UN Debate"; "UN Rioting Laid to Pro-Africans," *New York Times*, February 16, 1961; "The Disgraceful Spectacle at the UN," *Atlanta Daily World*, February 17, 1961.

5. Brenda Gayle Plummer, *Rising Wind: Black Americans and U.S. Foreign Affairs, 1935–1960* (Chapel Hill: University of North Carolina Press, 1996), 302–3; Meriwether, *Proudly We Can Be Africans*, 234.

6. "Negroes Picket U.N. without Riots," *Washington Post*, February 17, 1961; Meriwether, *Proudly We Can Be Africans*, 234.

7. "Riot in Gallery Halts UN Debate," 1.

8. UPI wire report, quoted in Meriwether, *Proudly We Can Be Africans*, 233.

9. "Negroes Picket U.N. without Riots," A12.

10. "Hoodlums," *New York Times*, February 17, 1961.

11. "Negroes Picket U.N. without Riots," A12.

12. Urquhardt, *Ralph Bunche*, 37–64; Charles P. Henry, *Ralph Bunche: Model Negro or American Other?* (New York: New York University Press, 1999), 48–65.

13. "U.N. Offices Remain under Heavy Guard," *Washington Post*, February 18, 1961, A6.

14. "Riots in Gallery Halts UN Debate."

15. "NAACP Press Release," February 16, 1961, Series A, Box 34, Library of Congress, Washington, D.C.

16. Meriwether, *Proudly We Can Be Africans*, 234.

17. P. L. Prattis, "Horizon," *Pittsburgh Courier*, March 4, 1961, A9.

18. James L. Hicks, "The Apologists," *New York Amsterdam News*, February 25, 1961, 8.

19. Ibid.

20. Warren Hall, "An Old Trick," *New York Amsterdam News*, March 25, 1961, 11.

21. Grace Johnson, "At Long Last!" *New York Amsterdam News*, April 1, 1961.

22. D. Parker, "He Can't Wait," *New York Amsterdam News*, April 1, 1961, 8.

23. Meriwether, *Proudly We Can Be Africans*, 235.

24. Manning Marable, *Race, Reform, and Rebellion: The Second Reconstruction in Black America* (Jackson: University of Mississippi Press, 1984), 95–108; Meriwether, *Proudly We Can Be Africans*, 148–49.

25. Stanley Crouch, *The Artificial White Man: Essays on Authenticity* (New York: Basic Civitas, 2005).

26. "Board of Directors Minutes," February 13, 1945, Records of the NAACP, Series II, Box A135, Library of Congress, Washington, D.C.; W. E. B. Du Bois to Roy Wilkins, February 28, 1945, Records of the NAACP, Series II, Box A240, Library of Congress, Washington, D.C.; Gerald Horne, *Black and Red: W.E.B Du Bois and the Afro-American Response to the Cold War, 1944–1963* (Albany: State University of New York Press, 1985), 27–28.

27. Horne, *Black and Red*, 28–30; Plummer, *Rising Wind*, 133; Penny Von Eschen, *Race against Empire: Black Americans and Anti-Colonialism* (Ithaca: Cornell University Press, 1997), 76–77.

28. Horne, *Black and Red*, 28–30; Von Eschen, *Race against Empire*, 76–77.

29. W. E. B. Du Bois, "San Francisco," *Crisis*, June 1945; Horne, *Black and Red*, 33–39; Plummer, *Rising Wind*, 125–65.

30. W. E. B. Du Bois, "A Forum of Fact and Opinion," *Pittsburgh Courier*, April 25, 1936.

31. David Levering Lewis, *W.E.B. Du Bois: The Fight for Equality and the American Century, 1919–1963* (New York: Henry Holt, 2000), 420–27.

32. Ibid., 511–15.

33. W. E. B. Du Bois, "Pan-African Movement," April–May 1945, Spingarn Papers, Box 30, Library of Congress, Washington, D.C.; Meriwether, *Proudly We Can Be Africans*, 66.

34. "Board of Directors Minutes," April 9, 1945, Records of the NAACP, Series II, Box A135, Library of Congress, Washington, D.C.

35. "Minutes of the Pan-African Congress Meeting," July 12, 1945, Records of the NAACP, Series II, Box A6, Library of Congress, Washington, D.C.

36. Ibid.

37. Ibid.

38. Walter White to W. E. B. Du Bois, July 31, 1945, Records of the NAACP, Series II, Box A135, Library of Congress, Washington, D.C.

39. "Board of Directors Minutes," September 10, 1945, Records of the NAACP, Series II, Box A241, Library of Congress, Washington, D.C.

40. W. E. B. Du Bois to Walter White, November 14, 1946, Records of the NAACP, Series A, Box 241, Library of Congress, Washington, D.C.

41. Plummer, *Rising Wind*; Von Eschen, *Race against Empire*; Mary Dudziak, *Cold War Civil Rights: Race and the Image of American Democracy* (Princeton: Princeton University Press, 2000); Thomas Borstelmann, *The Cold War and the Color Line: American Race Relations in the Global Arena* (Cambridge, Mass.: Harvard University Press, 2001).

42. Meriwether, *Proudly We Can Be Africans*, 1–10, 200–207.

43. Robert Weisbord, *Ebony Kinship: Africa, Africans, and the Afro-American* (Westport, Conn.: Greenwood Press, 1973), 181–86; P. Olisanwuche Esedebe, *Pan-Africanism: From Idea to Movement, 1776–1963* (Washington, D.C.: Howard University Press, 1982), 76–82.

44. Plummer, *Rising Wind*, 72–73, 218–20.

45. Ibid., 28–29.

46. The analysis was generated by two coders working independently to screen news content related to India and Ghana for expressions of linked-fate. The intercoder reliability was 94 percent. In the 6 percent of cases in which the coders did not agree on whether the item contained an expression of linked fate, I adjudicated the disagreement by serving as a third coder.

47. Coretta Scott King, *My Life with Martin Luther King, Jr.* (New York: Holt, Rhinehart, and Winston, 1969), 155.

48. The analysis was generated by two coders working independently to screen news content related to Ethiopia and Ghana for characterizations that portrayed these nations as "primitive," "savage," "uncivilized," "barbarous," or some similar construction. The intercoder reliability for this study was 98 percent. In the 2 percent of cases in which the coders did not agree on whether the item contained such content, I adjudicated the disagreement by serving as a third coder.

49. Martin Meredith, *In the Name of Apartheid: South Africa in the Post-War Period* (London: Hamilton, 1988), 54–56.

50. Leo Kuper, *Passive Resistance in South Africa* (New Haven: Yale University Press, 1957), 99–106.

51. Ibid., 106–11.

52. For an excellent brief summary of the interactions between the government and the protesters, see Meriwether, *Proudly We Can Be Africans*, 103–6.

53. Ibid., 104.

54. Ibid.

55. Ibid., 106.

56. Thomas Karis, *From Protest to Challenge: A Documentary History of African Politics in South Africa, 1882–1990* (Pretoria: UNISA Press, 1997), 484–86.

57. Thomas Borstelmann, *Apartheid's Reluctant Uncle: The United States and Southern Africa in the Early Cold War* (New York: Oxford University Press, 1993), 77–80.

58. Robert B. Edgerton, *Mau Mau: An African Crucible* (New York: The Free Press, 1989), 63–66.

59. David Throup, *Economic and Social Origins of the Mau Mau, 1945–1953* (Athens: Ohio University Press, 1988), 3–11.

60. Edgerton, *Mau Mau*, 1–41.
61. Throup, *Economic and Social Origins*, 3–11.
62. Wunyabari Maloba, *Mau Mau and Kenya: An Analysis of a Peasant Revolt* (Bloomington: Indiana University Press, 1993), 24–44.
63. Ibid., 45–59.
64. Edgerton, *Mau Mau*, 41–68.
65. Maloba, *Mau Mau and Kenya*, 70–77.
66. Ibid., 81–85; Edgerton, *Mau Mau*, 105–6.
67. Adam Hochschild, *King Leopold's Ghost: A Story of Greed, Terror, and Heroism in Colonial Africa* (New York: Houghton-Mifflin, 1999), 1–46.
68. Ibid.
69. Ibid.; Roger Anstey, *King Leopold's Legacy: The Congo under Belgian Rule, 1908–1960* (London: Oxford University Press, 1966), 1–36; Meriwether, *Proudly We Can Be Africans*, 210.
70. Meriwether, *Proudly We Can Be Africans*, 210.
71. Ibid.
72. Donald Young, *Politics in the Congo: Decolonization and Independence* (Princeton: Princeton University Press, 1965), 297–300; Thomas Kanza, *The Rise and Fall of Patrice Lumumba: Conflict in the Congo* (Boston: G. K. Hall, 1972), 33–40.
73. Kanza, *Rise and Fall*, 152–64. Young, *Politics in the Congo*, 307–57.
74. Kanza, *Rise and Fall*, 162–64.
75. Ibid., 173–78.
76. Ibid., 182–94.
77. Meriwether, *Proudly We Can Be Africans*, 216–17.
78. Kanza, *Rise and Fall*, 236–60.
79. Meriwether, *Proudly We Can Be Africans*, 218–19.
80. Kanza, *Rise and Fall*, 265–324.
81. See, for example, Plummer, *Rising Wind*, 167–217.
82. "An Important Message from Paul Robeson," *Spotlight on Africa*, February 25, 1952.
83. "Harlem Speaks for South African Freedom," *Spotlight on Africa*, April 14, 1952; "Harlemites Picket for South Africa's Freedom," *Atlanta Daily World*, April 8, 1952.
84. "An Important Message from Paul Robeson," 1.
85. William Alphaeus Hunton to Reverend Donald Harrington, March 21, 1952, William Alphaeus Hunton Papers [hereafter Hunton Papers], Box 1, Schomburg Center for Research in Black Culture, New York Public Library, New York [hereafter NYPL].
86. George Houser to William Alphaeus Hunton, March 28, 1952, Hunton Papers, Box 1, Schomburg Center for Research in Black Culture, NYPL.
87. "Harlemites Protest," *New York Amsterdam News*, April 5, 1952.
88. Ibid.
89. Mary McLeod Bethune, "Words of South African Racists Are Compared with Hitler's Mein Kampf," *Chicago Defender*, July 26, 1952, 10. See also Meriwether, *Proudly We Can Be Africans*, 113.
90. Bethune, "Words of South African Racists," 10.
91. "Powell Asks Cut in Aid to Kenya," *Baltimore Afro-American*, July 11, 1953, 8.
92. "Resolution on Kenya," Brotherhood of Sleeping Car Porters to the AFL Annual Convention, September 1953, Box 123, Brotherhood of Sleeping Car Porters Papers, Library of Congress, Washington, D.C.
93. Ibid.
94. A. Philip Randolph to President Dwight David Eisenhower, June 17, 1953, *Foreign Relations of the United States, 1952–1954* (Washington, D.C.: U.S. Government Printing Office, 1955), 2:42–43.

95. "Resolution on Kenya," Records of the NAACP, 1, 1951–1955 supplement, 8/233, 12/239-40, Library of Congress, Washington, D.C.

96. Meriwether, *Proudly We Can Be Africans*, 137.

97. Thomas J. Noer, "Segregationists and the World: The Foreign Policy of White Resistance," in *Window on Freedom: Race, Civil Rights, and Foreign Affairs, 1945–1988*, ed. Brenda Gayle Plummer (Chapel Hill: University of North Carolina Press, 2003), 141–63.

98. "Nixon, Powell, Diggs to Ghana Celebration," *New York Amsterdam News*, February 16, 1957; Ethel Payne, "World's Notables See Ghana Born," *Chicago Defender*, March 9, 1957.

99. Ethel L. Payne, "King Gets Bid to DC from Nixon in Accra," *Chicago Defender*, March 6, 1957.

100. A. P. Randolph, "Can Ghana Make It?" *New York Amsterdam News*, March 30, 1957, 1.

101. Ibid.

102. Ibid.

103. Quoted in "Ghana, with Eventful Past, Looks Forward to the Future," *Atlanta Daily World*, March 13, 1957, 2.

104. Stan Grant, "King Asks Nixon's Aid in Ghana," *New York Amsterdam News*, March 9, 1957; Payne, "King Gets Bid."

105. See Gerald Gill, "Ain't Gonna Shuffle No More," in *The Eyes on the Prize*, ed. Clayborne Carson, David J. Garrow, Gerald Gill, Vincent Harding, and Darlene Clark Hine (New York: Penguin Books, 1987), 442–43; Marable, *Race, Reform, and Rebellion*, 97–99; Harold Cruse, *Rebellion or Revolution?* (New York: William Morrow, 1968), 206–7, 213–15; Debbie Louis, *We Are Not Saved: A History of the Movement as People* (Garden City, N.Y.: Anchor Press, 1970), 296–97.

CHAPTER 5. "WE ARE A POWER BLOC"

1. See, for example, Robert Singh, *The Congressional Black Caucus: Racial Politics in the U.S. Congress* (Thousand Oaks: Russell Sage, 1998), 70–95; Katherine Tate, *Black Faces in the Mirror: African Americans and Their Representatives in the U.S. Congress* (Princeton: Princeton University Press, 2003), 73–96.

2. Indeed, this incident was only the second time in the twentieth century that Congress took such action. See Gary L. Galemore, "Congressional Overrides of Presidential Vetoes," Congressional Research Service, Report 95-1137, Washington, D.C., October 16, 1996, 1. For an account of how the potential of an override created deep anxieties in the Reagan administration, see Chester A. Crocker, *High Noon in Southern Africa: Making Peace in a Rough Neighborhood* (New York: W. W. Norton, 1992), 329.

3. Alvin B. Tillery Jr., "Black Americans and the Creation of America's Africa Policies: The De-Racialization of Pan-African Politics," in *The African Diaspora: Old World Origins and New World Self-Fashioning*, ed. Carol Boyce Davies, Isidore Okpewho, and Ali Mazrui (Bloomington: Indiana University Press, 1999), 526–53.

4. Yossi Shain, *Marketing the American Creed Abroad: Diasporas in the U.S. and Their Homelands* (New York: Cambridge University Press, 1999), 163–64; Tony Smith, *Foreign Attachments: The Power of Ethnic Groups in the Making of American Foreign Policy* (Cambridge, Mass.: Harvard University Press, 2000), 71–72; Ronald Walters, "The African Growth and Opportunity Act: Changing Foreign Policy Priorities toward Africa in a Conservative Political Culture," in *Foreign Policy and the Black (Inter)national Interest*, ed. Charles Henry (Albany: SUNY Press, 2000), 17–37.

5. Ronald Walters, "African-American Influence on U.S. Foreign Policy toward South Africa," in *Ethnic Groups and U.S. Foreign Policy*, ed. Mohammed E. Ahrani (New York: Greenwood, 1987), 65–83; Hanes Walton, *African American Power and Politics: The*

Political Context Variable (New York: Columbia University Press), 352–69; Smith, *Foreign Attachments*, 61–63.

6. For an excellent discussion of this method, see Beth Leech, "Asking Questions: Techniques for Semi-Structured Interviews," *PS: Political Science and Politics* 35, No. 4 (2002): 665–68.

7. See, for example, Kenny Whitby, *The Color of Representation: Congressional Behavior and Black Interests* (Ann Arbor: University of Michigan Press, 1997), 86–87; Tate, *Black Faces in the Mirror*, 37–40. For other works in which this assumption is implicit, see Carol M. Swain, *Black Faces, Black Interests: The Representation of African Americans in Congress* (Cambridge, Mass.: Harvard University Press, 1993); David T. Cannon, *Race, Redistricting, and Representation: The Unintended Consequences of Black Majority Districts* (Chicago: University of Chicago Press, 1999); David Lublin, *The Paradox of Representation: Racial Gerrymandering and Minority Interests in Congress* (Princeton: Princeton University Press, 1999).

8. Quoted in Marguerite Ross Barnett, "The Congressional Black Caucus," in *Congress against the President*, ed. Harvey Mansfield Sr. (New York: Praeger, 1975), 35.

9. Quoted in ibid.

10. William L. Clay Sr., *Just Permanent Interests: Black Americans in Congress* (New York: Amistad Press, 1993), 117.

11. See, for example, Richard F. Fenno, *Congressmen in Committees* (Boston: Little, Brown, 1973), xiii–xvii; David R. Mayhew, *Congress: The Electoral Connection* (New Haven: Yale University Press, 1974), 87–97, 92–97; Kenneth A. Shepsle, *The Giant Jigsaw Puzzle: Democratic Committee Assignments in the Modern House* (Chicago: University of Chicago Press, 1978).

12. Mayhew, *Congress*, 13.

13. Nelson Polsby, Miriam Gallaher, and Barry S. Rundquist, "The Growth of the Seniority System in the U.S. House of Representatives," *American Political Science Review* 63 (September 1969): 787–807; David Rohde, *Parties and Leaders in the Post-Reform House* (Chicago: University of Chicago Press, 1991), 5. For a statement of the importance of cracking the seniority system for the long-term success of the CBC, see Lucius J. Barker and Jesse McCorry Jr., *Black Americans and the Political System* (Cambridge, Mass.: Winthrop Publishers, 1976), 299–301.

14. Shepsle, *Giant Jigsaw Puzzle*, 112–28; See also Barbara Sinclair, *Majority Leadership in the U.S. House* (Baltimore: Johns Hopkins University Press, 1983), 1–3, 22–23.

15. James Buchanan and Gordon Tullock, *The Calculus of Consent* (Ann Arbor: University of Michigan Press, 1962), 144–46; Fenno, *Congressmen in Committees*, 58, 165–66; James T. Murphy, "Political Parties and the Pork Barrel: Party Conflict and Cooperation in House Public Works Committee Decision Making," *American Political Science Review* 68 (March 1974): 169–85.

16. Dianne Pinderhughes, *Race, Ethnicity and Chicago Politics* (Urbana: University of Illinois Press, 1987), 267.

17. For an account of how Oscar De Priest began the tradition of challenging segregation within the institution of Congress, see "De Priest Jolts Congress," *Chicago Defender*, March 31, 1934, 10. On Adam Clayton Powell's efforts to overturn these rules, see Singh, *Congressional Black Caucus*, 73; Charles V. Hamilton, *Adam Clayton Powell, Jr.: The Political Biography of an American Dilemma* (New York: Macmillan, 1991), 178, 186–87.

18. Singh, *Congressional Black Caucus*, 79–84; Tate, *Black Faces in the Mirror*, 108.

19. Telephone interview with the Honorable William L. Clay Sr. (D-Mo.), member of Congress 1968–2000, May 12, 2002. See also Clay, *Just Permanent Interests*, 174–81; Nadine Cohodas, "Black House Members Striving for Influence," *Congressional Quarterly Weekly Report*, April 13, 1985, 675–81.

20. Telephone interview with Clay.

21. Alex Poinsett, "The Congressional Black Caucus: Five Years Later," in *Black Americans and the Political System*, ed. Lucius Barker and Jesse McCorry Jr. (Cambridge, Mass.: Winthrop Publishers, 1976), 291.

22. Swain, *Black Faces, Black Interests*, 167.

23. Ibid., 218.

24. Robert Dahl, *Congress and Foreign Policy* (New York: Harcourt, Brace, 1950), 10–23.

25. Ibid., 13.

26. Ibid., 58.

27. Ibid., 13–14.

28. Fenno, *Congressmen in Committees*, 9–13.

29. Ibid.

30. Hamilton, *Adam Clayton Powell, Jr.*, 178, 186–87.

31. Wil Haygood, *King of the Cats: The Life and Times of Adam Clayton Powell, Jr.* (Boston: Houghton-Mifflin, 1993), 113.

32. Clay, *Just Permanent Interests*, 75–76; ibid., 117.

33. Swain, *Black Faces, Black Interests*, 34–35.

34. Quoted in Edward T. Clayton, *The Negro Politician: His Success and Failure* (Chicago: Johnson Publishing, 1964), 73.

35. James Q. Wilson, "Two Negro Politicians: An Interpretation," *Midwest Journal of Political Science* 4 (1960), 346–39; Hamilton, *Adam Clayton Powell, Jr.*, 480–81; Singh, *Congressional Black Caucus*, 47; Tate, *Black Faces in the Mirror*, 126.

36. The importance of the Chicago machine within the national Democratic Party forced the southerners who dominated the Committee on Committees to allow Dawson to become the first black person to chair a standing committee in the history of the House of Representatives. See Wilson, "Two Negro Politicians," 356–59.

37. Hamilton, *Adam Clayton Powell, Jr.*, 139–199, 480–81; Singh, *Congressional Black Caucus*, 47–48.

38. Hamilton, *Adam Clayton Powell, Jr.*, 175–99.

39. Ibid., 332–38.

40. Ibid., 259–313.

41. Interview with Randall Robinson, president of TransAfrica and former legislative aide to Representative Charles Diggs, April 23, 1998, Washington, D.C. See also Randall Robinson, *Defending the Spirit: A Black Life in America* (New York: Dutton Press, 1998), 90–94; Clay, *Just Permanent Interests*, 86–87.

42. Black Americans in the middle of the twentieth century used the phrase *race man* to describe someone who championed the causes of the black race before white Americans. St. Clair Drake and Horace Cayton provide the first serious interrogation of the importance of the phrase as a cultural and political construct in the black community; see their *Black Metropolis: A Study in the Life of a Northern City* (New York: Harcourt Brace, 1945), 390–92. For an excellent meditation on the importance of the concept, see Hazel Carby, *Race Men* (Cambridge, Mass.: Harvard University Press, 1998).

43. Haygood, *King of the Cats*, 195; Carolyn P. Du Bose, *Charles Diggs: The Untold Story* (Arlington, Va.: Barton Publishing, 1998), 40–43, 79.

44. Brenda Gayle Plummer, *Rising Wind: Black Americans and U.S. Foreign Affairs, 1935–1960* (Chapel Hill: University of North Carolina Press, 1996), 247.

45. Adam Clayton Powell Jr., *Adam by Adam: The Autobiography of Adam Clayton Powell, Jr.* (New York: Dial Press, 1971), 102–6.

46. Adam Clayton Powell Jr. to Maxwell Rabb, Secretary to the Cabinet, February 2, 1955, Central Files, Dwight David Eisenhower Library, Abilene, Kansas [hereafter DDEL].

See also Powell, *Adam by Adam*, 103–5; Hamilton, *Adam Clayton Powell, Jr.*, 241; Haygood, *King of the Cats*, 199–200; Plummer, *Rising Wind*, 250.

47. W. K. Scott, Assistant to President Eisenhower, to Maxwell Rabb, February 16, 1955, Central Files, DDEL. See also Hamilton, *Adam Clayton Powell, Jr.*, 245; Haygood, *King of the Cats*, 200; Plummer, *Rising Wind*, 250–51; Penny Von Eschen, *Race against Empire: Black Americans and Anti-Colonialism* (Ithaca: Cornell University Press, 1997), 170; Thomas Borstelmann, *The Cold War and the Color Line: American Race Relations in the Global Arena* (Cambridge, Mass.: Harvard University Press, 2001), 96.

48. Powell and Eisenhower developed a personal fondness for one another and a solid working relationship on civil rights issues during Eisenhower's first year in office. See Powell, *Adam by Adam*, 96–97.

49. Ibid., 103–4; Hamilton, *Adam Clayton Powell, Jr.*, 241–43; Haygood, *King of the Cats*, 201–2; Von Eschen, *Race against Empire*, 170; Plummer, *Rising Wind*, 250; Borstelmann, *Cold War and the Color Line*, 96.

50. Hamilton, *Adam Clayton Powell, Jr.*, 242.

51. Ibid., 243; Haygood, *King of the Cats*, 202–3.

52. Homer Bigart, "Powell Tells Asia about U.S. Negro; Red Newsmen Find Him off the 'Line,'" *New York Herald Tribune*, April 18, 1955.

53. Richard Wright, *The Color Curtain: A Report on the Bandung Conference* (New York: World Publishing, 1956), 177–79; Hamilton, *Adam Clayton Powell, Jr.*, 242–43; Haygood, *King of the Cats*, 203; Von Eschen, *Race against Empire*, 170.

54. "Mr. Powell at Bandung," *Baltimore Afro-American*, April 30, 1955. See also Von Eschen, *Race against Empire*, 171.

55. James L. Hicks, quoted in Von Eschen, *Race against Empire*, 171.

56. Ibid., 171; Hamilton, *Adam Clayton Powell, Jr.*, 248; Haygood, *King of the Cats*, 202–3.

57. Powell, *Adam by Adam*, 118–19.

58. Hamilton, *Adam Clayton Powell, Jr.*, 244.

59. Adam Clayton Powell Jr., "My Mission to Bandung: How Washington Blundered," *Nation*, May 28, 1955, 455; Powell, *Adam by Adam*, 107–8. See also Plummer, *Rising Wind*, 249–53.

60. In the months following the Bandung episode, Powell requested that Eisenhower name him to the official U.S. delegation headed to the Ghanaian independence ceremonies in early 1957. The decision to send the delegation represented a major shift in U.S. strategy vis-à-vis the new states of the Third World. Because his performance at Bandung had played a major role in pushing the administration in this new direction, Powell believed that he was due some official recognition at the event. See Hamilton, *Adam Clayton Powell, Jr.*, 281; Haygood, *King of the Cats*, 224.

61. In my interviews with them, both Representative Clay and Randall Robinson commented to me that Representative Diggs had told them that Powell was instrumental to his developing an internationalist perspective when he entered the Congress in 1955.

62. Thomas J. Noer, *Cold War and Black Liberation: The United States and White Rule in Africa, 1948–1968* (Columbia: University of Missouri Press, 1985), 49; Plummer, *Rising Wind*, 246; Borstelmann, *Cold War and the Color Line*, 109.

63. Haygood, *King of the Cats*, 224; Hamilton, *Adam Clayton Powell, Jr.*, 281–82.

64. The speaker of the House, Representative Sam Rayburn (D-Tex; 1913–1960), blocked Powell's appointment to the delegation by threatening officials at the Department of State with a loss of funding. Rayburn made this move to punish Powell for endorsing Eisenhower in the presidential election of 1956. See Hamilton, *Adam Clayton Powell, Jr.*, 280–81; Haygood, *King of the Cats*, 224.

65. Maxwell Rabb to Sherman Adams, Assistant to President Eisenhower, February 4, 1957, and Sherman Adams to Maxwell Rabb, February 8, 1957, Central File, DDEL; Haygood, *King of the Cats*, 224.

66. Du Bose, *Charles Diggs*, 65.

67. Clay recounted in his interview with me that, when he entered the Congress in 1968, Diggs's colleagues on the Foreign Affairs Committee affectionately referred to him as "Mr. Africa" because of his vast knowledge of the issues in U.S. foreign relations in the region and his campaign to raise the profile of the continent in committee proceedings. See also Singh, *Congressional Black Caucus*, 82; Du Bose, *Charles Diggs*, 122.

68. *New York Times*, February 4, 5, 14, and 15, 1967. See also Dean Rusk, *As I Saw It* (New York: W. W. Norton, 1990), 589–90; Shelly Leanne, "African-American Initiatives against Minority Rule in South Africa: A Politicized Diaspora in World Politics," PhD diss., Oxford University, 1994, 267–68.

69. A number of written accounts substantiate this tradition. See Raymond W. Copson, *The Congressional Black Caucus and Foreign Policy: 1971–1995* (Washington, D.C.: Congressional Research Service, 1996), 6–9; Du Bose, *Charles Diggs*, 96; Ronald Dellums, *Lying Down with the Lions: A Public Life from the Streets of Oakland to the Halls of Power* (Boston: Beacon Press), 122.

70. Telephone interview with Clay.

71. See, for example, Representative Shirley Chisholm (D-N.Y.; 1969–1983), "Remarks on Racism in U.S. Foreign Policy," 91st Congress, *Congressional Record*, 35406.

72. Interview with the Honorable Louis Stokes, member of Congress (D-Ohio), 1969–1998, June 13, 1998, Washington, D.C.

73. Both Fenno and Mayhew believe that members of Congress are primarily interested in engaging in legislative behavior that bolsters their chances for reelection. At the same time, however, their writings acknowledge that members of Congress will sometimes engage in behavior that is less likely help with their reelection in order to make good public policy. See Fenno, *Congressmen in Committees*; Mayhew, *Congress*. Keith Krehbiel, by contrast, sees legislative behavior as driven primarily by a desire to share information within the institution; *Information and Legislative Organization* (Ann Arbor: University of Michigan Press, 1991).

74. The 1969 Nixon administration review of U.S. foreign policy devotes several passages to Diggs's influence on Capitol Hill. See U.S. National Security Council, National Security Study Memorandum 39, Annex 6, 15–16, National Security Archive, George Washington University, Washington, D.C., Document S.A. 00379.

75. Robert Kinloch Massie, *Loosing the Bonds* (New York: Doubleday, 1997), 301–2; Andrew J. DeRoche, "Standing Firm for Principles: Jimmy Carter and Zimbabwe," *Diplomatic History* 23, no. 4 (1999), 662.

76. As it now stands, the literature about this change points only to disagreements over domestic policy issues. See Marguerite Barnett, "The Congressional Black Caucus," in *The New Black Politics: The Search for Political Power*, ed. Michael B. Preston, Paul L. Puryear, and Lenneal J. Henderson (New York: Longman, 1982), 37; Poinsett, "Congressional Black Caucus," 291–93; Singh, *Congressional Black Caucus*, 76–78.

77. Telephone interview with Clay.

78. See, for example, Barnett, "Congressional Black Caucus," 39, 1982 [n. 77]; Singh, *Congressional Black Caucus*, 79–80.

79. The reform movement that swept the House of Representatives in the early 1970s diminished the power of committee chairs. For accounts of the reform movement, see Burton Shepard, *Rethinking Congressional Reform* (Cambridge, Mass.: Schenkman, 1985); Rohde, *Parties and Leaders*, 17–39.

80. Because tight control over the committee system was the primary source of the Dixiecrats' power in the House, these reforms significantly enhanced the ability of CBC members to navigate in the institution. See Singh, *Congressional Black Caucus*, 79–81.

81. Barnett, "Congressional Black Caucus," 37–39, 1982 [n. 77]; Singh, *Congressional Black Caucus*, 76–81; Tate, *Black Faces in the Mirror*, 37–40.

82. Massie, *Loosing the Bonds*, 474.

83. Ibid., 385–86.

84. Charles Diggs, "The Afro-American Stake in Africa," *Africa* (November 1975), 57.

85. Massie, *Loosing the Bonds*, 387, 404–6.

86. Ibid., 386–88.

87. See, for example, Diggs, "Afro-American Stake in Africa," 57.

88. Singh, *Congressional Black Caucus*, 52–54.

89. Philip V. White, "The Black American Constituency for Southern Africa, 1940–1980," in *The American People and South Africa: Public, Elites, and Policy-Making Process*, ed. Alfred O. Hero Jr. and John Barratt (Lexington, Mass.: D.C. Heath), 94–95; Francis N. Nesbitt, *Race for Sanctions: African Americans against Apartheid, 1946–1994* (Bloomington: Indiana University Press, 2004), 98–99.

90. White, "Black American Constituency," 94–95; Sanford J. Ungar, "South Africa in the American Media," in *The American People and South Africa: Public, Elites, and Policy-Making Process*, ed. Alfred O. Hero Jr. and John Barratt (Lexington, Mass.: D.C. Heath), 25–46; Congressional Black Caucus, "The African American Manifesto on Southern Africa," *Freedomways* 16 (1976): 216–21.

91. Telephone interview with Clay.

92. Mayhew, *Congress*, 61–67.

93. Massie, *Loosing the Bonds*, 473, 497–98; Nesbitt, *Race for Sanctions*, 98–110.

94. Interview with Stokes.

95. Massie, *Loosing the Bonds*, 404; Nesbitt, *Race against Sanctions*, 102.

96. Massie, *Loosing the Bonds*, 405.

97. Ibid., 404–6; Nesbitt, *Race for Sanctions*, 97–107; Randall Robinson, *Defending the Spirit: A Black Life in America* (New York: Dutton, 1998).

98. Massie, *Loosing the Bonds*, 405–6.

99. Robinson, *Defending the Spirit*, 90–97. See also Nesbitt, *Race for Sanctions*, 104.

100. Pauline H. Baker, *The United States and South Africa: The Reagan Years* (New York: Ford Foundation-Foreign Policy Association, 1989), 27–30; Massie, *Loosing the Bonds*, 558–60; Nesbitt, *Race for Sanctions*, 105–21.

101. Baker, *United States and South Africa*, 29–30; Massie, *Loosing the Bonds*, 558–60; Nesbitt, *Race for Sanctions*, 123–28.

102. Massie, *Loosing the Bonds*, 560; Nesbitt, *Race for Sanctions*, 124–27.

103. Interview with Robinson.

104. Peter J. Schraeder, *United States Foreign Policy toward Africa: Incrementalism, Crisis and Change* (New York: Cambridge University Press, 1994), 228–31; Baker, *United States and South Africa*, 30–44; Massie, *Loosing the Bonds*, 523–80; Walton, *African American Power and Politics*, 364–65.

105. For more on the role that Representative Dellums played in the sanctions movement, see Dellums, *Lying Down with the Lions*, 121–49; Nesbitt, *Race for Sanctions*, 138, 147–48, 150–51. On Diggs's indictment and exit from Congress, see Massie, *Loosing the Bonds*, 474–75.

106. Telephone interview with the Honorable Ronald V. Dellums (D-Calif.), member of Congress 1969–1998, October 11, 1998. Emphasis in original.

107. Dellums, *Lying Down with the Lions*, 138.

108. The member who lost the reelection was Representative Alton Walton Jr. (D-N.Y.). His loss had nothing to do with his voting record or the fact that he sponsored a sanctions bill. Indeed, Walton, who went to Congress through a special election, served only the last two months of the term of a vacated seat before a slate of more experienced and popular local politicians challenged him in the general election. See Tate, *Black Faces in the Mirror,* 58–59.

109. Telephone interview with Clay.

110. Ibid.

111. Tate, *Black Faces in the Mirror,* 59.

112. Telephone interview with Dellums. For secondary accounts that bolster Dellums's interpretation, see Baker, *United States and South Africa,* 39–44; Massie, *Loosing the Bonds,* 558–619.

113. Telephone interview with Clay.

114. Massie, *Loosing the Bonds,* 597–621; Nesbitt, *Race for Sanctions,* 138–49.

115. Massie, *Loosing the Bonds,* 558–619.

116. Telephone interview with Clay.

117. Nesbitt, *Race for Sanctions,* 150–51.

118. Singh, *Congressional Black Caucus,* 70–95; Tate, *Black Faces in the Mirror,* 73–96.

119. Interview with the Honorable John Lewis (D-Ga.), member of Congress 1987–present, October 11,1997, Washington, D.C.

120. Interview with Mel Foote, president of the Constituency for Africa, May 7, 1998, Washington, D.C.

121. Interview with the Honorable Earl F. Hilliard (D-Ala.), member of Congress 1993–2003, October 10, 1997, Washington, D.C.

122. "Remarks by Representative Jim McDermott (D-WA)," Overseas Development Council, Conference on African Economic Recovery, press release, June 12, 1996, Washington, D.C.; House of Representatives, African Growth and Opportunity Act of 1996, 104th Congress, 2nd Sess., H.R. 4198, *Congressional Record* 142, no. 135, daily ed., September 26, 1996, E1725.

123. William H. Lash III, "Textile Trade Instead of Aid," *Journal of Commerce,* July 7, 1997; John Maggs, "African Trade Bill Faces Fight in Senate," *Journal of Commerce* February 27, 1998; John McCaslin, "Nation: Inside the Beltway," *Washington Times,* July 20, 1999; Heidi Przybyla, "Africa Bill Draws Rally of Supporters," *Journal of Commerce,* March 19, 1999.

124. McCaslin, "Nation."

125. See, for example, Walters, "African Growth and Opportunity Act," 17–37.

126. Representative Sanford Bishop (D-Ga.), 106th Congress, 1st Sess., *Congressional Record* 145, no. 101, House Documents, July 16, 1999, H5708.

127. Interview with Representative Carolyn C. Kilpatrick (D-Mich.), May 14, 1999, Washington, D.C.

128. I conducted a differences of means test using SATA statistical software ver. 9. I compiled the data on the thirty-six congressional districts by merging the Bureau of Labor Statistics aggregate data sets on the economic environment in metropolitan statistical areas and counties. The results of the test are statistically significant at the $P < 0.05$ level.

129. For excellent primers on logistic regression techniques, see Alfred Demaris, *Logit Modeling: Practical Applications* (New York: Russell Sage, 1992); David Hosmer and Stanley Lemeshow, *Applied Logistic Regression* (Danvers, Mass.: John Wiley and Son, 2000).

130. I coded the variables used in the logistic regression analyses as follows: AFLCIO is a continuous variable ranging from 0 to 100 that reflects a ranking of the CBC members' voting records on issues that the AFLCIO deems critical for U.S. labor; %BLACK is

a continuous variable ranging from 0 to 100 that reflects the size of the black population in the districts of CBC members; MEDINCOME is a continuous variable that reflects the median income in the districts of CBC members; MOV1998 is a continuous variable that reflects CBC members' margins of victory in the 1998 midterm election; SOUTHREG is a dummy variable for the southern region (coded 1 for districts in the South and 0 for all others); UNEMPLOYMENT is a continuous variable ranging from 0 to 100 that reflects the size of the jobless population in the districts of CBC members.

131. Hosmer and Lemeshow, *Applied Logistic Regression*, 74–79.

132. Barnett, "Congressional Black Caucus," 1982 [n. 77], 40–50; Poinsett, "Congressional Black Caucus," 291–92; Swain, *Black Faces, Black Interests*, 37–44; Singh, *Congressional Black Caucus*, 74–85; Tate, *Black Faces in the Mirror*, 104–10.

133. Swain, *Black Faces, Black Interests*, 218.

CONCLUSION

1. Louis Gerson, *The Hyphenate in Recent American Politics and Diplomacy* (Lawrence: University of Kansas Press, 1964); Alexander DeConde, *Ethnicity, Race and American Foreign Policy: A History* (Boston: Northeastern University Press, 1992).

2. The meaning of term *transnationalism* is somewhat contested within the social sciences. For insights into this debate, see Stephen Vertovec, "Conceiving and Researching Transnationalism," *Ethnic and Racial Studies* 21, no. 1 (1999): 447–62. Most political scientists subscribe to the view that transnationalism encompasses any political behavior intended to forge or reify the bonds of fealty to a faraway ancestral or adopted homeland. For studies in political science that use this definition, see Samuel P. Huntington, "The Erosion of American National Interests," *Foreign Affairs* 76, no. 5 (1997): 28–50; Yossi Shain, *Marketing the American Creed Abroad: Diasporas in the U.S. and Their Homelands* (New York: Cambridge University Press, 1999); Tony Smith, *Foreign Attachments: The Power of Ethnic Groups in the Making of American Foreign Policy.* (Cambridge, Mass.: Harvard University Press).

3. See, for example, Ronald Walters, "African-American Influence on U.S. Foreign Policy toward South Africa," in *Ethnic Groups and U.S. Foreign Policy*, ed. Mohammed Ahrani (Westport, Conn.: Greenwood Press, 1987), 65–83; Hanes Walton, *African American Power and Politics* (New York: Columbia University Press, 1997), 352–69; Elliott P. Skinner, *African Americans and US Policy toward Africa 1850–1924: In Defense of Black Nationality* (Washington, D.C.: Howard University Press, 1992); Penny Von Eschen, *Race against Empire: Black Americans and Anti-Colonialism* (Ithaca: Cornell University Press, 1997), 69–122; Smith, *Foreign Attachments*, 60–64.

4. Robert D. Putnam, "Diplomacy and Domestic Politics: The Logic of Two-Level Games," *International Organization* 42 (1988): 427–61.

5. Desmond S. King and Rogers M. Smith, "Racial Orders in American Political Development," *American Political Science Review* 99, no. 1 (2005): 75–92.

6. See, for example, Michael Dawson, *Behind the Mule: Race and Class in African-American Politics* (Princeton: Princeton University Press, 1994); Rodney Hero, *Latinos in the US Political System: Two-Tiered Pluralism* (Philadelphia: Temple University Press, 1992); Katherine Tate, *Black Faces in the Mirror: African Americans and Their Representatives in Congress* (Princeton: Princeton University Press, 2003).

7. For an excellent introduction to the use of path dependence in political science research, see Paul Pierson, *Politics in Time: History, Institutions, and Social Analysis* (Princeton: Princeton University Press, 2004), 17–54, 79–103.

8. For examples of this literature, see Gabriel Sheffer, "Ethnonational Diasporas and Security" *Survival* 36 (1994): 60–79; Yossi Shain, "Multicultural Foreign Policy," *Foreign Policy* 100 (1995): 69–87; Huntington, "Erosion of American National Interests," 28–50.

For references to the black American experience, see Bernard Magubane, *The Ties That Bind: African-American Consciousness of Africa* (Trenton: Africa World Press, 1989); Ronald Walters, "African-American Influences," 65–83.

9. Putnam, "Diplomacy and Domestic Politics."

10. Huntington, "Erosion of American National Interests," 28–50; Bruce D. Porter, "Can American Democracy Survive?" *Commentary* 96 (November 1993): 37–40; James Schlesinger, "Fragmentation and Hubris: A Shaky Basis for American Leadership," *National Interest* 49 (fall 1997): 3–10.

11. See, for example, Charles Mathias Jr., "Ethnic Groups and Foreign Policy," *Foreign Affairs* 59, no. 5: 975–98; Huntington, "Erosion of American National Interests," 32–33.

12. George W. Shepard Jr., "Introduction," in *Racial Influences on American Foreign Policy*, ed. George W. Shepard Jr. (New York: Basic Books, 1970); DeConde, *Ethnicity, Race and American Foreign Policy*; Shain, *Marketing the American Creed Abroad*.

13. Herschelle Challenor, "The Influence of Black Americans on U.S. Foreign Policy toward Africa," in *Ethnicity and U.S. Foreign Policy*, ed. Abdul Aziz Said (New York: Praeger, 1981); Shain, *Marketing the American Creed Abroad*.

14. Patricia Gurin, Shirley Hatchett, and James S. Jackson, *Hope and Independence: Blacks' Response to Electoral and Party Politics* (New York: Russell Sage Foundation, 1989); Dawson, *Behind the Mule*; Katherine Tate, *From Protest to Politics: The New Black Voters in American Elections* (Cambridge, Mass.: Harvard University Press, 1994), 23–29.

15. Dawson, *Behind the Mule*, 57.

16. Ibid., 58.

17. Carol Swain, *Black Faces, Black Interests: The Representation of African Americans in Congress* (Cambridge, Mass.: Harvard University Press, 1993); Richard Fenno, *Going Home: Black Representatives and Their Constituents* (Chicago: University of Chicago Press, 2003); Tate, *Black Faces in the Mirror*.

18. Tate, *Black Faces in the Mirror*, 127.

19. Fenno, *Going Home*, 7.

20. Kevin Gaines, *Uplifting the Race: Black Leadership, Politics, and Culture in the Twentieth Century* (Chapel Hill: University of North Carolina Press, 1996), 1–19.

21. Swain, *Black Faces, Black Interests*, 167.

22. See, for example, Walters, "African-American Influence."

23. Alvin B. Tillery Jr., "Black Americans and the Creation of America's Africa Policies: The De-Racialization of Pan-African Politics," in *The African Diaspora: African Origins and New World Identities*, ed. Isidore Okpewho, Carol Boyce Davies, and Ali A. Mazrui (Bloomington: Indiana University Press, 1999), 504–25.

24. For an excellent study of the ambivalence that black Americans show toward African immigrants, see Shayla Nunnally, "Limiting Blackness or Ethnic Ordering: African Americans' Diasporic Linked Fate with West Indian and African Peoples in the US," *Du Bois Review*, forthcoming.

25. Richard Fenno, *Congressmen in Committees* (Boston: Little, Brown, 1973), 3–9.

26. For recent studies of African immigration to the United States, see April Gordon, "The New Diaspora: African Immigration to the United States," *Journal of Third World Studies* 15, no. 1 (1993): 79–103; Yanyi K. Djamba, "African Immigrants in the United States: A Socio-Demographic Profile in Comparison to Native Blacks," *Journal of Asian and African Studies* 34, no. 2 (1999), 211–18.

27. Reuel Rogers, "Race Based Coalitions among Minority Groups: Afro-Caribbean Immigrants and African Americans in New York City," *Urban Affairs Review* 39, no. 3 (2004): 283–317; Evrick Brown, "The Caribbean Nation State in Brooklyn Politics: An Examination of the UNA Clarke Major Owens Congressional Race," in *Race and Ethnicity in New York City*, ed. Jerome Krase and Ray Hutchinson (New York: Elsevier, 2004), 221–45.

See also Curtis L. Taylor, "Brooklyn Politics in Flux: Caribbean Migration Is Bringing Change to Area Long-Controlled by African-Americans, Whites," *New York Newsday*, September 19, 2004, A37.

28. Sheldon Stryker, "Identity Salience and Role Performance: The Relevance of Symbolic Interaction Theory for Family Research," *Journal of Marriage and the Family* 30, no. 4 (1968): 558–64; Dawson, *Behind the Mule*, 56–72.

Index

Adams, Henry, 24–28
Address to the Nations of the World, 46
African Blood Brotherhood (ABB), 82, 84
African Growth and Opportunity Act (AGOA), 2–3, 5, 125–26, 145–47
African Methodist Episcopal Church (AME), 29–30, 39; Bethel Church, 18
African National Congress (ANC), 111–12
Allied Powers, 47
American Colonization Society (ACS), 17–20, 25, 31–32
American Federation of Labor (AFL), 81, 85–86, 121, 146
American Negro Labor Congress (ANLC), 83, 86
American Negro Leadership Conference on Africa (ANLCA), 95, 97–99, 133
Americans for South African Resistance (AFSAR), 120
Americo-Liberians, 31–32, 65
Arkansas Refugees, 30–31

Battle of Adowa, 67, 70
Belgium, 99, 114–16
Berlin Conference, 108, 115
Bethune, Mary McCloud, 104, 120
Bishop, Sanford, 125–26
Black Forum on Foreign Policy, 137
Black Panther Party, 102
Black Star Lines, 55–59
Briggs, Cyril, 82, 84
Brown vs. Board of Education of Topeka Kansas, 93
Bruce, Blanche K., 28–29, 33
Bunche, Ralph Johnson: apologizes for black protestors at UN, 99; career in academia and politics, 101; on Ghana's independence, 123; NAACP committee on Pan-African Congress, 105–7; reaction to apology in the black press, 101–2
Butler, Matthew, 39–41; Butler emigration bill, 44–45
Byrd Amendment, 135–37

Cadet, Elizer, 61–62
Clark, Tom, 73

Clay, Henry, 17–18
Clay, William L., 127–28, 133, 136–41
Cleveland, Grover, 40
Cockburn, Joshua, 55–57
Cold War, 6, 11, 72–75, 93
Communist Party-International, 82–83
Communist Party-USA, 73, 80, 82–89
Comprehensive Anti-Apartheid Act (CAAA) of 1986, 126, 140–44
Congo Crisis, 100–101, 108, 114–17
Congressional Black Caucus (CBC), 2, 7; affect of the Free South Africa Movement on, 139–40; formation of and early history, 127–30, 133; growth in membership, 143–45; internal divisions over AGOA, 125, 145–47; passage of CAAA, 126; strategic approach to anti-apartheid activism, 133–38
Council on African Affairs (CAA), 72, 104, 106; media coverage of, 91–93; persecution during Red Scare, 73–75; response to Defiance Campaign, 119–20
Counter-Reconstruction, 22–25
Crummel, Alexander, 14–16
Cuffe, Paul, 16–18, 22
Cuthbert, Marian, 90

Daily Worker, 87
Daniels, Samuel, 68
Dawson, Michael, 6, 15, 18
Dawson, William L., 130–31
Declaration of Independence, 19
Delany, Martin, 26, 35; criticism of Liberia, 36; debate with Douglass over patronage, 27–28, 32; emigrationist views, 36–37; exploratory mission to Nigeria, 36
Dellums, Ronald V., 139–41, 153
Democratic Party, 22–23, 130, 136–37
DePriest, Oscar, 89, 129
Diagne, Blaise, 47
Dickstein, Samuel, 88
Dies, Martin, 88–89
Diggs, Charles: chairman of subcommittee on Africa, 134–35; election and early years in Congress, 130–32; formation of the Congressional Black Caucus, 127; leader of

INDEX

Diggs, Charles (*continued*)
  campaign for sanctions bill, 129, 133–34; patron of the Free South Africa Movement, 138–39; protests USS *Roosevelt* stopover in South Africa, 133; resignation from House of Representatives, 139
Douglass, Frederick: debate with Delany over patronage, 27–32, 36; endorsement of John H. Smyth for diplomatic post, 35; opposition to the Butler Bill, 41; support for U.S. recognition of Liberia, 21
Drummond, Eric, 62
Du Bois, W.E.B.: conflicts with UNIA, 61–62; coverage of Garvey in *Crisis* magazine, 43, 50–53; engagement with Liberian diplomatic corps, 64–65; expelled from the NAACP, 73; founder of NAACP, 47–48; joins CAA, 73; negative views of Communist Party-USA, 83; Pan-African Congress Movement, 46–47, 78, 103–6; resigns from the NAACP, 78; San Francisco conference on the United Nations, 104

Eason, James W.H., 43
Eisenhower, Dwight David, 74, 93, 131–32
Ethiopia, 46, 65–66
Eufaula Riot, 23–24

Federal Bureau of Investigation (FBI), 58
Fifteenth Amendment, 22, 40–41
Fish, Hamilton, 27, 33
Ford, James, 86
Forten, James, 18
Fourteenth Amendment, 22
Frazier, Henry, 24
Free South Africa Movement (FSAM), 139–41, 153

Garnett, Henry Highland, 31
Garvey, Marcus Mosiah, 42; Booker T. Washington's influence on, 49; conviction for fraud, 54–56; coverage of in the black press, 52–55; early life in Jamaica, 48; petitions League of Nations, 60–63; relations with Americo-Liberians, 61–62; rivalry with W.E.B. Du Bois, 50–51, 60–62; studies in London, 47–48; Universal Negro Improvement Association, 49–52; views on communism, 84–85
Ghana, 122–23
Grant, Ulysses S., 22, 27, 32
Great Depression, 67, 76
Great Migration, 80

Hamid, Sufi Abdul, 68–70
Hammarskjold, Dag, 117
Harding, Warren, 64
Harrison, Benjamin, 40
Hastie, William, 105–7
Hayes, Rutherford B., 35, 40
Hayes-Tilden Compromise, 15, 28
Height, Dorothy, 97
Hill, Elias, 27
Hilliard, Earl F., Sr., 144–45
Houser, George, 97
House Un-American Activities Committee (HUAC), 88–89
Hull, Cordell, 67, 77
Hunton, William Alphaeus (CAA), 120

India, 108–10
International Labor Defense (ILD), 67, 83
Italian-Ethiopian War, 65–68, 71; African-American response to, 69–70, 76–78

Jackson, Jesse, Jr., 1–3, 5, 146
Johnson, Charles S., 65
Johnson, Gabriel Moore, 63
Johnson, James Weldon, 51–52
Johnson, Lyndon Baines, 133
Johnson, Mordecai Wyatt, 89, 120
Joint Select Committee to Investigate the Affairs in the late Insurrectionary States, 23–24

Kansas: exodus movement to, 41
Kansas-Nebraska Act, 36
Katanga Province, 116–18
Kennedy, John F., 11, 74, 95–98
Kikuyu ethnic group (Kenya), 112–13, 121
Kilpatrick, Carolyn C., 146
King, C.D.B., 61, 65
King, Coretta Scott, 109
King, Martin Luther, Jr., 109, 123–24
Ku Klux Klan, 23–24, 60

Leadership Conference on Southern Africa, 138–39
League of Nations, 62–63, 70, 77
Leopold II (King of Belgium), 115
Lewis, John, 144
Liberia: ACS role in founding of, 19–20, 29; attempts to recruit blacks from the U.S., 14–15, 38; diplomatic relations with U.S., 14, 20–21, 45, 64–65, 118; forced labor crisis, 65, 102
Liberia Fever, 17, 24–25, 32–34

Liberian Joint Stock Steamship Company, 37–38
Lincoln, Abraham, 14, 37
Logan, Rayford, 105
Lumumba, Patrice, 99, 114, 116–18

Malcolm X (El Haj Malik Shabazz), 102
Marke, George, 62
Mau Mau uprising (Kenya), 108, 110, 112–14, 121–22
McCormack, John, 88
McDermot, James ("Jim"), 145
McKay, Claude, 82–83
Miller, Kelly, 50, 85–86
Minor, Robert, 86
Mississippi Plan, 23
Moore, Richard, 84
Murphy, Frank, 89

National Association for the Advancement of Colored People (NAACP), 6, 11, 47, 49, 59; avoids persecution from HUAC, 89–91, 93; conflict with Communist Party-USA over Scottsboro Boys, 86–88; conflict with Du Bois over Pan-African Congresses, 75–77, 103–6; expels W.E.B. Du Bois, 73; interactions with UNIA, 51–53; passes resolution to condemn violence of the Mau Mau uprising, 121; response to Italy's invasion of Ethiopia, 67, 76; support for Liberia, 64–65; support for Truman's national security policies, 78–79; use of Cold War frame to push for decolonization in Africa, 93–95
National Emigration Convention, 36
Negro Sanhedrin Conference, 83–86
New Deal, 88–89
Nixon, Richard M., 96, 123, 132
North American Free Trade Agreement (NAFTA), 1–2, 145

Padmore, George, 105–6
Painter, Nell Irvin, 8, 25–26, 33
Pan-African Congress Movement, 46–47, 51, 60–63, 75–76, 104–7
Parrot, Russell, 19
Pickens, William, 51, 53, 87
Pickering, Timothy, 16–17
Powell, Adam Clayton, Jr.: defends Eisenhower administration at Bandung Conference, 131–32; hosts rally in support of Defiance Campaign, 120; introduces bill to cut military aid to British forces in Kenya, 121; serves as mentor to Charles Diggs, 132; strategies for gaining influence in House of Representatives, 131
Public Advisory Council on Africa (PACA), 96–97

Radical Republicans, 23
Rainey, Joseph, 127
Randolph, A. Philip, 50, 53, 63, 70, 120–23
Reagan, Ronald, 140
Red Scare, 6, 78–79, 98
Rhodesia, 111, 135
Robeson, Paul, 73–74, 79, 118–19
Robinson, Randall, 139
Roosevelt, Franklin Delano, 67, 77
Roosevelt, Theodore, 45
Rusk, Dean, 97–98

Sampson, John H, 39
San Francisco Conference on the UN Charter, 104
Schwellenbeck, Lewis B., 72–73
Scottsboro Boys, 86–88
Scott v. Sanford (1857), 20
Selassie, Haile, 66–70
Sierra Leone, 16–17
Skinner, Elliot, 16, 62
Smyth, John H., 35
Soviet Union, 81, 85, 117
Stokes, Louis, 134, 136, 138
Sumner, Charles, 21
Swain, Carol, 8, 129, 148, 153

Taft, William Howard, 69
Tanner, Benjamin T., 29, 33, 39
TransAfrica, 139
Truman, Harry S.: Cold War security measures adopted by, 72–73; coverage by the black media, 74–75, 91–92; delivers speech to NAACP convention, 92; desegregates U.S. armed forces, 92
Truman Doctrine, 73–74, 78, 90–94
Tuner, Henry McNeal, 37–39, 44
Turner, James Milton (abolitionist and first black diplomat to Liberia): appointed minister resident to Liberia, 32; conflicts with Americo–Liberians over emigration, 33–35; paternalistic attitudes toward black masses, 34–35; role in Republican Party politics, 32–33

United Nations, 72, 99–100, 103–4, 112, 117
Universal Negro Improvement Association (UNIA), 49–51, 67, 70, 84; communists

Universal Negro Improvement Association
  (UNIA) (*continued*)
    speak at UNIA convention, 84–85; composition of membership, 53–54; contacts with the League of Nations, 62–63; efforts to acquire land in Liberia, 63–64; record as a business, 55–57; reorganization after Garvey's imprisonment, 59–60

Versailles Peace Conference, 47, 51, 60–63, 76
Virginia House of Delegates, 18
Voting Rights ACT of 1965, 124, 127, 142

War of 1812, 16–17

Washington, Booker T., 41–42, 44–47, 79
White, George, 127
White, Walter, 77, 88–90, 104
White League, 22
White Line Campaign (Mississippi), 23
White Man's League, 23
Wilkins, Roy, 101, 105
Williams, G. Mennen, 95–98
Williams, George Washington, 115
Williams, Henry Sylvester, 46, 105
Wilson, Woodrow, 47, 85
Windom, William, 26

Yergan, Max, 73

www.ingramcontent.com/pod-product-compliance
Lightning Source LLC
Chambersburg PA
CBHW062000251125
35956CB00029B/772